The
South Asian
Religious Diaspora
in Britain, Canada,
and the
United States

SUNY series in
Religious Studies

Harold Coward, editor

The South Asian Religious Diaspora in Britain, Canada, and the United States

edited by
Harold Coward,
John R. Hinnells,
and
Raymond Brady Williams

STATE UNIVERSITY OF NEW YORK PRESS

Published by
State University of New York Press, Albany

© 2000 State University of New York

For information, address the State University of New York Press
State University Plaza, Albany, NY 12246

Production by Kristin Milavec
Marketing by Michael Campochiaro

Library of Congress Cataloging-in-Publication

The South Asian religious diaspora in Britain, Canada, and the United
    States / edited by Harold Coward, John R. Hinnells, and Raymond
    Brady Williams.
        p. cm. — (SUNY series in religious studies)
    Includes bibliographical references and index.
    ISBN 0-7914-4509-7 (alk. paper). — ISBN 0-7914-4510-0 (pbk. :
alk. paper)
    1. South Asia—Religion. 2. South Asia—Emigration and
immigration. 3. South Asians—Great Britain—Religion. 4. South
Asians—Canada—Religion. 5. South Asians—United States—Religion.
I. Coward, Harold G. II. Hinnells, John R. III. Williams, Raymond
Brady. IV. Series.
BL1055.S68 2000
200'.89'914—dc21
                                                        99-39476
                                                        CIP

10 9 8 7 6 5 4 3 2 1

*To the memory of those
who worked for the
independence of India*

Contents

Acknowledgments

The idea for this book was born in the minds of the three editors in a discussion at the 1995 Annual Meeting of the American Academy of Religion. Authors were recruited and they met to present first drafts of their chapters at a seminar hosted by the School of Oriental and African Studies (SOAS), University of London, in November 1996. Faculty and graduate students from SOAS and other British universities attended and helped with the critique. Authors then revised their chapters for presentation in this volume.

This book could not have appeared without the support of the SOAS Centre of South Asian Studies (University of London), the Centre for Studies in Religion and Society (University of Victoria, British Columbia), and the Wabash Center (Wabash College, Crawfordsville, Indiana). Special thanks are due to Barbara Lazoi for arranging the meeting at SOAS, and to Ludgard De Decker at the Centre for Studies in Religion and Society for preparing the manuscript for publication.

Introduction

South Asian Religions in Migration

A Comparative Study of the British, Canadian, and U.S. Experiences

John R. Hinnells

Academics in various subjects, Sociology for example, have studied Asian communities in the Western world for decades. The existence of these groups has often been used by scholars of religion to legitimate Religious Studies, as opposed to the traditional emphasis on Christian Theology, on the grounds that Asian religions now have immediate relevance to the Western world because of their visible presence here. But these two trends did not interact much until the end of the 1980s. Sociological, anthropological, political, and other studies have rarely taken significant account of the religious beliefs and practices of the communities studied, and Religious Studies has commonly focused on the classical (and thereby ancient) literature of the religions in the "old countries." Until recently, the diaspora groups have been considered marginal to the study of the "main" religion, and they have been viewed as peripheral in studies of Western religion. In Sociology, and other disciplinary studies, the focus has been on the problems encountered by migrant groups, such as prejudice in the workplace, in housing, and in public places. Undoubtedly there have been problems, but to focus so much on that dimension of the ethnic minority experience, has resulted in the impression that the groups themselves are to be seen as problems. The vitality, social contributions of, and spirituality within the groups were overlooked. In the 1960s and early 1970s, the era when South Asian migration grew, most outside commentators assumed the second and third generations would inevitably and increasingly assimilate into the host society. That has not happened. As various chapters in this book show, the visible evidence of South Asian religions in the West is far greater in the late 1990s than it was before, not only in the form of splendid new temples and mosques, but also in the more common wearing of turbans and the *hijab*, and in the number and range of religious ceremonies performed in the communities. Why that has happened is discussed in the chapters that follow. Behind this publicly visible front are a myriad of diverse forms of religious activity. Workers in race relations who neglect the religious dimension of the ethnic minorities are neglecting what the members of those groups commonly consider significant. Many researchers report that their informants have commented that they believe they have become more religious after migration than they were before, because religion is an important part of individual and community identity. The growth in the studies of migrant religions in the 1990s is therefore a welcome scholarly development.

New or developing subjects commonly have problems with their technical vocabulary, and their methodology. The first paragraph deliberately used a number of terms that are common in the media, and in academic works, but which specialists in the field would consider highly ambiguous if not questionable and dubious. Perhaps the most debated terms are "race" and "ethnicity." The term "race" has widely been taken to imply a biologically determined set of characteristics that condition personality type, abilities, and so on. Although racial prejudice is now officially banned in most Western countries, the presuppositions behind the offensive and invalid theories, at their most potent in the work of Hitler, are not far beneath the surface of some popular and official attitudes. In order to avoid the pejorative associations of "race" many writers have turned to "ethnicity," usually interpreted as a shared sense of history, language, culture, or religion. In popular usage, however, "ethnic" has come to be identified with "Black" or "Third World." A famous international chain store, for example, has an "ethnic jewelry" section, but includes only items derived from what some term "underdeveloped" countries. But all people have their own "ethnicity," be that Derbyshire, English, mid-Western, and so forth. A vivid example of the vagueness with which the term "ethnicity" is used is the 1991 British census, which listed among ethnic categories not only Indian, and so on, but also "White"—despite the number of different White British ethnic and national groups (Welsh, Scottish, Irish, as well as many continental Europeans, Americans, etc.) living in the British Isles. There are many more terms that have to be questioned. "Migrant groups" is naturally offensive to the many young British/ Canadian/ American Hindus, Sikhs, Muslims, and so on, who were born in the West, see their future here, and identify with the country of their birth, as well as with their religious or cultural heritage. The term "host" community has also been challenged. What is "the host" community? Most recent migrants find the wider White society anything but a host, it is often alien, prejudiced, and vocal extremists call for repatriation. The effective hosts are members of their own community. The word "community" has frequently been questioned. Certainly there is nothing corresponding to the (South) Asian community, and rarely a single entity such the Hindu, Muslim, Sikh, or Zoroastrian community—there are Gujarati or Bengali movements; diverse branches of the Islamic tradition, and so on. The divisions, be they religious, caste or class, "ethnic," cultural, national may be more significant to the people under discussion than the universalizing "Hinduism," Islam and so forth. Similarly the concept of "culture" has been described as a vague and meaningless, if common, reification (Baumann 1996). Is there a phrase that can be used as an umbrella term? Hinnells 1996 argued for the term *diaspora religions* to indicate those groups that have a sense of being a minority, commonly an oppressed minority, living in an alien culture at a distance from the "old country." This has been objected to not only on the grounds that it is a term derived from the field of Biblical Studies, but also because it is not appropriate for many religious groups. Christians, for example, have a sense of a holy land, but British and American Christians from the major denominations can hardly be described as living in a diaspora. What of Muslims living away from Arabia, but where they are a majority, for example in South East Asia? Perhaps one may be in a religious majority but in a cultural diaspora (e.g., Indian Christians in the United States)?

Another question of definition relates to the phrase "New Religious Movements." This is true in the study of religion as a whole, but comes to the fore with the study of Asian religions in the West. What from one perspective may be seen as a New Religious Movement, for example, ISKCON, can from another be seen as the modern expression of classical Indian teaching. In one sense definitions are concerned with drawing the appropriate boundaries around subjects, but there are times when strictly drawn boundaries are artificial. The lack of an accepted technical vocabulary does not necessarily indicate a sloppy academic discipline, it can also be a sign of a subject that is new and changing rapidly. Although this book deals with some of these definitional issues in passing, it does not address them directly because there is already a rich literature on such questions. But it is important to point to the debates.

What is different about this book is that it seeks to study the phenomena comparatively in two senses: (1) comparatively between the religions and (2) comparatively between three Western countries. Comparative Religion has often been seen as a vague subject, characterized by generalizations and a lack of specialist understanding, which inevitably undermines any conclusions drawn from the material. However, the value of comparison is that it identifies not only what is common, but also, and perhaps more importantly, what is distinctive or characteristic of a particular phenomenon. There is a saying in Comparative Religion: He who knows one, knows none. If a person studies only one religion, say Christianity, then he or she cannot be said to be studying religion, only Christianity. Equally, if one studies only, say, Hindus in the United States, one is not studying diaspora/transnational religion, only Hindus in the United States. That may be a valid field of study in its own right, but in order to understand what is distinctive about Hindus in the States it is increasingly recognized that one has to study "both ends of the migration chain," that is, the old and the new countries. Taking the argument one stage further, perhaps a degree of triangulation is necessary, that is, the study of the old country and a comparison of two diaspora groups. This book takes that approach much further by comparing six religious movements—Hinduism, Islam, Indian Christians, Indian New Religious Movements, Sikhism, and Zoroastrianism—in three countries—Britain, Canada, and the United States. A single chapter each is devoted to South Asian Christians, Zoroastrians, and the New Religious Movements in the three countries. Hinduism, Islam, and Sikhism are considered separately for each of the three countries. Not only are the authors specialists in their respective fields, scholars who have done fieldwork in the groups they write about, there is also a logic and coherence behind the structure of the book. The focus is on religions from the Indian subcontinent and how these different groups from a related background have fared in three Western countries sharing a common (English) language and with an interwoven history. The study is, therefore, of six religions in related Western environments. So although the subject matter is broad, it is also focused. It is the first attempt at such international collaboration in this field. The book grows out of two meetings, the first at the American Academy of Religions in Philadelphia in 1995, and the second a workshop at the School of Oriental and African Studies (SOAS) in London in 1996. At the latter, participants circulated their papers in advance, were given five minutes to identify what they considered the key issues, and these were then discussed for forty minutes. There were further debates at the end of each section (on Britain, Canada, and the United States) and at the conclusion of the Workshop on what are the distinctive experiences of Hindus, Muslims, Sikhs, and so on, and what is specific to the British, Canadian, and United States contexts. Authors produced the final text of their chapters in the light of these discussions. There has, therefore, been considerable interaction between contributors. Of course, there are still differences of emphasis and treatment because the religions and the countries are different, as are the research backgrounds of the various scholars. However, this scholarly debate identified a series of themes that bind what might have been a very disparate book into a logical whole.

The themes that emerged as significant for many, if not most, religions studied were: the significance of the distinctive histories of migration in the different countries; the consequences of life in the new world for religious practice, exemplified, for example, in sacred space, institutional, public, and private worship; the effects of public policy in the various countries on the minorities (e.g., multiculturalism, religious and higher education); strategies of adaptation; generational issues; relations with the old country, and the place of women in the religions in the West. The emphasis may vary between chapters, sometimes the issues appear as headings and sometimes not, but each chapter addresses them to the extent that they are appropriate for the subject under discussion.

What has emerged is a rich diet of ingredients, blended into a balanced, wholesome menu. Clearly, there are problems encountered by all the religions in each country. The role of women is one which has already been mentioned. There are related issues, notably marriage. However westernized South Asians, young or old, may be, when the time of marriage approaches the force of traditions becomes potent. In different ways and to different degrees, inter-marriage commonly emerges as a major issue. Whatever the teaching against caste in classical Sikh literature, in practice *jati* becomes crucial for many Sikhs. Similarly among Muslims, although conversion of marriage partners is part of the tradition, Gujarati or Bengali ties may become prominent when marriage plans are made. The impact of Western education is another important issue, not least because South Asians value education so highly. In Canada and the United States it was overwhelmingly the well-educated South Asians who were the original migrants. Although this was less true of the early Indian settlers in Britain, the second generation pursues higher education to a far greater extent than do the White Anglo-Saxon majority. The question of how to integrate traditional values and westernized attitudes is a common concern. In the 1970s scholars wrote of the second generation as "caught between cultures." More recently Ballard has suggested that one should view the South Asian young in the West as "skilled cultural navigators," people who move comfortably between the culture of home and wider society, just as bilingual people switch easily between languages (Ballard 1994). Hinnells 1995 suggests there is truth in both positions with regard to different groups within any community. However the young react, the problems, tensions, and opportunities that face each tradition in the West are similar.

Although caution was expressed above concerning an overemphasis on the problems encountered by diaspora or transnational religions, nevertheless there are religious problems encountered by South Asians in the West that have not yet been fully addressed. Several authors in this book refer to the difficulties posed by the pressures of working life in the West, by the pattern of the working week and of public holidays. One of the most profound set of problems is associated with death and bereavement. Western funeral parlors and undertakers are not equipped to allow for the various death ceremonies that are important for the different religions. The time allocated at crematoria, the enormous (insurmountable?) problems associated with purity and pollution in a Western environment, which almost by definition is seen as impure, confront the grieving with yet greater distress. The inability to observe hallowed tradition can be a cause of guilt, however illogical such an emotion may be. Similar, though usually less acute, problems may be associated with childbirth and suffering (both physical and psychological). The West therefore confronts the various groups with substantial religious and personal problems.

Western public policies affect the internal structures and self-perceptions of the members of the various South Asian religions. Several authors comment on how the American laws governing charitable status determine community structures of internal management with committees, Memoranda of Agreement and Incorporation, the role of leaders, and so forth. In Britain there is a further problem posed by the fact that religious education is a core part of the state school syllabus. Apart from the fact that this may inculcate Christian values, even where Asian religions are part of the syllabus the image and emphasis that are conveyed can determine the self-perception of young Hindus, Muslims, and so on. The obvious example is the priority given to doctrine and "scriptural" texts, rather than to family practices and values. Interfaith dialogue can produce a similar result. The goal, clearly, is to spread understanding and thereby tolerance, but the emphasis on "faith," as in the common phrase "the faith communities," gives a particular Christian slant to what is seen to be the essence of religion. The widespread Western assumption that to be effective, prayers must be understood, the stress on congregational worship, all result, in the view of many scholars, in the protestantizing of non-European religions.

Western images of South Asian religions impact on the communities in different ways. The hostile stereotyping of religions inevitably triggers antagonism and an understandable reassertion of tradition. The obvious example of this is the all too common media image of Muslims as fundamentalist fanatics. A different example is the Western image of all Sikhs as bearded wearers of turbans resulting in the idea that the only "true" Sikhs are those who grow beards and wear turbans. A third interaction is that between Western scholarship and the traditional members of the religion, best exemplified in the conflicts between "orthodox" Sikhs in Canada and the United States and the distinguished scholar Hew McLeod, discussed in two chapters in this book. Increasingly younger Asians are studying their heritage at Western universities. What the long-term impact of that will be, and how it will affect relations between this Western-educated youth and leaders in the old countries has yet to be seen. There can be little doubt that what happens in the diaspora will, for better or worse, have an influence on the religion in the old country.

There is one term that has not yet been examined, but which has to be: what is meant by "the West"? Edward Said challenged Western stereotypes of "the Orient," in particular the imperialist simplification of a unitary phenomenon, as a false reification (Said 1974). Equally one might question the concept of "the West." America is east of Australia, and Britain is east of America. The Europocentric map projection of the world locates Australia on the bottom right, as an eastern country. But in the popular use of the term "the West" Australia and New Zealand would be included. Their omission from this book was simply a question of time and space, but on grounds of principle perhaps they should have been included as a fourth example of English speaking "Western" countries. It would, however, be simplistic to suggest that there is any such entity as "the West." It was said above that there is much that binds Britain, Canada, and the United States together, for example, language and an interwoven history. But it has often been said that Britain and the United States are two countries divided by a common language. As there is much in common, so there is much that is different between the countries, for example, Britain has a state Church, with all that entails regarding government. It has even been questioned whether a non-Christian could be a prime minister. The only Jew to obtain that position was Disraeli, and he converted to Christianity (Saghal and Yuval-Davis 1992: 12). In Britain, the Prime Minister recommends the name of candidates for bishoprics to the head of state, the Queen. How would a Muslim or Sikh do that? In the United States there has been a strong demarcation between state and church, yet religion has a far higher public profile in the United States than in Britain, with a higher number of active Christians, both in absolute and proportional terms. Christian groups have had much more influence in U.S. elections for the presidency than in Britain. As the following chapters indicate, Muslims and Zoroastrians have established continental "America-wide" umbrella organizations that include both Canada and the United States. But despite their close relations, there are significant differences between the two countries. The obvious one to highlight in this book is the contrast between the Canadian multiculturalism and the American melting-pot theory. It must immediately be said that the U.S. government has moved beyond that early policy, but it remains a significant part of the South Asian groups' perception of that country, because it is seen as such a threat to the preservation of identity. But what is also important for this book is the different groups that have settled in the three countries. The history of migration to the three countries is different. Migration in Britain dates back to Roman times; until the twentieth-century migration to Canada and the United States was almost wholly European. The South Asian migration to Britain was earlier than that to the American continent, but was different in other ways also, as detailed in the chapters below. Briefly it came with all the presuppositions, on both sides, which grew out of the Empire. Because of Britain's needs, those who migrated were almost all single, young, male manual workers, reinforcing imperial perceptions of Indians as coolies. (Asian) Indian religion was first seen in the States as a consequence of the World Parliament of Religions in Chicago and was perceived as a mystical, meditative religion. When Asian migration developed to Canada and the United States in the 1960s, instead of attracting "the tired, the poor and the huddled masses," as it is said on the Statue of Liberty, it was the highly educated professionals and the scientists who came. The history and demography of the migration is therefore different. And so also is the wider context of the history of immigration. In Britain, the South Asians are, apart from the Irish, the major non–Anglo-Saxon ethnic group. Apart from Chinese (mainly from the ex-British colony Hong Kong), there are no large East Asian groups in Britain. In the United States, the South Asians are just one group among Latin Americans, East and South East Asians, and a much larger Black African population than in Britain or Canada. Immigration in the United States is a far more varied mosaic than it is in Britain. Canada is, in this regard, somewhere in the middle between the other two countries.

Various authors look to the future developments in the diaspora religions in the West. The first point to make is that in all three countries it seems certain that numbers will increase. Although primary migration has been reduced in the United States and Canada, and especially in Britain where it has virtually ceased, the age profile of all the groups is such that numbers will increase. Although the numbers of births per family tends to reduce to Western norms as communities become more established, the fact that young people far exceed the numbers of elderly means that the birth rate exceeds the death rate. As the numbers grow and the number of economically successful individuals increases, so the resources available to the religions increases. Two contrasting trends may be discerned. On the one hand, through increased international travel, not only to the old country but to other diaspora groups, and through telecommunications and the Internet, the process of globalization becomes more evident. Among some, the demand is for an emphasis on the religious ideals and the curtailing of "simply" ethnic traditions. There is therefore a quest for a pure Islam, Hinduism, and so forth. How that "true" religion is perceived varies. In some cases there is a trend toward what may be seen as a "sanitized" form of the religion, one thought to be more acceptable in the West, for example, a Hindu emphasis on the Gita and Gandhi rather than on purity laws. The *sampradaya*, or the guru lineage (e.g., Sai Babha), is also an increasingly popular tradition, not least because of the educational and community infrastructures that these movements have evolved. On the other hand, increased resources mean that unlike in the early years of settlement there was less need for different groups to share centers. For example, in the 1960s it was not uncommon to find Indian cultural centers that housed not only images of the various Hindu gods, but also pictures or statues from Sikhism and Jainism. The political tensions in India during the 1980s, as well as increased resources, resulted in separate Sikh centers. But this trend has developed further as more regional Gujarati or Tamil centers have grown. Whether the future communities will be more global or regional in nature, or a mixture of both, is unclear at the dawn of the third millennium.

The importance of the diaspora groups, and their impact back in the old country, seems almost certain to grow. Leading teachers from the old countries are often invited to the West, and when not present in body they are seen on the video screen. Similarly, Western leaders visit the old country where they are sometimes seen as important and successful people, who have something to offer to the old country. Whereas it used to be thought that it was people in the old country who preserved the traditional religion, and the diaspora was a force for change, various writers in this book report that in some instances it is the diaspora groups who prove more resistant to change as they seek to preserve their identity in a sea of change. Those of us who were active in the study of diaspora religions in the 1960s did not foresee the vitality, and strength, of the religions that would characterize these groups at the end of the millennium.

There are, of course, more common experiences and differences than this short introduction has identified. But perhaps enough has been written to indicate, in broad brush strokes, some of the questions, issues and themes addressed in this book with its breadth of scope, but clear focus. For a fuller picture, the reader is invited to study the following chapters!

This intellectual collaboration grew out of the shared interests and friendship of the three editors. They would like to thank the contributors for their scholarly cooperation, the good spirit in which the meetings took place, and the bodies that sponsored them. The Workshop at SOAS was sponsored by the British Academy, the Spalding Trusts, and by SOAS.

────────────── **BIBLIOGRAPHY** ──────────────

Ballard, R. (ed.) (1994). *Desh Pardesh, the South Asian Presence in Britain.* London: Hurst.

Baumann, G. (1996). *Contesting Cultures: Discourses of Identity in Multi-ethnic London.* Cambridge: Cambridge University Press.

Hinnells, J. R. (1995). *Zoroastrians in Britain.* Oxford: Clarendon Press.

Hinnells, J. R. (1996). *A Handbook of Living Religions.* Oxford: Blackwell.

Said, E. (1978). *Orientalism.* London: Routledge and Kegan Paul.

Sahgal, Gita and Yuval Davis, Nira (1992). *Refusing Holy Orders: Women and Fundamentalism in Britain.* London: Virago Press.

1

South Asian Christians in Britain, Canada, and the United States

Raymond Brady Williams

Syrian Malankara Christians from India gather each Sunday near Blackfriars Bridge in London for worship in their beautiful sanctuary designed by Sir Christopher Wren in St. Andrew-by-the-Wardrobe. They are part of a diocese that includes Britain, Europe, and Canada and maintain close relations with sister dioceses in the United States and the Gulf States. Members of their church family and of their extended families stretch from Kerala to many countries on several continents. They constitute transnational families and transnational churches made possible by the rapidity of contemporary migration and communication. Elinor Kelly uncovered a similar network of transnational families (she calls them "transcontinental families") while working in a village in Gujarat: "Gradually, as they told their stories and discussed the pros and cons of the different countries where they worked, I realized that . . . my country was only one of a number of options which they would consider in order to earn the cash which should flow as remittances into their villages. . . . I soon realized that I was experiencing something else which all the literature on Asian communities in [the West] had somehow failed to convey" (1990:252).

The new reality of immigrants is driven by technology. A vision of one world linked together by almost instantaneous communication is rapidly being realized by modern technologies, but a consciousness of the spiritual and social unity lags behind. Nevertheless, the movement of Indian Christian immigrants to Britain, Canada, and the United States is part of a worldwide pattern of migration that brings Christians and those of other religions together in new transnational groupings. The thesis is that Christian immigrant communities constitute and exemplify new transnational groups whose identity is shaped by the necessities of their new, individual settled location and by new relationships emerging since 1965 among transnational religious communities in the United States, Britain, and Canada.

South Asian Christians bring several societies into a single social field that relates India to the Gulf States, Great Britain, Canada, the United States, and other countries as well. These relations emerging among migrants at the close of the twentieth century generate a new transnational approach to the study of migration and migrants "who develop and maintain multiple relations—familial, economic, social, organizational, religious, and political that span borders . . . and take actions, make decisions, feel concerns, and develop identities within social networks that connect them to two or more societies simultaneously" (Glick Schiller, Basch, and Blanc-Szanton, 1992:1–24). Immigrants with transnational relations are able to maintain several identities and to express these at times and in ways that are most advantageous to them in adapting to current circumstance and in preserving options for the future. One result of this transnationalism is the necessity of remapping the social and religious fields of the new immigrants to the West.

Religion is a major aspect of creating and maintaining identities across geographical and national boundaries because of the transcendent character of religious claims. It is increasingly evident that immigrants are maintaining transnational ties in ways different from the earlier immigrants, demanding new perspectives on the transnational vitality of religions and religious life. Both the practice and the study of religion, and especially Christianity, have developed methods and agencies reflecting the migration and ecumenical character of religious groups, but the experience and study of immigrants in the nineteenth and early twentieth centuries did not reveal the same transnational character of religion experienced by the new immigrants. The situation calls for a new sociological description of the lived reality and social fields of Christian immigrants and of the vitality of their relationships within and between several societies, and it demands a new conceptualization of ecclesiology that will take into account new forms of church interactions.

The two tracks for migration since 1965 are education and family reunification, and these are regulated by the vagaries of immigration laws and policies in each country. Nevertheless, as one immigrant explained, "Education is the universal passport." Medical education is the most common passport for Indian Christians, especially nurses' training as the primary passport for female immigrants to North America. A unique and the most important aspect of the immigration of Christians from India is the role of Christian nurses. Of 256 South Asian Christian women at North American national family conferences completing a survey, 182 identify themselves as nurses. Ten of the women are physicians. The typical pattern is that the woman gains certification and immigration status as a nurse and then either brings her spouse and children under family reunification provisions of the immigration law or returns to India for marriage in order to sponsor her spouse to immigrate. A significant number of the men follow their spouses into the hospitals as medical technicians or counselors.

Nurses are not explicitly mentioned in the third preference category of the United States Immigration Act of 1965, which states that "profession" shall include, but not be limited to, architects, engineers, lawyers, physicians, surgeons, and teachers of various types. The ascendancy of registered nurses to the third preference classification came about through case law ("Matter of Gutierrez in Visa Petition Proceedings A-17653997, July 5, 1967, in *Administrative Decisions under Immigration and Nationality Laws of the United States*, XII, 418ff).[1] They filled a niche created by the decline of women attending North American nursing schools. An uneven distribution of both physicians and nurses made the situation critical in some inner-city hospitals, which undertook recruiting campaigns reaching out to the Philippines and to India to attract physicians and nurses. In 1978 the National Council of State Boards of Nursing and the Commission on Graduates of Foreign Nursing Schools created tests of nursing and English language competencies to be administered twice a year in cities around the globe, making it easier for nurses to get visas. Missionaries would have been astonished to know that so many of their students would eventually serve in inner-city hospitals in North America.

To a great extent, the relative presence and distribution of Christians among South Asian immigrants in Britain, Canada, and the United States results more from the weight given to professional competence in immigration laws and regulations and from the level of difficulty foreign nurses face in gaining certification than on other push-pull factors of migration. The general perception among South Asians is that tests for certification as a nurse are stringent in Britain, which explains why there are more physicians than nurses among South Asian Christians in Britain. Many South Asian physicians took much of their training in Britain.

The Christians are the only South Asian group coming to North America carried by women. Gender roles in immigration are reversed. In most South Asian families of immigrants (except those from East Africa, relatively few of whom are Christians), a man with high educational and professional qualifications either studied in the West or was offered a job in a business or a position as a physician in a residency program. Then the man either went back to India for an arranged marriage and to bring a bride back with him or he sent for his spouse and children to join him. Among Indian Christians, however, women gain permanent resident status, earn the higher salary, provide for family security—especially was this the case during the economic recession in the mid-1980s when many husbands lost their jobs as factory workers and engineers—and now the women enjoy secure professional status. The incongruence between gender roles in India, where the man is lord over the family, home, and church, and the claims South Asian Christian women have to prominence, because they typically have a higher professional status and provide more income, creates tensions that require skillful and sometimes painful negotiation in both families and churches. The church is the only location outside the home where the new relationships can be named and negotiated. Renegotiation of gender roles as an important part of both individual and group identities often makes church meetings of immigrants lively, tearful, and effective.

Representational Strategies

A number of representational strategies with different rhetorics are evident among immigrant groups, both religious and secular, determining boundaries that form the basis of negotiation between immigrant groups and with the settled society. Boundaries are maintained by such aspects of group experience as language, rituals, cuisine, dress, organizational structure, beliefs, and other communicative aspects of customary behavior. Representational strategies are closely related to the formation and preservation of personal and group identity, so different strategies can be primary in various contexts. "I am an Indian . . . a Keralite . . . a Knanaya Syro-Malabar Catholic . . . a surgeon . . . a Canadian" all imply intricate applications of strategies. Hence (and this is a most important point), the strategies are not exclusive for individuals, but they are determinative for groups. Because religion can be so important in providing a transcendent basis for the formation and preservation of personal and group identities for immigrants, religious organizations are involved in boundary creation and maintenance representing several strategies.

Individual representational strategies are common in the early stages of immigration. An individual or family sustains religious commitment through private devotion in the home. Christian parents in several churches in India have clearly defined traditional roles as religious specialists in the home, presiding over morning and evening prayers, for example. A variation of the individual strategy is that new immigrants participate in parishes of established churches, often those in communion with their church in India—Mar Thoma Christians in a Church of England parish, Methodists with a Methodist congregation in the United States, or Plymouth Brethren with an assembly in Canada. A different individual strategy is to discontinue Christian activities and commitments. Migration provides an opportunity both to revise or to reject religious and other commitments, thereby reshaping personal identity. The individual strategies lead to a form of what is usually referred to as assimilation, in this case, into an established Christian group or into the dominant secular ethos.

An ecumenical strategy is one in which Christians from several churches and geographic areas in India unite in new congregations, such as the India Christian Fellowship or the National Association of Indian Christians. A common pattern is that families attend one of the established churches regularly, but attend a Christian gathering with immigrants from India once a month or on Sunday evenings, attempting to attain, as it were, the best of both worlds through dual membership. One attraction is the opportunity to discuss with other Christians the common immigrant experience of trying to maintain elements of Christian devotion and ethos from India while adjusting to a new culture and raising British, Canadian, or American children. Another attraction is the desire to join together in projects that will support evangelistic or other Christian activities and institutions in India.

Regional-linguistic representational strategies (ethnic) are closely related to language, because churches are often the only place outside the home where the native language of Malayalam, Gujarati, Hindi, Tamil, Telugu, or Kanada can be spoken and where many aspects of the accompanying identity can be enjoyed in cuisine, dress, leadership styles, and music. This is the most powerful strategy of adaptation for the first generation. The strategy is often combined with ecumenical and denominational strategies because here language is the unifying element that transcends denominational lines and because several churches in India are defined in part by regional-linguistic identity. Even where too few from any one region are present to sustain regular meetings or regional parishes, Keralites, Tamils, or North Indians gather for Christmas programs or other special events.

While it seems obvious that new religious groups would develop along *denominational* lines, reservations exist regarding the appropriateness of this term as a designation for new immigrant groups. The model is compelling because it is pervasive in both academic analyses and self-identification of North American Christian groups. Denominationalism may be an American Protestant creation, resulting from experiences of adaptation of earlier immigrants and subsequently, perhaps, superimposed on Christianity in India. Hence, denominational forms are immediately available, understood by people in the society, and supported by some governmental agencies, which understand and are comfortable with denominational affiliation. Networks of church affiliation and support are, along with families, primary manifestations of the new transnational Christian reality that establishes boundaries for

Christian immigrants and connects them with "brothers and sisters" in several countries.

Variables of Social Location

Adoption of a representational strategy or a combination of more than one depends on the individual's history and commitments, the dynamics of the immigrant group in a given location, and permissions and encouragements that are part of the ethos of immigrants' new residence, which vary considerably even within the same country. A number of variables of social location influence selection of adaptive strategies similar to the influence of environmentally directed effects in scientific models. Several variables influence both the selection of representational strategies and their viability: length of residence, population density, transition of generations, and majority/minority status. Each of these is affected significantly by size of country, changes in immigration law, and administrative decisions.

Changes in migration patterns that are both remarkably unforeseen when changes in immigration laws are made and then difficult to trace produce dramatic results. Few would have predicted, for example, that inclusion of nurses in certain immigration categories would lead to Syro-Malabar rite Catholic missions in North America. Availability of professional certification and advancement for immigrants and their children dictates Christian migration patterns. South Asian Christian migration to Britain occurred earlier than in North America, predominantly professionals who were educated in British universities. The Mar Thoma parishes claim a large number of physicians who were trained in Britain and "stayed on." They established themselves and their families prior to the formation of South Asian congregations or the arrival of priests, so they regularly joined Anglican parishes or other congregations. Remnants of colonial days, such as the Indian YMCA, provided some facilities for Christian immigrants. Fewer Christian nurses were part of the East African migration to Britain and Canada; hence, nurses constitute a smaller proportion of the Christian women in Britain than in North America. British Indian families have aged into the second and third generations further than in North America. Few Christians are migrating to Britain both because of the difficulty of gaining entrance and because the United States seems to be the preferred location in the transnational movement.

Christians constitute a small minority of immigrants to Canada from India. In the 1990 Canadian census, for example, there were only 395 Catholics and 1,155 Protestants identified, and 132,045 Eastern non-Christians (and among Punjabis, 130 in United Church, 110 Pentecostal, 60 Baptist, 35 Presbyterian, 130 Anglican, 190 Jehovah Witness, and 10 Eastern Orthodox).[2] Christian immigrants perceive themselves as occupying various levels of minority status in the West, and that affects relations with other Christian groups and with the larger society.

These strategies and variables led to a variety of congregations in urban areas like Toronto. A Pentecostal immigrant started the Indian Christian Assembly in the late 1960s and a Baptist founded a Chaplaincy to Asians in the early 1970s. By 1990 Keralites had established eleven main churches and two smaller groups in the Toronto metropolitan area: Mission of St. Thomas the Apostle (Catholic), St. Gregorious Orthodox Church, St. Thomas Orthodox Syrian Church, St. Mary's Syrian Church, St. George Orthodox Church, the Canadian Mar Thoma Church, Zion Gospel Assembly, the International Mukti Mission, Grace New Covenant Pentecostal Church, World Revival Prayer Fellowship, Full Assembly of God (Pentecostal), and the India Gospel Assembly of Brethren (John, 1990, 113–19).

Although the Indian Christian communities in Canada and the United States share the foundation of professionals admitted in the 1970s, many in the medical field, different patterns of immigration now occur. The United States allows for family reunification, so congregations grow both through natural means and the regular arrival of family members from India. Canada does not formally allow for family reunification, so the main provision allowing new Christian immigrants is the provision for people bringing wealth to invest. The number of new Christian immigrants is smaller in Canada than in the United States, with the result that Christian churches and congregations there are often joined in South Asian Christian dioceses and councils with those in the United States.

The Churches

A result of recent migrations is that one can now trace in the West the long history and many elements of the complex social, regional, and theological reality of Christians in India. Groups claim descent from missionary activity of the Apostle Thomas, a fourth century

Syrian entry, the Portuguese Latin orders, the Protestant missionaries (some of whom immigrants now visit in nursing homes in London, Toronto, or New York), and indigenous evangelical and Pentecostal revivalists. Among the groups represented in the West are the St. Thomas Christian groups—the Syrian Orthodox Church, the Knanaya Orthodox Diocese, the Malankara Orthodox Syrian Church, and the Mar Thoma Church, Catholics in three rites—Latin, Syro-malabar, and Syro-malankara; and several Protestant groups— Church of South India, Methodists, Brethren Assemblies (Plymouth Brethren), Pentecostals, Church of the Brethren, ecumenical, and language-based independent congregations. Three provide illustrations of the experience of Christian immigrants in the West.

Mar Thoma Church

Bishops of the Mar Thoma Church joined with those of the Church of South India in opposing the creation of congregations, parishes, and dioceses in the West. They reasoned that, because the Mar Thoma Church is in full communion with the Anglican Church, all pastoral services could be provided by Anglican bishops and parishes and that children in the second and third generation would be well served by Anglican parishes and priests. Bishops first urged that members join local parishes. They did not oppose special gatherings for festivals, such as Christmas, or continued loyalty to the Indian traditions and customs. Nevertheless, their ecumenical strategy was overwhelmed by the needs of the immigrants, by the attraction of language and ritual, and by the threat of "sheep stealers" who used these to attract immigrants.

Mar Thoma prayer groups were established, then congregations, followed by parishes and a diocese. Clerical assistance for these growing missions came from Mar Thoma priests studying in seminaries and graduate schools. They entered the United States as exchange scholars (on J-1 visas) along with their families (on J-2 visas) and resided in seminary housing. Many of these priests became extremely busy and overworked as they responded to the needs of these prayer groups and missions by flying around the country on weekends to provide for regular worship and pastoral assistance. The students came on official assignment by the synod for graduate training and returned to India at the completion of their studies, so a constant turnover and long periods without leadership characterized the 1970s.

The first official parish was recognized in New York in 1977 and those in Chicago and Houston the next year. An annual national youth conference began in 1980 and was followed by the first family conference in 1983. After a great deal of pleading and persuasion, leaders in Kerala approved the organization of a zonal council of Mar Thoma Churches that became the prototype for the diocese recognized in 1988.

The Mar Thoma Church in the West is the largest and most successful of those from the St. Thomas tradition. It has twenty-nine parishes and one congregation in the United States, six in Canada, and two in Britain. The relative strength and unity of the Mar Thoma Church in America results from the high quality of the priests sent to the West and from the pastoral rotation system of assigned priests. Mar Thoma priests accept ordination to the church as a whole and not to a single parish, and both in India and America they participate in a regular rotation system that assigns them to a new location about every three years. Hence, Mar Thoma priests, unlike other Protestant clergy from India, are not permanent residents in the West. Approximately a hundred Mar Thoma priests currently serve in India, having lived with their families for three years abroad.

The Mar Thoma Church in the United States has grown rapidly since the official recognition of a Zonal Council in 1982. By 1993 the diocese had 37 parishes and two congregations and identified over 3,000 families with 11,160 members—9,676 in the United States, 941 in Canada, and 543 in the UK. (See Table 1 in the endnote.)[3] Note that the relative size in the three countries may also be typical of other Christian groups, even though the other churches are smaller. Formal establishment of the new diocese in 1988 and the appointment of a resident bishop are responses to past growth, present strength, and future potential for growth. The Mar Thoma Pradhinidthi Mandalam appointed Zacharias Mar Theophilus as resident bishop of the Diocese of North America and the UK in October of 1993, and in 1994 he moved to the diocesan headquarters in Richboro, Pennsylvania.

Now that the church is on solid footing in North America, discussions revolve around how to become a witnessing and serving church. The question is asked, "How can the Mar Thoma Church and the immigrants make significant contributions to Western society?" Leaders urge congregations to change their focus from matters internal to the church, which have necessarily occupied their attention in years immediately following immigration, to the needs of society at large.

Malankara Orthodox Syrian Church

Thomas Mar Makarios is the founding metropolitan of the North American diocese of the Malankara church. He was a student at the Orthodox Seminary in Kottayam and received a World Council of Churches fellowship to study at Lincoln College in England in 1958–1959. He also studied for a summer in Geneva at the World Council of Churches. He enjoyed the benefits of scholarships that were readily available in the 1950s and early 1960s for priests and deacons to study in Britain or North America. As is the case with several who now serve in Western dioceses, he earned graduate degrees from Western theological schools: Nashota House and Union Theological Seminary (Virginia). While serving as metropolitan, he has taught part-time at Alma College in Michigan. When he resigned from his position in the early 1990s and returned briefly to India as secretary to the Catholicos, Mathews Mar Barnabas was sent from India to serve the church.

After Mar Barnabas had been in America for a few months in 1992–1993, the Catholicos and the synod decided that he should be officially designated as metropolitan of the diocese. They believed that because he is a very senior bishop and one known for his personal piety and humility, he would attract the allegiance of both priests and congregations. The return of Mar Makarios to reside in Buffalo, New York, precipitated tension. In an attempt to bring harmony, the Catholicos first appointed Mar Makarios as metropolitan of Canada and Europe (a position of relatively little significance because relatively few members are there) and Mar Barnabas as metropolitan of the United States. When that did not reduce tension, the Catholicos decided that administration should be in the hands of Mar Barnabas, but Mar Makarios should be designated "Senior Metropolitan" of the North American Diocese and continue as metropolitan of Britain and Europe. The result is that two metropolitans stand poles apart as symbols of potentials in the future of the church of becoming too American or too Indian. One future involves a strategy of rapid westernization of the liturgical, administrative, and social aspects of the church's life. The other attempts to maintain close ecclesial and theological relations with the mother church in Kerala.

A distinct contrast with the Mar Thoma Church is that priests and deacons of the Malankara Orthodox Church are permanent residents, and almost all of them have secular employment and serve the congregations only part-time. Fifty-three priests and thirteen deacons are in the United States diocese and three are in Canada. A few travel across boarders to serve small congregations or prayer groups, including the two or three small groups in Britain. The priests immigrated on their own as professionals, as spouses of nurses, or for family reunification. Hence, the Catholicos and synod in Kerala have little authority over them. The parishes are generally small and divide often, in part because so many priests are available to attract the allegiance of disgruntled members who form new congregations. While preserving the Orthodox rituals and Malayalam, now almost a sacred language, parishes and congregations lack a unified vision of their role in the West.

Pentecostal Churches

The largest annual South Asian Christian conference in North America is held cooperatively by several Pentecostal Churches—the Indian Pentecostal Church (IPC); the Church of God of Cleveland, Tennessee; the Assemblies of God; and independent congregations. More than 3,500 Pentecostals from some 175 Malayalee Pentecostal churches gathered in Chicago over the Fourth of July weekend in 1994 for the twelfth Malayalee Pentecostal Conference of North America. Initiatives to establish a national council of Indian Pentecostals have not yet been successful, but the annual conference continues as a witness to their common origins in India and to their previous cooperation in founding churches in North America. They claim that no doctrinal differences separate the Keralite Pentecostal churches, only organizational differences (with the exception of the Ceylon Pentecostal Mission). Hence, the first Keralite immigrants formed Pentecostal churches in the major cities that served people from the various group, and the annual conference grew out of that cooperation.

As the number of Keralite Pentecostals increases in urban areas, the congregations divide and reconstitute themselves, resulting in many relatively small congregations. Several leaders estimate that New York has over fifty Keralite Pentecostal churches, but no one knows how many. A factor contributing to divisiveness is that a larger number of pastors live in the United States than there are congregations. Fewer South Asian Pentecostals are in Britain than in North America. A wide range of preparation for ministry is found among the pastors. Some were certified pastors in India; others were "called" to the ministry after immigration. Some have graduate seminary degrees; others have only apprenticeship training or a few courses in Bible colleges. A few are full-time pastors; most work at secular jobs as well. All feel that they are called to ministry and have the charismatic authorization.

The IPC has the largest number of Indo-Christian churches in both India (over 2,000) and in the United States (approximately 55, with 60 to 75 pastors), and these relatively large churches exercise the greatest influence on the annual conferences. The Assemblies of God of Springfield, Missouri, have approximately 20 South Asian congregations and 40 pastors in North America. The pastors enjoy options of maintaining their ordination in Kerala or transferring their ordination to a state district of the Assemblies of God, so organizational affiliation is diffuse. A few were ordained by American churches before immigrants established their congregations and procedures for ordination. The Church of God of Cleveland, Tennessee, recognizes 22 Keralite congregations and approximately 32 pastors. The Church of God of Anderson, Indiana, has mission work in South India from which a few individuals immigrate, but no separate churches exist in the West. Many independent Pentecostal congregations attract members from various groups and exhibit elements of the sectarian affiliation of the pastor or of the majority of members. No one knows the exact number of South Asian Pentecostal churches in Britain and North America.

Major Issues

Experiences of recent immigrants in wrestling with the potentials and problems in contemporary society—for example, underemployment, marital disputes, disrespectful children—are similar to those in the society at large, but immigrants tend to interpret them as peculiar to their immigrant status. The experience is different for contemporary immigrants, in part because of rapid mobility and communication that creates new transnational dynamics. Moreover, both the diverse racial, ethnic, and religious character of the migrants and the ethos of the settled societies that they enter are very different from those of earlier generations. Christian immigrants from India occupy an interesting liminal status in this situation, being in each of the three countries both like and unlike the nominal Christian majority. Hence, some common issues arise but with different aspects for new immigrants from India, for Christians, and for those in the three Western contexts.

Assimilation to What? and How? or Whether?

Christians from India leave one form of minority status, facing the necessity to establish new relationships with the rest of society. The movement is complex because, although Christians are a small minority in South Asia, some of these immigrants come from areas like central Kerala where the Christian ethos is strong, if not dominant. New immigrants often visualize Western countries as "cities set on a hill" where the Christian ethos will be dominant, and are greatly disappointed and troubled. One suspects that the formation of Indian Christian churches and organizations arise out of that disappointment. When they look for Christian groups to which to relate, they find different constellations in Britain, Canada, and the United States. The stage of secularism and disestablishment of Christianity (in a *de facto* sense rather than *de jure)* is different in the three contexts. In general, the South Asian Christian community in Britain is older both in age and length of residence than in North America. New immigrants will assimilate to some social group—settled Christian communities, secular society, perhaps an ethnic group. The absence of Christian activity implies a form of assimilation via other activities and commitments. The relative size of the South Asian Christian community and its dispersed character make it unlikely that a distinctly South Asian Christianity will develop in Britain or Canada. The few congregations and occasional fellowship meetings of denominational or language-based groups, which now welcome very few new immigrants, will not sustain Western forms of Indian Christianity. Those in Britain and Canada are appendages to the larger and growing community in the United States. As long as new immigrants are admitted, a form of South Asian Christianity will develop and, perhaps, contribute to the developing colorful melange of new American Christianity.

Transmission of Tradition and Translation of Ritual and the Word

A young man who came from India with his parents as a small child is no longer able to converse in an Indian language, but he stands watching a videotape of himself at five years of age speaking to his parents in a language he has now forgotten. Such amnesia is at the heart of the process of forgetting and remembering that is the transmission and reformulation of tradition in immigrant communities. Yet the continuity and discontinuity between the past and the present provides the fragile basis on which people project and attempt to weave a future.

Three modes of communication of cultural messages are through written and oral language, the communicative aspects of customary behavior in gesture or ritual or gesture, and the modification of material culture into symbols. Word and ritual are two dominant elements of Christian tradition, and religious groups distinguish themselves by giving priority to one or the other. Some believe that the communication through verbal and written discourse is most effective, and therefore emphasize the Word of God, a preaching ministry, the Sunday School, and study groups. Others emphasize ritual, the symbolism of ancient liturgy in movement, color, and sound. Certainly, all South Asian Christian groups employ both modes of transmission, but the various groups can be placed on a scale based on relative emphasis placed on each mode.

Older immigrants remember when the change took place in the verbal language of the liturgy from Syriac or Latin to the Indian languages, and some South Asian services still preserve snatches of Syriac as the sacred language of Jesus. Parents can remember worshiping in a liturgy that was considered a sacred language and recognize that their children face a situation where Malayalam, Tamil, or Telugu are becoming sacred languages. The difference is, however, that in the earlier situation the distinction was between the priests who understood the meaning of the sacred language and the laity who did not, but now the distinction is between the parents who understand and the children who do not. Parents remember not understanding the Syriac, but nevertheless growing to love the liturgy, and hope that their children will come to love the services in Indian languages that they only partially understand. Some churches conduct all their meetings in Indian languages, while others make a distinction between liturgical speech (usually in an Indian language) and nonliturgical speech (often in English). Differences between Indian English and that spoken in the three countries create difficulty in finding or translating teaching materials for the children. Those prepared in India seem stilted, but those prepared in the West seem not to catch the essence of Indian Christianity and different English usage between Britain, Canada, and the United States is evident.

The beauty and power of the ritual do prove effective for some people even though they may not be able to explain details of interpretation; for example, the censer as the womb of Mary, the fire inside symbolic of Jesus, and the chains representing the Holy Trinity. Some leaders and parents argue that it is not necessary for people to be fluent in either the verbal language or symbolism of liturgy in order for ritual to be efficacious. The parents expect priests from India to perform the liturgy well, evoking the same beauty and power that they experienced while growing up in India, but they hope that the priests or others will also be able to interpret the meaning to the young people so that children will share their allegiance to the ancient rites. Part of the attraction of the charismatic movement is the revaluation of both language and gesture in Pentecostal meetings. Ecstatic speaking in tongues involves both a deconstruction of speech and its elevation to a level removed from domination by either Indian or Western syntax. Stylized Pentecostal gestures are themselves a ritualized deconstruction of rituals.

Save the Children

Periods of immigration empower religion as providing a transcendent basis for personal and group identity. Selection of representational strategies depending on the variables mentioned above depends on the parents' judgment of which of those available will best help them transmit both Christian faith and devotion and ethnic identity to their children. A few urban areas in Britain and Canada attract a sufficient number of South Asian Christians to support strong ethnic or denominational churches. Others widely scattered rely on occasional gatherings for religious festivals, such as Christmas, or visits of bishops or preachers from India to transmit a "taste of Indian Christianity." Otherwise, they rely on the already existing churches and organizations for support in the Christian training of their children. The South Asian Christian community in the United States is growing through both natural means and continued immigration. That is the reason that numerous parishes and congregations develop and that infrastructures of dioceses, councils, denominations—indeed, American forms of South Asian Christianity—are developing in the United States and through transnational networks are influencing Christianity in other Western countries.

Family and Friendship

Tensions between the generations flow from different rubrics of social interaction dominant in India and the West, and these tensions affect most immigrants and their religious organizations. First-generation immigrants carry in their minds a social network and modes of relationships formed by the primacy of family; second and third generations are shaped by Western individualism, which is, in effect, a transfer from the social rubric of family to that of friendship. Note the irony in the statement almost ubiquitous, at least in the United States, "My husband/wife is my best friend." How does a South Asian deal with this confusion of categories and the implied preference for friendship?

The flash points are dating and marriage. Dating is regarded by the young people as primarily a matter of friendship, but by the parents as primarily a threat to family. Negotiations of these dangerous shoals are intense, and gatherings of South Asian Christians are primary contexts outside the home where families can discuss the issues and obtain assistance. South Asian Christians in North America have just reached the age when marriages of the second generation are taking place, so it is too soon to know what shape the marriages will take. The models are traditional arranged marriage, semi-arranged marriage, and love marriage. An aspect of the transnational character of the new immigrants is that the marriage network now stretches across several countries and continents. Boundaries of Christian and ethnic groups are both formed and tested in the process of marriage.

Leadership

It is difficult to generalize about Christian leadership in the West—because the roles and training of Christian religious leaders are so diverse—except to say that Christians are the only immigrants from South Asia who brought their religious leaders with them in the early days of immigration. Why? (1) A significant number are spouses of nurses; (2) they possessed good skills in English, having lived, studied, and worshiped in contexts where English was common; (3) scholarships brought a number of Christian leaders to study in the West, so they either "stayed on" or returned to familiar settings; and (4) Britain, Canada, and the United States are attractive destinations for many migrants, but especially so for Christian leaders. Most, however, gained their primary religious socialization in India and approach Western congregations with strong role identities, behavior patterns, and expectations. Some of the skills and behavior patterns that are effective in India do not translate so well, particularly in dealing with youth socialized in the West. Parents want a little bit of India; youth want a priest who can understand them and speak to their situation in their own terms.

Very few young people from immigrant families are in training for the ministry, no theological school in the West is designated for any South Asian church, and no theological school is prepared to attend to South Asian Christianity and its needs. It is still unclear what form of training is appropriate for a minister in the new transnational context. Seminary education in India would be difficult and might not prepare the student for return home. Education in the West would not prepare the student for ministry in India, and it might alienate the student from the Indian Christian tradition. An interesting exception here are Roman Catholic priests, who, as part of a self-conscious transnational church, seem able to move from country to country with greater ease. Bishops have sent a few priests from the Syro-Malabar and the Syro-Malankara rites to minister to immigrants. Because south India, especially Kerala, is the source of a large number of vocations, many have come to serve in settled Latin rite parishes. Calling and training religious specialists for the new transnational churches remain a great challenge.

Relations with Churches in India

Structures developed to administer congregations in a small area or region of India are expanding, sometimes enduring great stress, to reach around the world. Disciplines developed to lead farmers in villages of Kerala toward Christian maturity are made available to (or imposed on, depending on one's perspective) young professionals and second-generation children in Houston, London, and Toronto. Symbols shaped by centuries of use in India are truncated and reinterpreted to be meaningful throughout a transnational church. It is increasingly necessary to develop a genuinely comparative perspective in the study of South Asian Christianity, one that will take account of both the diverse contexts of the churches in India, the Gulf, and North America and the new complex relationships that these churches establish between East and West.

The presence of Christians from India in the United States is part of a new pattern of relationship between Asian Christianity and North American Christianity within a new transnational Christianity that is exemplified also among immigrants from Korea, China and Taiwan, and Southeast Asia. The older colonial pattern involving Western missionaries going to evangelize South Asians is now less viable, both because of the weakening and redirection of energies of most American mainline churches and because of Indian governmental restrictions on granting visas to missionaries. Christian immigrants to North America generally hold positive views of missionaries and their accomplishments, coming as they do from segments of South Asian society less influenced by liberation theology, even while recognizing that the Indian church can no longer rely on Western missionaries. A second pattern of relationship developed in the second half of the twentieth century in relationships between British and American denominations and their "partner churches" in South Asia, especially through denominational world mission boards. The communication and assistance moves between West and East at the level of ecclesiastical bureaucrats and institutions, with little contact between congregations or individuals. A third pattern is aborning, a new relationship established by immigrants in several countries with the congregations and ecclesiastical structures back home.

Underneath the church bureaucracies that help keep international lines of communication open, there are developing between Christian immigrants and their Christian "brothers and sisters" networks that are as yet largely unnoticed or unappreciated by those involved in missions or ecumenical affairs. The relationship becomes much more complex, as must the structures developing out of the relationship, a complexity more congruent with the new transnational character of the churches. It seems likely that the networks established by immigrants will be the most important for sustaining relationships between North American churches and South Asian Christians—and with Christians in other parts of Asia as well. At present, however, the lines are crossed and mixed messages are being sent and received because the patterns established in earlier decades remain and have not been transformed or replaced by new patterns of transnational Christian relations. That transformation remains an important task for the churches as they prepare for a new century.

Conclusion

Both ecclesiastical reflection and academic study must now take account of the transnational aspect of religious groups. Both the practice and the study of religion, and especially Christianity, developed methods and agencies reflecting migration and ecumenical character of religious groups, but the experience and study of old immigrants did not reveal the same transnational character of religion experienced by the new immigrants. The situation calls for new studies of the lived reality and social fields of Christian immigrants and of the vitality of their relationships within and between several societies, and it demands a new conceptualization of ecclesiology that will take into account new forms of church interactions.

The challenge to religious groups in North America and Britain, in common with other social groups, is to create and maintain boundaries within which individuals can fabricate their identities and preserve continuities with the past. These can become either workshops or prisons. Can religion provide materials, perhaps newly conceived and worked, with which groups can build porous boundaries, ones strong enough to sustain personal and group identity but sufficiently permeable to allow easy, natural, nonthreatening movement among groups that will cause cooperation and goodwill to abound?

————— NOTES —————

1. At issue in the case of a nurse trained in the Philippines was whether "Registered Professional Nurses" included in the professional category those without a baccalaureate degree. The ruling was: "On the basis of these considerations it is concluded that a nurse may be considered as a member of the professions if she has been awarded a diploma or certificate signifying successful completion of a program for professional nurses conducted by an accredited hospital or independent school, or has attained a baccalaureate degree or an associate degree in nursing, as described in the Occupational Outlook Handbook" (Administrative decisions under immigration and nationality laws, XII:420). This opened the door for nurses from India who were trained in approved mission or government hospitals.

2. Statistics Canada. *Religions in Canada*. Ottawa: Industry, Science and Technology Canada, 1993. 1991 Census of Canada. Table 7 in Population by Selected Religions and Sex, showing Mother Tongue, p. 220. The fact that only Punjabi is singled out from among the languages of India is a significant indicator of the difference in migration patterns affecting distribution of religion. Gujaratis and Keralites are prominent in United States immigration.

3. **Table 1.** Mar Thoma Christians in the West in 1993

AREA	# OF FAMILIES	# OF PARENTS	# OF CHILDREN	TOTAL
U.S.	2,591	5,058	4,618	9,676
Canada	248	507	434	941
UK	162	303	240	543
Total	3,001	5,868	5,292	11,160

Adapted from *Mar Thoma Messenger* 1993, XII.

———————————— **BIBLIOGRAPHY** ————————————

Firth, C. B. (1960). *An Introduction to Indian Church History*. Bangalore: Christian Literature Society.

John, George M. (1990). "The Kerala Christian Community in Metropolitan Toronto." *Polyphony* XII:113–119.

Kelly, Elinor. (1990). "Transcontinental Families—Gujarat and Lancashire: A Comparative Study of Social Policy." In *South Asians Overseas: Migration and Ethnicity*, eds. Colin Clarke, Ceri Peach, and Steven Vertovec, pp. 251–67. Cambridge: Cambridge University Press.

"Matter of Gutierrez in Visa Petition Proceedings A-17653997, 5 July 1967. In *Administrative Decisions under Immigration and Nationality Laws of the United States*, XII, 418ff.

Schiller, Nina Glick, Linda Basch, and Christina Blanc-Szanton (eds.) (1992). *Towards a Transnational Perspective on Migration: Race, Class, Ethnicity, and Nationalism Reconsidered*. Annals of the New York Academy of Sciences, 645. The New York Academy of Sciences.

Statistics Canada. "Religions in Canada." *Ottawa: Industry, Science and Technology Canada, 1993*. 1991 Census of Canada. Table 7 in "Population by Selected Religions and Sex, Showing Mother Tongue," p. 220.

2

The Zoroastrian Diaspora in Britain, Canada, and the United States

John R. Hinnells

This chapter will consider the situation of Zoroastrian communities in the three countries including education issues, links with the old countries, then at the patterns of religious thought and practice of Western Zoroastrians, their strategies of adaptation, and perceptions of public policy. Although there is no separate piece on the place of women, their role in the various communities is discussed under a number of headings. But first a word is necessary on theoretical issues.

Some Methodological Comments

This chapter is based on fieldwork in all three countries, in Britain mostly in London; in Canada mostly in Toronto and Vancouver; in the United States mostly in Los Angeles, Chicago, New York, and Houston. In each center, I studied the records such as minutes of committees, newsletters, and so on. A survey questionnaire was circulated in 1986 that yielded 483 responses in Britain, 325 in Canada, and 589 from the United States. This represented approximately one-quarter of formal members of Zoroastrians in these countries. In Britain 240 structured in-depth interviews were undertaken.[1] There is much methodological debate over the relative merits of quantitative versus qualitative data collection, historical research versus anthropological fieldwork. This research attempted to use all of these methods to obtain a rounded picture of diaspora Zoroastrians.[2] No scholar is free of bias, and it is important to articulate mine. Apart from California where the Iranian community was especially helpful, my sample is weighted toward the Parsis. Most of my earlier research was with the Indian community where I am better known. Further, Iranian Zoroastrians and Parsis in several American centers were in dispute in the 1980s, so questionnaires distributed through the centers were responded to mostly by Parsis. In a volume on South Asians this weighting is not as significant as it would be if the work was on the total Zoroastrian community. Within Parsi communities my main contacts tend to be with people of my generation (i.e., the over 50s), though many younger Zoroastrians are also friends. Through my Bombay contacts I tend to be linked with the orthodox sections of the community, though again I have many "liberal" Zoroastrian friends. It has been a conscious life-long decision to avoid involvement in Parsi religious disputes, despite requests to comment on religious controversies. I share in the current anthropological agonizing over the influence of outside scholars on the groups we study (see Luhrman 1996: Ch. 7).

A Brief Historical Introduction

A group of Zoroastrians sailed from their Iranian homeland to escape fierce Muslim persecution and settled in India in the tenth century. They remained mostly in Gujarat in security and insignificance until the arrival of European traders (Boyce 1979). From the seventeenth century they migrated first to Bombay and thence around the world as traders. In the eighteenth century they went to China, then in the nineteenth century to Sind, Britain, and East Africa. The majority of British Zoroastrians arrived with other South Asian migrants in the 1960s. A number came from East Africa and Pakistan, but most came from Bombay. Also in the 1960s and 1970s Indian and Pakistani Parsis migrated to America as part of the South Asian migration to the New World (Hinnells 1994b). The earliest Associations were founded in 1964–1965 in Toronto, Vancouver, Chicago, New York, and California. From the late 1970s some Zoroastrians left Iran with the rise of the Islamic Republic. A few settled in Britain, most moved to Vancouver, New York, and California (Writer 1994). At the end of the millennium there are approximately 5,000 Zoroastrians in Britain (mostly near London), approximately 4,500 in Canada (mostly in Toronto), and 6,500 in the United States (about 2,000 in California, but Houston is probably the fastest growing U.S. community).

There are two main formal bodies in Britain. The Zoroastrian Trust Funds of Europe (ZTFE), founded in London in 1861, is the oldest of Britain's Asian communities. The other main British based organization is the World Zoroastrian Organization (WZO), formed in 1980, which has mainly educational and charitable concerns. It is in dispute with ZTFE, mainly due to personality clashes. But there are religious differences. The latter is more liberal (e.g., concerning the participation of non-Zoroastrian spouses), whereas the former is more heavily influenced by the typically traditional East African Parsis (Hinnells 1996a). There is an umbrella organization for both Canada and the United States, the Federation of Zoroastrian Associations of North America (FEZANA) which, in collaboration with four local associations in Canada[3] and seventeen associations in the United States,[4] organizes congresses, youth activities, religious education ventures, and publishes a widely read journal. There are two Zoroastrian buildings in Canada (Toronto and Vancouver), and four in the United States (Chicago, New York, and two in California).

The Current Situation

The demographic profiles in the three countries are different. Generally the numbers of male/female members are roughly equal, though there are more males in the scattered groups in each country. The families usually stay in the larger centers, presumably to help their young meet coreligionists. The Canadian and especially the U.S. communities are typically younger than the British communities, with 14 percent of London Zoroastrians over the age of 65, compared with 1 percent in Chicago and the scattered American groups, and generally under 6 percent throughout the continent.

The different age profile is due to the longer history of the British community. As there are so few elders in the West, the birth rate exceeds the death rate. Most Western Zoroastrians are married. The number of single persons is generally under 20 percent. Few respondents in any country had three or more children, most had only one or two, but on average only one in five families had no children.

Zoroastrians in any country have always taken advantage of educational and professional opportunities presented to them. In Iran they were denied such rights until the twentieth century, but under the Pahlavi dynasty they were significant achievers in business, education, and the professions. In India, they are highly educated. Most details are available for the Bombay community. There, the Parsis have a literacy rate of approximately 98 percent; approximately 25 percent of males and only slightly less of females go to university and consequently achieve high social status (Karkal 1984). It has been the educated professionals who have migrated westward, notably doctors, lawyers, engineers, and in the United States a high number of scientists. They are justly proud of their achievers. Three Parsis have been elected as Members of the British Parliament, the first, Dadabhoy Naoroji, as early as 1892; they have provided famous musicians (Zubin Mehta and Freddy Mercury); novelists (Rohinton Mistry has had two novels short-listed for the prestigious Booker prize, in 1991 and 1995); and Parsis have held high diplomatic office. The first Indian High Commissioner in London was a Parsi, as are Palkiwalla the former Indian ambassador in the United States, and Marker the Pakistan ambassador in Washington and then at the United Nations.

The educational levels of the British Zoroastrians is remarkable: 68 percent had a university or college education and 24 percent have proceeded to postgraduate study. The figures for Canada are even higher, 72 percent and 23 percent respectively, and still higher in the United States where approximately 90 percent have been to University and in some places some 50 percent have undertaken postgraduate study. In Britain and Canada the majority are arts graduates, in the United States they are predominantly scientists. The career consequences are that between a third and half of Western Zoroastrians are in executive-class employment. The employment figures vary not only between countries, but between cities. New York (52%), the scattered American groups, and Chicago have the highest, London (29%) and the scattered British groups (18%) the lowest proportion of executives.

So the United States has the youngest, the mostly highly educated, and the most scientifically inclined Zoroastrian population. In Canada, the Zoroastrian population is younger and better educated than the British community, but the latter two countries have attracted arts rather than science graduates. There are also some ethnic variations: Iranian Zoroastrians are more numerous in the United States and Canada than in Britain. The East African Parsis are found mostly in Britain, a few in Canada, but very few in the United States.

My research suggests that those who practice the religion less tend to be the young, highly educated, scientists, single, and out-married Zoroastrians, in comparison with those who finished their education at the school level, especially where that schooling was in the old country, the arts graduates, the recently migrated and the in-married, above all those who had children (Hinnells 1994a, 1996a and 1996b). Given these different demographic patterns between the three countries, one would expect to find different religious patterns among Zoroastrians in the three countries.

Informants from the first generation commonly assert that they practice their religion more after they migrated than they had before, because it represented a bond with their heritage. The survey evidence is, in broad terms, that two-thirds of respondents kept in regular contact with Zoroastrians overseas (the figure is naturally lower for those born in the West) and with Zoroastrians in the same country. A similar proportion of Parsis said that they prayed daily and wore the sacred shirt and cord, *sudre* and *kusti* (these are less commonly worn in Iran). Obviously Zoroastrians in scattered groups met coreligionists less frequently; but more Zoroastrians in Canada and the United States tended to keep in contact with fellow Zoroastrians than do British Zoroastrians. The explanation, I suspect, is that they are more recent migrants and the ties are closer. But that is not the sole explanation. More U.S. and Canadian Zoroastrians said that they read Zoroastrian literature regularly than British respondents did (50% in Canada, California 56%, and scattered U.S. groups 45%, compared with 25% in Britain). This may be due to the high level of education characteristic of American Zoroastrians. But that is unlikely to be the major reason because the educational level of British Zoroastrians is also high. It may be that more American groups produce good newsletters. But this raises the question, Why have American Zoroastrians done this? The question will recur in the section on the Perception of Public Policy below.

Intermarriage is a subject of intense debate among Zoroastrians (Kharas 1993). When this research was undertaken, there were more intermarrieds among the scattered groups in each country (roughly one in four marriages were out-marriages), but otherwise only London (16%), Chicago (17%), and New York (13%) had over 10% of their people married out. However, anecdotal evidence suggests that recently the rate of out-marriage has increased, especially in the United States, and particularly in the scattered groups where young Zoroastrians rarely meet coreligionists who may be potential spouses. Attitudes to intermarriage vary between and within countries. It is strongly opposed in Britain (33% of respondents objected strongly). In California an even higher proportion objected (46%), a proportion almost certainly explained by the number of Iranian Zoroastrians there who are especially keen to preserve their identity. In Houston 42 percent similarly objected. That is a center which often emerged in the survey as being traditional (Hinnells 1988). By contrast fewer objected to intermarriage in the scattered groups, in which ever country they lived, presumably they accepted the high probability of such out-marriages in their circumstances. But also in Chicago and New York fewer than 20 percent expressed objections. It is presumably no coincidence that it is these two cities that have the highest proportions of the very well educated; for Hinnells 1994a and Kharas 1993 both found incidence, and approval, of intermarriage most common in this group.

The issue of conversion is related to that of intermarriage. Although some Iranians accept the possibility of conversion, very few Parsis do. There has only been one public initiation of a person who was not of Zoroastrian descent, Joseph Peterson in New York in 1983, which was highly controversial. The typical Indian Parsi arguments regarding conversion are: (1) it is psychologically damaging to change the religion into which you were born; (2) some argue we are born into the religion God considers appropriate for our development in the sequence of rebirth, and it is therefore wrong to change it; (3) as salvation is achievable through all religions, conversion is unnecessary; and (4) conversion is often linked to missionary endeavors and these have caused more persecution and death than any other force in human history. There is little doubt that ideas of caste have also influenced Parsi thinking. The problem has arisen in the diaspora concerning the acceptance into the religion of non-Zoroastrian spouses and their offspring. Although this is not allowed in India, and extremely rare in Britain (though WZO membership is open to them), in Canada and the United

States increasingly these family members, especially the children, are being quietly admitted to the community, mainly because of the fear of losing members, but also some have argued that to refuse initiation contravenes the American constitution on the freedom of religion (see further Hinnells 1987).

In terms of religious beliefs, generally two-thirds of respondents affirmed belief in an afterlife. The percentage variations were too small to draw major conclusions, other than there was a generally higher affirmation of the belief in Canada (68%) than among New York's highly educated professionals (58%). More distinctive patterns emerged with regard to rebirth (a belief many Indian Parsis have absorbed), which was strongest in Canada, notably Toronto (51%), and least among the educated groups in Chicago, New York (26%), and in California, for whose Iranian members this is not part of the heritage. Crucial practices for Zoroastrians in the old countries are the ceremonies and prayers for the dead. These are most commonly considered essential in London (43%), Houston (38%), and Canada (36%), and less commonly seen as important in Chicago and New York (18% and 24% respectively). In short, the centers with the highest concentration of highly educated scientists tend to be more liberal, and fewer of them assert the importance of traditional practices. London and Houston commonly appear as more traditional centers of Zoroastrianism, as do Canadian centers, notably Toronto. The Californian groups are different because of the numbers of Iranian Zoroastrians there. But the level of religious commitment (though not necessarily of religious knowledge in terms of history and theology) is generally high.

Worship and Religious Practice

If the level of religious practice is high, what is the nature of that practice? How does it relate to practices in the old country? For these questions the survey material is not especially helpful. The following account is based partly on records (e.g., the minutes of priestly gatherings and of panels at conferences on religious practice), but mostly on discussions with countless Zoroastrians in the centers named.

For the religion to be a link to the old country, and express individual and communal identity, there has to be a substantial degree of continuity. The fundamental value system impresses me as preserving the old traditions: the importance of the family; the priority given to charitable giving; the emphasis on individual responsibility; the distinctive sense of humor; the love of food, and so on. Much religious practice preserves the tradition: the daily prayers; the use of the sacred language of Avestan in worship; the reverence for fire; the concern for purity; the prayers for the dead; and the observance of major festivals.

Yet change is also inevitable. The absence of a consecrated pure temple in the three countries means that the higher, or inner, liturgies cannot be performed. Nor is there a permanently burning fire before which devotions may be offered. In each Zoroastrian building there is a separate prayer room. Although these are not fully consecrated as a temple would be, something of the temple ritual is translated for use in these prayer rooms, which in one sense function as temporary temples.

For Parsis the first question is Who may enter? Because of the strict purity laws, non-Zoroastrians cannot enter fire temples in India. Iranian Zoroastrians do not restrict entry and this has caused friction in the West. But the problem is more complex. Debate focuses particularly on allowing non-Zoroastrian spouses and their children to enter the prayer room when they have not been initiated. On the one hand they are necessarily impure as non-Zoroastrians, because they do not observe the purity laws or say the preparatory *sudre/kusti* prayers. For traditional Parsis, the sacred fire radiates holy power, and non-Zoroastrians are considered vulnerable because they do not have the spiritual protection of the prayerfully donned *sudre* and *kusti*. In London, when a non-Zoroastrian was invited to a *jashan* (a ceremony discussed below), and given a place of honor at the front, there was consternation, both about defiling the fire and the risk to the guest. Guidance was sought from one of the orthodox Bombay High Priests. His advice was that a person could attend the ceremony when it was not in a temple, providing they kept a distance from the fire.

Other Zoroastrians, however, think it is important that spouses and children of intermarried Zoroastrians should be welcomed into the prayer rooms so that the next generation will remain in the religion. Such Zoroastrians also tend to believe it is important that other non-Zoroastrians, notably those involved in interfaith activities or academics, may enter the prayer rooms in order to increase sympathy for Zoroastrians.

The balance between these opposing views again varies between and within countries. Broadly speaking, the British Zoroastrians are more inclined to the traditional point of view, partly because of the influence of the East African Zoroastrians, but also because of the higher proportion of older people in Britain. In general terms, U.S. Zoroastrians are more inclined to the "liberal" position, perhaps because of their level of Western education. But this is too simple a picture of the United States, because the Chicago community is more liberal (for demographic reasons, and because of the influence of their leading priest) than the group in Houston (Hinnells 1988). The latter do not have a building or prayer room, but they are more traditional in their attitude to non-Zoroastrians in domestic ceremonies where the sacred fire burns. In Los Angeles, where the building was funded and run by Iranian Zoroastrians, non-Zoroastrians are welcomed as they are in Chicago. In Toronto and Vancouver non-Zoroastrians are admitted. There are also differences between generations. The survey figures indicate that generally it was the westernized, innovative individuals who migrated in the 1960s, who have had a long time to settle, who are most inclined to allow non-Zoroastrians to enter the prayer room. The more recent arrivals, still close to the old traditions, although they are younger and may be expected to be more liberal, are often stricter on this issue. But it is not simply a question of age. A higher proportion of young people born in the West compared to the 1960s settlers want to keep the prayer rooms for Zoroastrians only. As one teenage Zoroastrian girl in Toronto put it to me in conversation: "Every day I am in a multicultural environment. I want one place where I can go and be myself."

There is, however, one time in the year, *muktad* (or *Farvardigan* as Iranians know it), when the *fravashis* (heavenly selves) of the dead are invoked and few Zoroastrian groups welcome non-Zoroastrians. Anything associated with death, the presence and victory of evil, is a time when purity laws are crucial. This has caused problems when traditional priests have asked non-Zoroastrian spouses to leave the room during the recital of prayers. This caused a deep division in London when the English wife of a deceased leading Parsi was asked to leave, although she had been welcomed by the previous leadership. The difficulties of preserving purity in an impure environment, in a country lacking the properly demarcated sacred space, pose both practical, theological, and personal problems.

Questions of sacred space and community boundaries arise in connection with funeral grounds. The primary motivation in founding the London Association was to acquire a funeral ground, and this has been important in other groups also, for example, Vancouver. Death poses special problems for traditional Parsis. They were brought up to believe that as the earth, fire, and water are sacred and that burial, cremation, and disposal at sea involve the pollution of the holy. In India, and previously in Iran, the religious funeral has taken the form of the exposure of the corpse in *daxmas*, or Towers of Silence, to be consumed by vultures, with the bones bleached by the sun then disposed of in a pit at the center of the *daxma*. No such Tower exists outside the Indian subcontinent— their use was discontinued in Iran in the 1960s at the wish of the Shah. Small Indian communities that cannot maintain a *daxma* sometimes use stone coffins to prevent pollution of the earth. Neither of these options is available in the West. Some Western Parsis have their bodies flown to India for a *daxma* funeral, but that is costly and difficult to arrange speedily. The common practice is to cremate the body and, where possible, inter the ashes in a Zoroastrian cemetery. Inevitably such a practice is rationalized, and many argue that unlike ancient practices, modern crematoria do not involve polluting a flame, because the body is consumed by intense heat generated by electricity. The largest and oldest Zoroastrian funeral ground in the West is near London. It has been laid out to resemble, as far as the climate allows, a Persian garden, the symbol of paradise, and has at its center a replica of a monument from ancient Persia. There is, in other words, an attempt to define the space by traditional markers. Some of the grave architecture seeks to evoke Zoroastrian traditions with representations of a fire altar on the headstone and images of liturgical objects.

Death ceremonies present further problems. There are important ceremonies to be offered for the deceased, especially in the first three days when, according to tradition, the soul faces its judgment. These require a fully consecrated temple and a permanently burning ritual fire. Such rites cannot be practiced in the West, though meeting to pray for the deceased is not uncommon. The families therefore pay for these ceremonies to be performed on their behalf in India. Having lived with Zoroastrians at a time of bereavement, my impression is that grief is compounded by guilt because the mourners are unable to do what they have been conditioned from infancy to believe is the "right" thing for the deceased. Whether such guilt is reasonable is not the point. Bereavement is a time not of reason but of emotion. Zoroastrians who live near a Zoroastrian cemetery can perform some of the rites at the funeral ground (the London one, for example, has a special building for prayers), but for American Zoroastrians lacking such facilities the difficulties are acute. The time allocated at crematoria is so short, and the facilities at funeral parlors so limited, that the prayers which should be offered at the committal cannot be said. They may be said at home, but that distances the bereaved from their tradition because some of the prayers should be said close to the funeral site.

The absence of a temple is not the only factor for change in diaspora Zoroastrian worship. Some of the rites are easily preserved. Because the religion originated among nomads, many practices can be continued without buildings. For Parsis the most important rites are the *sudre/kusti* prayers, traditionally said five times each day. Even if not said so often, they are said regularly by many, as the Survey figures quoted above show. They take about five minutes and remind Zoroastrians of their duty to commit themselves to good and to fight evil. A number of devout Zoroastrians also keep a *divo,* a small oil lamp, to remind them of the divine, for all fire is sacred, not just the temple fire. But the social needs of diaspora groups are different from those in the old countries and these affect worship.

In the old countries Zoroastrians commonly live in discrete areas. In Bombay and Karachi there are charitable housing colonies so that religion is something caught not taught, it is part of daily life and is reinforced by constant contact with coreligionists. That is not the case in the West. In Britain, the Zoroastrians are concentrated near London so that they can meet at Zoroastrian House. But in Canada and the United States they have not usually concentrated in one area. Because of their career patterns, they have moved where their work has taken them. The vastly greater distances make meetings with fellow Zoroastrians more difficult. A social program, be it a "pot luck" supper, a lecture, or dance, is significant as a means of networking, not only in the search for marriage partners, but also for reaffirming identity. Worship has to meet a similar need. In the diaspora, congregational worship is more important than in the old country. In India, temple worship is essentially a personal pilgrimage to go and stand alone (even if others are present in the temple) before the fire and to receive the divine blessing. In the diaspora, there is also a need for religious practice that brings scattered individuals together as a group. To this end there are two rites common in the West: the *boi* ceremony and the *jashan.* These merit discussion.

The *boi* ceremony is performed five times daily in a temple to "feed" the permanently burning fire. The rite consists of preparatory *sudre/kusti* prayers, and the priest laying sweet smelling sandalwood on the fire and reciting the ancient Litany to the Fire. In the old country Parsis may like to attend the temple when such a ceremony is being performed, but they are not expected to. The purpose of a temple visit is not to observe the priest feeding the fire, but to stand in the presence of the divine. The *boi* ceremony is transplanted from a temple setting to prayer rooms in the diaspora as a communal event for people to attend. The fire is specially lit and allowed to go out afterward. It is a focal event observed by a congregation on important occasions.

The *jashan* is a part of the ancient tradition, practiced in modern Iran and India. The intention of the ritual can be modified by the choice of certain prayers, so it may be used to celebrate a public event (e.g., there was a large public thanksgiving *jashan* in Bombay at the end of the Second World War); when moving into a new home; it may be the focus of the installation of a new high priest when his fellow priests present him with shawls as a recognition of his authority. Because it can be celebrated in any clean place, it is not dependent on temple availability. Like all Zoroastrian ceremonies, it requires the presence of a fire, but not an ever burning one, so it can be lit for the occasion. Normally several priest perform the *jashan,* but one priest may function. The physical restrictions of Western life do not, therefore, restrict its observance. On major occasions, in the diaspora, *jashan* attracts large congregations, to observe and through it receive divine blessings. What is happening is not the creation of a new liturgy, but the yet greater importance of a traditional and "portable" ceremony, around which the faithful can congregate.

There are seven main Zoroastrian festivals, the New Year and six seasonal, agricultural, festivals. The importance of the agricultural festivals declined in urban Bombay, but they remained important for Iranian Zoroastrians. In the West, Iranian Zoroastrians are reminding Parsis of part of their forgotten tradition. Such festivals may include some of the ceremonies mentioned above, but the focal point is the sharing of food, usually funded in memory of a deceased loved one. Their function as a congregational activity, performed independently of a temple, again makes them especially appropriate for diaspora groups. When they are observed varies.

There are three calendars observed by Zoroastrians. The majority of Indian Parsis observe the *Shenshai* calendar; but in the seventeenth century they realized this differed from that observed in Iran, and so a group calling themselves the *Qadmis* (Ancients) campaigned for the adoption of the Iranian calendar. In the early twentieth century a reform movement, the *Faslis,* introduced a new calendar to accord with the Western Gregorian calendar. The structure of the religious year is the same in each, but because of past differences in intercalation the festivals fall on different days.

In the diaspora, but not in the old country, there is a trend toward adopting the *Fasli* calendar because it coincides with the calendar of wider society. But that puts a religious time difference between Western Zoroastrians and their coreligionists in the old countries.

Strategies of Adaptation

Some strategies of adaptation in worship and death practices have already been mentioned, but other measures are needed and taken. Because of the different demographic profiles between Zoroastrians in the three countries, the emphases of these strategies varies slightly. An important issue among diaspora communities is religious leadership (Hinnells 1996a). The Zoroastrian priesthood is based on patrilineal descent. In the old countries priests are not salaried but are paid for ceremonies performed, and the fees have not increased alongside twentieth-century prices. It is, therefore, generally an impoverished profession, though some charities have recently sought to ameliorate the problem. The priestly training requires prodigious efforts to memorize the many lengthy liturgies, efforts that leave little space, temporally or intellectually, for independent critical thought. (But it must immediately be said that there are some very scholarly priests, especially the high priests.) As a result of these two factors few young men of ability choose the priestly profession. However, they often undertake the first of the two initiations into the priesthood, so that the priestly lineage may be maintained, and then proceed to a secular education and career. A number of successful men of priestly lineage have then migrated to the West and it is they who function as priests in the diaspora. Few of them have ever functioned in a temple in the old country. Though there are notable exceptions, such as the late High Priest in London, Dastur Sohrab H. Kutar, and the most active of the current London priests, Ervad Rustom Bedhwar. As the priestly training received by almost all Western priests equips them to function only in the lower or more public rituals, and that training was given prior to puberty, so the liturgical and doctrinal knowledge of most Western priests is limited, however real their commitment to serve their people. Some of the sons of British and American priests have returned to India for their priestly training so that they can continue the priestly profession in the West. But some leaders are asking if it is necessary for future diaspora priests to have a Western education in Zoroastrianism to equip them to deal with the sort of questions the young Western educated people are asking.

It is rare for priests to take leadership roles in the Associations. A priest has been president of the Association in Toronto and London, but not elsewhere. The presidency of the larger bodies (FEZANA, WZO, ZTFE) and the local Associations has been in the hands of laypeople. Women as well as men have had leadership roles in all the larger bodies. One important quality of a President is not only good internal community relations, but also how they would represent the community to the outside world, for example, in interfaith activities. Religious education programs are usually organized by laypeople not the priests, but the latter may take the prayer classes for initiates. The communities are too small to fund the salary of a full-time priest, though an attempt was made in London. Because priests need to be free to travel at short notice, for example when deaths occur, many are retired people. The problems are greater in Canada and the United States than in Britain because of the distances involved. Lack of training, temple experience, and resources, and the pressure of secular daily life mean that the priests, however devoted, sometimes find it difficult to meet their people's spiritual needs. Reconciling the conflicting views on whether the religion must change (a view expressed most forcibly perhaps in the U.S.), or remain consistent with that in the old country (most strongly argued in Britain) makes their task yet more difficult. The impact of religious leaders from India, and occasionally from Iran, varies. Such visits are more frequent in the wealthier Canadian and U.S. groups. Some religious visitors have caused offence by pressing vigorously for the old traditions, especially by attacking intermarrieds. But my impression is that generally these visits function well in preserving links between the communities. The active participation of diaspora Zoroastrians in meetings in India, and religious tours of Iran, also mean that the influence is a two-way process. There are also diaspora links, for example British leaders often attend American congresses. Globalization is therefore a feature of contemporary Zoroastrianism.

Prominent in all three countries is a religious education program. Classes occur occasionally in the old countries, but in the West, the United States in particular, there is a conscious need to educate the young in Zoroastrianism if they are to be equipped to withstand the Americanizing influences encountered daily. At its annual conferences FEZANA consistently makes religious education a priority agenda item. As well as bringing priests and teachers from the old country, outside Zoroastrian scholars are also commonly invited to lecture and their publications are used. These steps were pioneered in Toronto, Chicago, and New York, but other associations soon followed, and in the 1990s such programs revived in Britain. The London-based WZO has, since its inception, organized academic seminars with approximately 50 percent of contributors being outside academics. The proceedings have been published regularly. So the education work is not limited to American communities, but it is the latter who set the pace partly because of the sort of people they are, and partly because of the particular dangers of assimilation they see in the United States. Youth camps, seminars, and sleep-over weekends have been organized from the early 1980s to enable the young to meet fellow Zoroastrians both with a view to seeking marriage partners, and to reinforce a sense of identity. In Canada and the United States, the different Sunday School groups often generate their own material, but there is also much networking. In the old countries religion is who you are, it has to do with community allegiance, blood, and genes. In the West there is more emphasis on what you believe. The doctrinal dimension of religion is considered important if religious allegiance is to be retained. This reflects on attitudes to worship and prayer. The younger generation want to know why a ritual is performed and what the words mean. Among many traditional Indian Parsis, the point of prayer is not to understand the words; indeed it is thought that understanding the meaning may be unhelpful because it makes a person think about the words, which reduces religion to mere human conceptual thinking. The point of prayers is that when offered in moral and physical purity, with devotion and intent, then the divine forces are "really" present. Others see prayer as a mantra that induces a trancelike state. Sacred prayers in the ancient Avestan language are words of spiritual power. Many young Western Zoroastrians fear that not knowing what the words mean results in "mumbo-jumbo." Be it in prayer or ritual, the young want to know "Why?" In this, and the development of congregational worship, can be seen a "protestantizing" process.

The Perceptions of Public Policy

The Zoroastrian perceptions of the three Western countries merits further discussion. Britain is typically thought of as a secular society where conversion to another religion is not a serious threat. The fact that religious education, which commonly means Christianity, is a core part of the state school syllabus means that young British Zoroastrians are exposed to Christian attitudes, for example about understanding the words of prayer, the emphasis on teachings, and congregational worship, as discussed above. But in my interview schedule British Zoroastrians were more likely to describe the British as cold, sexually immoral, and neglectful of family, than as religious. To some extent, therefore, the religious boundaries do not have to be emphasized. The United States is different in two ways. First, evangelical Christianity is more high profile than in Britain. Second is the image of the American melting pot. This concept was originally introduced to emphasize the aspiration that all communities make their contribution to American society. But many Parsis fear it implies the melt-down of their identity, and that they may be submerged in a wider "all American" group. The pressures for assimilation are commonly seen as considerable by U.S. Parsis. So although Zoroastrians consider Americans also to be sexually promiscuous and the drug culture is seen as a threat, the parents further fear that their young people will be seduced away from their heritage by the American dream. Because the threat is seen as great, the strategies are more developed than in 1980s Britain. My survey suggests that Canadian Zoroastrians typically feel less threatened by the wider society than do U.S. Zoroastrians, especially since the Canadian government emphasized its multicultural policies. Because minority groups are encouraged to preserve their traditions, they feel less need to draw a strict boundary between their ethnicity and their nationality. For example, the award of a substantial Ontario grant to refurbish the Toronto Zoroastrian House, with no conditions attached, reassured Zoroastrians that their religion was not threatened. Thus more Canadian Zoroastrians were willing to identify themselves as Canadian, than the U.S. Zoroastrians were willing to identify themselves as Americans. The British were in-between. There is a difference between London-based Zoroastrians and those in the scattered groups, with the latter affirming their British citizenship more strongly. This may be an indication of the type of person, the more educated professionals, who has moved away from London. It may also be that the higher levels of perceived ethnic discrimination in London engenders a sense of personal distance between Zoroastrians and White Anglo-Saxons.

The question of discrimination is an important one both in its own right and for its implications for the sense of identity. The city where most respondents said they faced discrimination was Toronto (49%), followed by the rest of Canada (44%), and London (42%). Approximately 35 percent of respondents in different U.S. cities said they had faced discrimination. But the situation is more complex than these figures at first suggest. Respondents who said that they had experienced discrimination were then asked whether they had faced it "Frequently," "Sometimes," or "Rarely" and whether it had been in connection with occupation, housing, education, or the police. In London 39 percent said they had faced discrimination frequently compared with only 23 percent in Toronto. In Canada and the United States, respondents thought that they had experienced discrimination specifically in the workplace. In Britain, by contrast, housing and education also appeared to be problems. Fifty-four percent of London respondents who sensed discrimination said they faced it frequently or sometimes (i.e., less than half said it was a rare experience) compared with only 18 percent in Toronto, and 20–30 percent in other American cities. My informants during my visits to Toronto confirmed these findings, saying it was not uncommon to face prejudice when seeking employment, but once you had proved yourself, the discrimination disappeared. Typically the people who said that they faced discrimination were the young, especially those born in the West, the well educated, those with successful careers, the East African Zoroastrians. This is in marked contrast to external stereotypes, which assume it is the less well educated, those who neither adapt nor speak English who experience discrimination. Respondents in all countries put the cause of discrimination down to color prejudice. My impression is that perceived discrimination typically reinforces community allegiance and the sense of identity, and distances the "victim" from wider society. But because this is a sensitive issue answers to surveys have to be treated cautiously. In my structured interview program in Britain, a number of Zoroastrians said that they had not faced discrimination, but later in the interview said they had suffered from "Paki-bashing." The experience of discrimination is, therefore, likely to be higher than these figures suggest. Some Zoroastrians resent the suggestion that they would be subject to discrimination. One interviewee dismissed the question briskly saying, "I'm above that sort of thing, because I am so westernized." This research suggests that he is as mistaken on who experiences prejudice as the usual stereotypes are.

Conclusion

Some American Zoroastrians believe that the future of the world's oldest prophetic religion lies not in the old world, but in the new. My research suggests that religious activity is greater among British Zoroastrians in the 1990s than at any other time in their history

(Hinnells 1996a). Some American newsletters have compared the migration to the West as the modern equivalent of the migration of Zoroastrians from Islamic Iran to India in the tenth century. Some attach symbolic significance to the fact that the next World Zoroastrian Congress, usually held every five years, is to be held in the year 2000 for the first time outside Iran or India. It is to be in Houston, Texas. However deep the ties with the old countries may be, and however real the threats posed by assimilation, by the melting pot, by discrimination, by westernizing or protestantizing tendencies, by factional divisions, by debates over change and continuity, nevertheless Western Zoroastrians typically feel optimistic about the future of the religion in the West. Indeed they believe that they will play a crucial role in the history of the religion in the third millennium.

--- NOTES ---

1. The postal survey was funded by the universities of Manchester and Oxford, the British Academy, and the Spalding Trusts; the interview schedule was funded by Manchester University and almost wholly carried out by Dr. Rashna Writer. The visits were funded by Manchester university, Tahempton Aresh, the Rivetna family, and the British Academy. The organization of the Canadian and U.S. surveys was organized by the Bhumgara family with the help of the relevant Zoroastrian Associations. In Britain substantial help was given in distributing the Survey by the Avari family and the Managing Committee of the Zoroastrian Trust Funds of Europe. The data were put on the computer by the Mehta family and with the help of the Regional Computer Centre at Manchester University. The work could not have been undertaken without the active support of the Associations in each country. I am deeply grateful to them all.

2. In Canada and the United States the sample is almost wholly based on contacts through the formal associations. The newer communities on the American continent probably have more complete membership records than the London Association has because migration to Britain has been spread over a longer period and is more diffuse. Of my British sample approximately half were not formal members of the Association. My California sample could be skewed, because the help I received in distributing the questionnaire there was particularly effective among the younger people and the Iranians. Figures for questions on religious practice

may be inflated as respondents may have replied in terms of what they believed they should do, rather than what they actually did. However, the questionnaires could be returned anonymously and so the need to give the "right" answer may not have been felt. The figures were confirmed in Britain by the detailed discussions of the structured interviews and by personal observations in each country.

3. These are at Alberta (Calgary and Edmonton); British Columbia, mainly Vancouver; Ontario, mainly Toronto; and Quebec, essentially Montreal.

4. These are in Arizona, Boston, three near Los Angeles, two near San Francisco, Chicago, Houston, Kansas, two in New York, Pennsylvania (mainly in Pittsburgh), Rosemont, Washington, and Washington State.

———————————— BIBLIOGRAPHY ————————————

Boyce, M. B. (1979). *Zoroastrians: Their Religious Beliefs and Practices.* London, Routledge, 3rd rev. reprint 1988.
Hinnells, J. R. (1987). "Parsi Attitudes to Religious Pluralism." In H. G. Coward (ed.), *Modern Indian Responses to Religious Pluralism* (pp. 195–233). New York: State University of New York Press.
———. (1988). "Zoroastrian Migration to the American Continent." In M. Treasureywalla (ed.), *Proceedings of the 6th North American Zoroastrian Congress* (pp. 19–49). Toronto: Zoroastrian Association of Ontario.
———. (1994a). "South Asia Diaspora Religion: Comparative Parsi Experiences." *South Asia Research* 14:62–110.
———. (1994b). "Modern Zoroastrian Diaspora." In J. Brown, R. Foot (eds.), *Migration: The Asian Experience* (pp. 56–82). London and New York: Macmillan.
———. (1996a). *Zoroastrians in Britain.* Oxford: Clarendon Press.
———. (1996b). "The Study of Diaspora Religion" and "Comparative Reflections on South Asian Religion in International Migration." In J. R. Hinnells (ed.), *A New Handbook of Living Religions* (pp. 682–89, 819–47). Oxford: Blackwell.
Karkal, M. (1983). *Survey of Parsi Population of Greater Bombay–1982.* Bombay: The Parsi Punchayet.
Kharas Fraser, H. (1993). *Intermarriage among Bombay Zoroastrians,* Manchester University Ph.D. thesis (unpublished).
Luhrman, T. (1996). *The Good Parsi.* Cambridge, Mass.: Harvard University Press.

Mistry R. (1991). *Such a Long Journey*. London: Faber and Faber, repr. New York, 1992.

———. (1995). *A Fine Balance*. Toronto: Faber and Faber, London ed. 1996.

Writer, R. (1994). *Contemporary Zoroastrians: An Unstructured Nation*. Lanham, New York: University Press of America.

3

New Religious Movements in the West Led by South Asians

Judith Coney

East and West are like two arms. Both together can uplift the world. West paid more attention to prosperity. East paid more attention to inside. But now modern science has brought all people together. That is . . . God's work.

—Ma Yoga Shakti

Concomitant with the immigration of South Asians into Canada, Britain, and the United States during this century and the increasing links between the regions has come an upsurge in the numbers of new religious movements (NRMs) in the West led by South Asians or inspired by the South Asian religious traditions.[1] To some, their presence is indicative of an increasing

Western interest in spirituality. Others view them less favorably. Nevertheless, drawn from every conceivable religious configuration from that area, whether this be within the Hindu, Jain, Islamic, Sikh, or the Sant Mat tradition, they have made a visible impact on the Western religious landscape.

Because of the large numbers of these movements in the West, this chapter does not attempt to provide an exhaustive description. Instead, groups are used to illustrate particular issues in relation to the reception of South Asian NRMs in Britain, Canada, and the United States. Beginning with an explanation of the term *NRM* and some indication of the numbers of groups in this category, an outline is given of the ways in which such movements have arrived in these countries. This is followed by a discussion of a few of the similarities and differences between these groups, and a brief examination of how their public image has been shaped. Despite the uniformity implied by this image, there are discernible differences in both their behavior and their treatment in the United States, Britain, and Canada, and the remainder of the chapter is devoted to elaborating these differences.

Definition and Numbers

The term *NRM* is most often attached to South Asian religious and spiritual groups that have appeared in the West since 1945, who have succeeded in gearing their message to attract a Western audience, and whose teachings and practices are generally perceived of as innovative or unorthodox in some way. This perception is held either by the parent traditions from which they are derived, or by Westerners, to whom they are unfamiliar. The term is rarely used by NRMs to describe themselves, as they are likely to see it as an inappropriate label that downplays either their connections to older traditions or their spiritual identities.

Among the academic community, NRM is used commonly to designate a broad range of new groups with South Asian roots, such as the Brahma Kumaris, Ananda Marga, Siddha Yoga, Sahaja Yoga, Sikh Dharm International, Transcendental Meditation, the Neo-Sannyas movement of Rajneesh, and the Sufi Order in the West, to name but a few.[2] As defined, it also covers the International Society for Krishna Consciousness (ISKCON), a movement that has played a significant part in the development of Hindu worship in all three countries. However, it was only formally instituted in 1966 in the United States, and its full-time devotees are mainly Western.[3] In addition, it includes organizations of devotees clustering around living avatars or divine figures such as Ma Amritanandamayi, Sathya Sai Baba, and Mother Meera, since all three attract substantial Western followings and none are initiated formally into an established lineage of teachers.[4]

NRM, however, is not usually applied to sectarian organizations with South Asian roots such as the Swaminarayan *sampradaya* or the Ahmaddiyya movement who, although perhaps considered unconventional or, in the latter instance, even heretical by some within their home traditions, were both founded in the nineteenth century and not in the West, and whose message is not geared to a Western audience. Also outside are such spiritual figures as the Sufi Pir Maroof, who involves himself in the mainstream religious activities of Muslims in Britain on a wide scale, and who has few, if any, Western followers.[5]

Notwithstanding such exceptions, the number of NRMs in the West still appears fairly large, although difficult to estimate precisely. There is no agreed point, for example, at which a group of disciples around a central figure becomes a "new religious movement." Nevertheless, it has been suggested that Britain has about 600 NRMs, whereas the United States is home to slightly more and Canada to only slightly less.[6] To counterbalance any impression of prolific expansion given by such figures, however, it should be noted that the NRMs under scrutiny are not increasing rapidly in size. Few are large in terms of members, and together they represent only a small fraction of the religious constituency in each of the three countries.

It has been estimated that in the first three decades since World War II as many as 5 percent of the adult population of North America participated in some way in the activities of an NRM (Wuthnow 1988, 1). Similarly, one expert has suggested: "Half a million have gone so far as to participate in a seminar, course or workshop or to spend at least several hours investigating an NRM" in Britain (Barker 1992,151). These figures, though, do not reflect those of committed, full-time membership. In a national survey in 1980, although 3 percent of Canadians expressed an interest in alternative religions, less than one-half of 1 percent were actually participating in any new religious activities and fewer still were fully committed (Bibby 1987). By the early 1990s, it was estimated that less than a tenth of 1 percent of all Canadians were participating actively in some way in an NRM (O'Toole 1996), although it may be that this revised figure has more to do with the accuracy of the estimate than with any real drop in numbers.

Such estimates concur broadly with those in the United States and Britain, where the numbers of adherents in relation to the total population remain small. It has been reported that there were just over 18,000 active members of new religions in Britain in the early 1990s, or somewhat less than half of 1 percent of the total population (Brierley and Hiscock 1993, 280–81).[7] Similarly, the best estimate of total membership of new religions in the United States places it between 150,000 and 200,000 individuals, or just over half of 1 percent of the total population (Melton 1992, 8). It must be remembered, too, that NRMs of South Asian origin, or South Asian-inspired, represent a lesser proportion of any of these figures.

Of these, Transcendental Meditation, although it is not always seen by practitioners as a religion, is among the most popular of the South Asian NRMs. There are between 10,000 and 20,000 current meditators in North America and perhaps as many as 6,000 new people every year taking the basic instruction in meditation in Britain (Barker 1992, 152). In 1988, Sikh Dharm International reported 139 centers in the United States and 11 in Canada. Between 5,000 and 10,000 Sikhs are associated with the movement in North America as a whole, out of a Sikh population of some quarter of a million, though there are only a few hundred in Britain. ISKCON estimates that there are about one thousand active devotees living full-time in Canada and the United States and a further 390 initiated devotees on their current lists in Britain.[8] Siddha Yoga, founded by Swami Muktananda, and Kripalu Yoga, founded by Yogi Amrit Desai, which both work with kundalini energy, have thousands of followers in the United States and Canada, though fewer in Britain. There are perhaps between 5,000 and 7,000 followers of Osho Rajneesh in Britain, Canada, and the United States. Most other South Asian movements are smaller, however, with membership figures in the hundreds rather than thousands in the West.

Patterns of Establishment

The routes by which these South Asian NRMs have reached the West are diverse. But, since 1965, the United States, due to its size and orientation toward religion, has had the largest number of NRMs and seen the establishment of more headquarters for NRMs from South Asia than any other Western country. Most commonly, once having put down roots in the United States, embryonic religious movements have then opened additional centers in Canada and Europe. The vast majority of South Asian NRMs in Canada especially, with a handful of notable exceptions, have originated elsewhere and are usually affiliated to a large international organization based abroad. However, not all groups conform to this pattern, nor are all movements established by the same route. Britain, for instance, with double the population of Canada, has also been a starting place for a number of spiritual movements from South Asia that have then spread to North America, such as the Brahma Kumaris and Sahaja Yoga.

The establishment of some is clearly connected to the arrival of the leader to live in a particular country. Thus, Sahaja Yoga started in England after its founder, Sri Mataji Nirmala Devi, moved there from India in 1970 because her husband took up a diplomatic post in London. Meetings were held in the houses of individuals interested in experiencing the "cool breezes" of the kundalini meditation she teaches, and an organization emerged gradually. Sahaja Yoga centers were then set up in both Canada and America. The leader of Sikh Dharm International, Yogi Bhajan, first arrived in Toronto, Canada, in 1968, but shortly thereafter moved to the United States to find work as a kundalini yoga instructor at the East West Center in Los Angeles, and began attracting followers. The organization he established spread subsequently back to Canada and, in a small way, to England (Tobey 1976, 5–30; Williams 1988, 144–51).

A. C. Bhaktivedanta Swami Prabhupada, the founder of ISKCON, arrived in America in 1965 and discovered a receptive audience in the hippies and drop-outs he met in New York and then San Francisco, hundreds of whom were captivated by the notion of staying high forever on Krishna Consciousness. The first Canadian ISKCON temple, in Montreal, opened in January 1967. In August the following year, three married couples were sent to London to start a preaching center there. They were given a large house, Bhaktivedanta Manor, by the Beatle George Harrison for the British headquarters in 1973.

Other movements have started as the result of tours undertaken by spiritual teachers with already established headquarters in South Asia. The Sant Mat leader, Kirpal Singh, embarked on one such tour of the United States in 1955 and so laid the foundations for a number of Sant Mat organizations with Western followers in the West, as well as Sant Mat-inspired organizations, such as Eckankar and MSIA (Melton 1992; Olson 1995), led by Westerners. Another movement that came out of the Sant Mat tradition, the Divine Light Mission, started in the United States after Westerners who had been initiated while traveling in India invited their 13-year-old spiritual leader, Guru Maharaj Ji, to visit the United

States in 1971 (Messer 1976, 52–72). Similarly, Swami Muktananda was persuaded by newly initiated American devotees in India to undertake a world tour in 1970, and after this visit several centers of followers were started before the formal establishment of Siddha Yoga in 1975 in the United States. Some movements have flourished because leading disciples have come to live in the countries. Swami Vishnu Devananda, one of a number of well-known disciples of Swami Sivananda Saraswati of Rishikesh, has founded several Sivananda Yoga Vedanta centers in America and is one of the few who have established Western headquarters in Canada, in Montreal. In 1976 the leader of Kundalini Maha Yoga, Dhyanyogi, brought a leading disciple, Anandi Ma, with him on an extended tour of the United States. Although he returned to India permanently in 1980, she stayed to build up support for the movement in America (Johnsen 1994, 58–72).

Others, however, have not required the presence of a leader to flourish in a new soil, at least initially. Although Mother Meera stayed for a short while in Canada in 1979 and has visited the United States briefly, she has never visited Britain herself. She is known there largely because of the media publicity generated in the early 1990s by an articulate and influential disciple. The teachings and miracles of Sathya Sai Baba were introduced to the West by immigrants from East Africa and South Asia and by Western travelers on the spiritual circuit of the East. The Neo-Sannyas movement of Osho Rajneesh was brought to Britain and North America by Western students, travelers and therapists who went to his *ashram* in Poona, became followers, and then returned to set up centers in their own countries in the mid 1970s. Rajneesh himself only traveled later to the United States in June 1981.

The Range of NRMs

Before turning to the impact which these movements have had since their arrival, it is important to look more closely at the groups themselves. Although they cover a vast range, in certain respects these NRMs tend to share some characteristics, in addition to their roots in the religious traditions of South Asia. They are commonly seen as deviant in relation to the mainstream, offer a "surer, shorter, swifter, or clearer way to salvation" (Wilson 1990, 205), and incorporate a strong experiential component. Often, they ask for higher levels of commitment than is usual for religious groups. All are led by figures who are seen to be especially spiritually endowed. Many look to the establishment of a new social order, and almost all are visibly syncretic, incorporating elements from traditions other than their own or from the New Age.

There are other similarities as well. As O'Toole (1996, 130) notes: "Canadian recruits typically resemble their American or European counterparts, and the attractions of NRM membership transcend national boundaries." Some of the more traditionally orientated groups, such as the Science of Spirituality from the Sant Mat tradition, reach out to Hindi and Punjabi as well as to English speakers in the West; Sathya Sai Baba is able to command strong, though far from universal, support from a wide range of communities; and ISKCON reports Gujurati, and to a lesser extent Punjabi, congregations of around a hundred thousand in North America and 50,000 in Britain. Nevertheless, full-time members of the majority of South Asian NRMs in the West are typically middle-class, well-educated Westerners. Despite stereotypical images of NRMs, which portray them as enlisting the wretched and lonely, most groups tend to find converts in the West from existing social networks. Moreover, some, including the Poona-based part of Rajneesh's Organization, the Brahma Kumaris and Siddha Yoga Dham, are strikingly affluent:

The temples, auditoriums and statuary [of Siddha Yoga] are opulent even by American standards and immaculately maintained. The setting is so lavish it is almost unearthly . . . "Yuppie yoga?" my guide laughs . . . "There are many people here who were never attracted to spiritual life until they met Gurumayi. She's created an atmosphere where they can feel comfortable—clean and beautiful and very Western in some ways." (Johnsen 1994, 78)

Others, however, are not, and any standardized profile of South Asian NRMs, tends to mask the huge diversity between groups. Some leaders, for instance, including Sathya Sai Baba, Ma Amritanandamayi, and Mother Meera, are nonexclusive, this stance being captured in the following conversation between a devotee and Mother Meera:

Q: All the Gods, all the paths, all the revelations are in the Mother. Does this mean that anyone in the world from

whatever background can be taught by you and awakened
to the Divine within the terms of their own religion, or
lack of it?

MM: Yes. My Light is everywhere.

(Mother Meera 1991, 51–52)

At the other end of the spectrum are groups that demand very high
levels of exclusive commitment from followers, especially those which
are communally based and offer themselves as alternative families
to devotees. In between, the majority of groups, particularly once
they have been established for some time, offer various levels of
participation to members. ISKCON, for example, began in the 1960s
as a community-based movement, with full-time devotees adopting
an entirely new lifestyle. Now, many devotees live outside the
temples, and have jobs in the "outside world," and the movement
encourages the participation of those who are not full-time.

There is also discernible variation in the extent to which a new
religion is really new in relation to the activities of its parent
tradition. Some of the new movements are clearly reinventions of
a particular tradition and are highly eclectic, often incorporating
strands from the New Age or Western values, as well as from older
traditions. Among these NRMs is the Sufi Order in the West. This
group was founded in 1910, by Hazrat Inayat Khan who was initiated originally into the Nizami branch of the Chisti Order in
India. With a vision to unite East and West, he subsequently went
to America, and later, in 1912, to England. Even at this early
juncture, Khan made two radical innovations. The first was to give
Western women important positions in the order; and the second
was to separate Sufism from Islam and declare it a universal teaching (Rawlinson 1993, 55). After his sudden death in 1927, the
movement split into factions and ceased to exist in America (Koszegi
1992). It was then revived in the 1960s, however, by Pir Vilayat
Khan, the founder's son. The latter is described in the movement's
own literature as a leader who:

offers an integrated vision of spiritual practices drawn from
the mystical dimensions of the Hindu, Buddhist, Zoroastrian,
Jewish, Christian and Islamic traditions. Pir Vilayat's published works include "Introducing Spirituality into Therapy
and Counselling" . . . and "Sufi Masters."

The movement sponsors the Omega Institute in the United States, which holds an annual New Age Symposium, and Pir Vilayat has introduced a religious ritual in which "reverence and gratitude is offered to all the religions with lighted candles and readings from their sacred scriptures" (Ibid. 1992, 214). The Sufi Order in the West, in other words, although incorporating elements of Sufism, has become a highly syncretic reworking of traditional Sufi teaching and practice.

Also innovative in some important respects is Sikh Dharm International. Yogi Bhajan has integrated unorthodox yogic practices, learned before his arrival in North America, into the movement. As a result, several respected Sikh leaders have left the movement and it has little contact with the mainstream Sikh community. His group has also been influenced by the New Age, and was associated in the 1980s with *Spiritual Community Publications*, an influential New Age publisher. Other movements, however, especially those with teachers who spend time in South Asia as well as in the West, tend to be much more conservative.

Still on the theme of diversity, NRMs can take different forms in different countries, for reasons that include relative economic strengths and the ways in which they become established. On the latter point, Sahaja Yoga is commune-based in both the United States and Canada because it was this type of organization that was set up initially in these countries. In Britain, however, it was built up though public meetings. Because of this difference in initial form, the pressure to live communally in Britain remains far less than in the other two countries.

Internal diversity can also be influenced by national identities, and followers in many international movements characterize their counterparts elsewhere, usually in jest, according to national stereotypes. This tendency is reflected in the following comments of two ISKCON devotees, the first from the United States:

British devotees often comment on how the Americans are more brash. I have observed that our British cousins are often more concerned with proper protocol and appropriate behavior of ladies and gentlemen. In North America, our Canadian devotees tend to feel overlooked by their big, southern neighbors. They are a bit sensitive about their national identity, as are many Canadians.

and the second from Britain:

> [Devotees from the United States] are brash, outspoken, ma-
> nipulative, more energetic but get themselves into trouble (re-
> member that many early leaders were from the United States).
> Canadians are more civilized Americans.

To sum up, then, although these movements have characteristics in
common, there is much variation between them. The internal ho-
mogeneity, which is so often assumed in relation to NRMs, is usually tempered by relative histories, economic factors, and national
contexts.

Popular Reactions to New Religious Movements

Despite the differences between the teaching, practices, and organization of new religious movements that have been outlined, it
is noteworthy that popular stereotypes attached to them show
them all in much the same light. Their portrayal in the media—
which is how most ordinary individuals know of their activities—
differs little in Canada, the United States, and Britain. Much of
the bad press that they have received can be attributed to the
activities of the anticult movement (ACM). For, as Beckford (1995,
103) notes: "the anti-cult movement presents journalists with
material which needs very little adaptation before it can be easily
digested by audiences."

The ACM began in the United States in 1971 as small grassroots
organizations of concerned middle-class individuals who, worried
for family members joining NRMs, sought to persuade politicians
and others of their view that these groups were not really religious
at all. Instead, they were: " 'cults,' pseudo-religious groups which
engage in destructive mind-control practices that subvert family
unity and individual autonomy" (Bromley and Shupe 1995, 222).
This view then spread to Canada and Britain where similar movements appeared. There seem to have been substantial links between
cult-watching organizations in the various countries. For instance,
an early ACM organization, the Council on Mind Abuse, was set up
in Canada in the early 1980s by Ian Howarth, who then moved to
Britain and established the Cult Information Centre along much
the same lines. Less visibly, members of groups in Britain and
Canada have consulted regularly with their counterparts in the
United States. As a result, a relatively cohesive ACM image of the

dangers of NRMs has been provided to the press and to other concerned individuals in each country.

Notwithstanding this image, however, differences in religious and cultural histories have meant that NRMs have both behaved and been treated, to an extent, in dissimilar ways in the United States, Britain, and Canada. These are now considered briefly in turn, especially in terms of the relationships between NRMs and other secular and religious institutions. To highlight these relationships, the treatment and development of two high-profile South Asian NRMs, the Rajneesh movement and ISKCON, are compared in the three countries. Usually, South Asian NRMs have received somewhat less publicity, maintained less controversial profiles and, therefore, received less state attention. However, an examination of these two groups highlights the different national responses to NRMs within Britain, Canada, and the United States.

NRMs in the United States

To some leaders of South Asian NRMs, the United States represents a materialistic, decadent society that must be purified. To others, it is a land of opportunity, full of sincere seekers thirsty for their teachings. Its popularity as a first destination for NRMs is due to a combination of factors, including its history of toleration toward marginal and sectarian groups, and the relaxation of immigration law in 1965. South Asian NRMs have tended to settle first along the East and West coasts of the United States, and move from there into the rest of the country.

The campaign of the ACM to classify NRMs as nonreligious groups is a product, at least in part, of the constitutional affirmation of the autonomy of religious groups in the United States. For the state to intervene, so the constitutional argument runs, it has to be persuaded that such groups are not bona fide religious organizations. In fact, the state has intervened increasingly in the affairs of NRMs in the last two decades (Beckford 1993). NRMs, for instance, are being required increasingly to conform to public policies in order to keep their tax-exempt status. Nevertheless, direct intervention in the affairs of South Asian NRMs has only occurred where there is suspicion of illegality, such as when Rajneesh was arrested for immigration violations in North Carolina by FBI agents who had monitored his flight out of Rajneeshpuram.

Typically, the social control of NRMs in the United States has been administered through the legal system. Exceptionally, a few

South Asian NRMs have had criminal charges brought against them. Leading followers at the Rajneeshpuram community in Oregon, who were denounced by Rajneesh, were convicted of poisoning members of a neighboring community. This had been done by sprinkling salmonella bacteria over salad bars in ten restaurants in order to affect the outcome of a crucial local election. Some were also convicted of conspiracy to murder Rajneesh's doctor and the U.S. Attorney, Charles Turner. Just as serious, the leader and some other members of the New Vrindaban community in Virginia, which has now been expelled from ISKCON,[9] have been convicted, among other charges, of arson, fraud, and conspiracy to murder. In all these cases, other followers testified for the prosecution.

Civil litigation, too, has limited South Asian NRMs' sphere of operations. For example, ISKCON has been restricted from soliciting for donations in public areas such as airports; and Rajneeshpuram was subjected to sustained attempts to have it declared illegal on the basis of zoning regulations. Some movements have also had large claims for civil damages made against them in the United States courts. Most seriously, they have been accused of brainwashing or kidnapping former members. Perhaps the most celebrated case involving a South Asian NRM is that of *George v. ISKCON* in 1974. Robin George, who was a minor when she joined the movement, and her mother sued ISKCON successfully for false imprisonment, libel, invasion of privacy, and the intentional infliction of distress. They were awarded $32 million, although this sum was later reduced substantially on appeal to the higher courts.

Such cases in the 1970s and 1980s did not help to incline public opinion favorably toward South Asian NRMs in the United States, despite support from the National Council of Churches of Christ in America on the grounds that "religious liberty is one of the most precious rights of mankind" (Eck 1987, 144). In the 1990s, however, a more tolerant attitude toward South Asian NRMs is gaining ground. For example, the American Psychological Association has rejected allegations that brainwashing techniques are being used in NRMs. Significantly, South Asian doctors played a role in persuading the Association that chanting, rather than being a component of "manipulative mind control," is part of Hindu practice. NRMs have also fought back through the courts. They have been so successful that the Cult Awareness Network, an umbrella ACM organization, was bankrupted in June 1996, leaving the movement in some disarray.[10]

Thus, notwithstanding the general damage done to relations between NRMs and the State by the ill-managed confrontation at Waco, Texas, in 1993 (Wright 1995), most South Asian NRMs are seen increasingly as legitimate religious organizations in the United States. Rajneesh's movement is an exception, and has declined rapidly in membership since the mid-1980s in the United States. The more conservative ISKCON, however, has gained the support of sections of the South Asian population, largely because of the respect it has won for its temple worship. It has worked hard to convey its message that it is an authentic exponent of Indian religion. This claim seems now to have been accepted.

NRMs in Britain

In Britain, in contrast, partly because of its history of constitutional links between Church and State, there is a widespread attitude of tolerant indifference toward mainstream religion, but a lack of understanding of religious fervor. As a result, the British "are accustomed to relegating spiritual enthusiasm to a category of, at best, eccentricity, and at worst, exploitation, [and] they distrust any and all would-be Messiahs, evangelists and gurus" (Beckford 1985, 239). Even so, in the 1980s South Asian NRMs enjoyed a more liberal relationship with outside agencies than their counterparts in the United States. Like all religious groups in Britain, they were allowed to have charitable status, with associated tax concessions. The government even assisted in the establishment of an impartial information agency about new religious movements, INFORM. This agency is based at the London School of Economics, part of the University of London, and has the senior cleric of the Church of England, the Archbishop of Canterbury, as its Patron.

This is not to say that South Asian NRMs in Britain met with no setbacks whatsoever in the 1980s. Rajneesh was refused a visa to land in England in 1986, for instance, after his expulsion from the United States, apparently on the advice of U.S. government officials. However, there have been no charges of murder or conspiracy leveled against any groups, although a guru who had left ISKCON in Britain, Jayatirtha, was murdered subsequently by another former follower.

In the 1990s, INFORM is still supported by the Church, one of its most active governors being the Canon of Southwark Cathedral.

Furthermore, British churches have engaged in interfaith dialogue with NRMs, especially with ISKCON. ISKCON has recently won a lengthy battle over the threatened closure of its largest temple because of infringements over planning regulations, and is viewed increasingly as a respected part of the Hindu community. Rajneesh's movement has also retained more members than in the United States. Especially noteworthy is their luxurious London "embassy," housed in a prime site close to Piccadilly Circus.

However, although the anticultist Ian Howarth was bankrupted in 1996 following legal action over his activities in Canada, this does not seem to have affected his ability to campaign. Moreover, before the general election in 1997, government views on NRMs appeared to be hardening. A Home Office Minister, the Rt. Hon. Thomas Sackville, was quoted as saying: "In the past the Home Office has seemed to give the impression that it is neutral and I very much regret this. We are anti-cult" (*Mail on Sunday*, 20 October 1996). Home Office funding for INFORM was stopped and has so far not been introduced under the new government. Against a background of an increasing lack of sympathy for NRMs in Continental Europe, it is not possible to say, therefore, that South Asian NRMs in Britain are no longer vulnerable.

NRMs in Canada

Like Britain, Canada has a longer history of South Asian immigration than the United States. Canada also stresses a policy of multiculturalism and tolerance. As elsewhere, the activities of a few can create a climate of apprehension around small religious movements generally. In October 1994, five charred bodies which were discovered in Canada, including that of the infant child of an ex-member, were identified as belonging to individuals with connections to a Neo-Templar group, the Order of the Solar Temple. Further deaths among members of the movement in Europe, and in Canada in 1997, heightened fears among the public and in the press about the activities of marginal religious movements generally. Nevertheless, the response of state and religious institutions toward NRMs in Canada has been, despite some ACM activity, generous and measured.

This moderate stance was typified in 1980 by the findings of the Hill Report, which had been commissioned by the Ontario government to investigate whether government action against NRMs was warranted. It recommended that research be done into reports of psychiatric problems arising from membership of NRMs and that victims of dubious practices be encouraged to go to law. However, it described the forced deprogramming of members of NRMs as "repugnant" (Hill 1980, 585), and concluded that no government action be taken in the form of a public enquiry into NRMs. In so doing, the report followed the recommendations of the United Church of Canada and of the Anglican Church of Canada. Both institutions opposed the regulation of NRMs and, instead, suggested that interfaith dialogue and increased education were more appropriate responses to their presence. To increase understanding about NRMs, and to counter biased media reports, the Canadian Council of Christians and Jews published an Ontario directory of NRMs in 1980, and the United Church of Canada put together an educational kit in 1982 (Eck 1987). In the 1990s, the Ontario database on the Internet provides an invaluable resource on NRMs and issues of public freedom. Although it is not financially supported by either state or church, it can be seen as a legacy of the tolerant attitude toward marginal groups that both have worked to promote.[11]

Unlike their counterparts in the United States, ISKCON devotees in Canada have never become involved in soliciting contributions in airports and so have faced no legal challenge over this issue. They have never been restricted from asking for donations or chanting in Canadian streets. Neither have they had to face the huge awards made against the movement in the law courts of their southern neighbors. As in the other two countries, and especially in Vancouver and Toronto, they are working hard to establish closer working relationships with the South Asian community. Osho Rajneesh, in contrast, and again apparently as a result of pressure from the United States, was refused a visa to land in Canada after his expulsion. However, his followers have had an easier time than those he left behind in Oregon as they have been less tarnished by the downfall of Rajneespuram. Fewer Canadians moved to Rajneeshpuram during the 1980s and fewer, therefore, had subsequently to rebuild their lives. However, there are also few new followers of Rajneesh in Canada, and the movement, to that extent, can be said to be in decline.

Concluding Remarks

This chapter has traced the arrival and development of South Asian NRMs in Britain, Canada, and the United States. It has suggested

that the impact they have had has been generated not so much by
their numbers, which are small, but by their success in attracting
Western members to what have been perceived of as deviant
lifestyles, and by the bad publicity they have received as marginal
and sometimes exclusive communities. Only rarely, as in the cases
of Rajneesh's movement and ISKCON, has such publicity been due
to dubious activities on the part of the groups themselves. In each
of the three countries, church-state relations, and the attitudes of
governments toward minority groups, have led to somewhat different treatments of the NRMs in their midst. Their modes of arrival
and the relative economic strengths of NRMs in Canada, the United
States, and Britain have contributed to further diversity in terms
of their establishment and interaction with the host country.

Relationships between South Asian NRMs and the wider South
Asian communities in the West have not always been easy, in any
of the three countries. Some South Asians express great frustration
at Western ignorance of the fact that not all gurus and swamis are
respected widely in South Asia. Such people fear that they will face
an increase of discrimination as part of a backlash against Eastern
religion in general, because of ACM-inspired antipathy toward
NRMs. Nevertheless, as we have seen, there is overlap between
South Asian and Western constituencies in certain organizations.
As arenas in which members of both can develop spiritually together, South Asian NRMs have a role to play in contributing to
good relations between these communities in a multicultural West.

NOTES

1. The author would like to express her appreciation to the British
Academy for their generous financial assistance in relation to this chapter,
and to Dr. Gordon Melton for supplying the latest material on NRMs in
Canada.

2. Readers are advised to consult Melton (1993) for details of the
histories, beliefs, and practices of all the movements that appear in this
chapter, as it remains by far the most comprehensive reference source on
NRMs in the West. Other accessible sources, though more limited in scope,
include Beit-Hallahmi (1993), Miller (1995), and Barrett (1996).

3. Because of its importance to Hindus, ISKCON is also dealt with
elsewhere in this volume by both Knott and Eck. Further, devotees

themselves dislike the label NRM, despite fitting the category. See Goswami (1995).

4. Although Sathya Sai Baba claims to be a reincarnation of Sai Baba of Shirdi and Mother Meera stayed for some time at the Sri Aurobindo Ashram.

5. As Lewis notes (1994, 82–83), Pir Maroof is specifically "critical of freewheeling, self-styled spiritual guides and insists on the importance for any pir to belong to an order, to have his own spiritual guide and to have his permission to initiate devotees."

6. See Stark (1993, 393) and Melton (1992, 7).

7. This figure is probably an underestimate, as it includes a figure of 10,000 devotees of Satliya Sai Baba, which could easily be doubled. Even so, the proportions are small.

8. These figures were kindly supplied in 1996 by devotees from the Philadelphia Temple in the United States and from Bhaktivedanta Manor, England.

9. These events occurred after the death of Prabhupada, when a number of gurus he had appointed had to be discharged on behavioral grounds.

10. The announcement was posted on CAN's web site, http:Hwww.xnet.com/-can.can.html, on 21 June 1996.

11. See http://web.canlink.com/ocrt/ocrt hp.htm

———————————— **BIBLIOGRAPHY** ————————————

Barker, E. (1992). *New Religious Movements: A Practical Introduction.* London: HMSO.
Barrett, D. (1996). *Sects, "Cults" and Alternative Religions: A World Survey and Sourcebook.* London: Blandford.
Beckford, J. (1985). *Cult Controversies: The Societal Response to the New Religions.* London: Tavistock.
———. (1993). "States, Governments and the Management of Controversial New Religious Movements" In E. Barker et al. (eds.), *Secularization, Rationalization and Sectarianism.* Oxford: Clarendon Press.
———. (1995). "Cults, Conflicts and Journalists." In R. Towler (ed.) *New Religions and the New Europe.* Aarhus: Aarhus University Press.
Beit-Hallahmi, B. (1993). *The Illustrated Encyclopedia of Active New Religions, Cults and Sects.* New York: Rosen.

Bibby, R. (1987). *Fragmented Gods: The Poverty and Potential of Religion in Canada*. Toronto: Irwin Publishing.

Brierley, P. and V. Hiscock (eds.) (1993). *UK Christian Handbook, 1994–1995 Edition*. London: Christian Research Association.

Bromley, D. G. and A. Shupe. (1995). "Anti-Cultism in the United States: Origins, Ideology and Organizational Development." *Social Compass* 42:2, 221–236.

Eck, D. (1987). "A Report from North America" in A. R. Brockway and J. P. Rajashekar (eds.). *New Religious Movements and the Churches*. Geneva: WCC Publications.

Glock C. Y. and R. N. Bellah (eds.) (1976). *The New Religious Consciousness*. Berkeley: University of California Press.

Goswami, M. (1995). "NRM Is a Four-Letter Word: The Language of Oppression." *ISKCON Communications Journal* 3:2:73–75.

Hill, D. (1980). *Study of Mind Development Groups, Sects and Cults in Ontario*. Toronto, Ontario: Office of the Special Advisor, Study of Mind Development Groups, Sects and Cults in Ontario.

Johnsen, L. (1994). *Daughters of the Goddess: The Women Saints of India*. Minnesota: Yes International Publishers.

Koszegi, M. (1992). "The Sufi Order in the West: Sufism's Encounter with the New Age" in M. Koszegi and G. Melton (eds.). *Islam in North America: A Sourcebook*. New York: Garland Publishing.

Lewis, P. (1994). *Islamic Britain*. London: I. B. Tauris & Co.

Melton, G. (1992). *Encyclopedic Handbook of Cults in America: Revised and Updated Version*. New York: Garland Publishing.

———. (1993). *The Encyclopedia of American Religions*, 4th ed. Detroit: Gale.

Messer, J. (1976). "Guru Maharaji and the Divine Light Mission." In C. Y. Glock and R. N. Bellah (eds.).

Miller, T. (ed.). (1995). *America's Alternative Religions*. Albany: State University of New York.

Mother Meera (1991). *Answers*. London: Rider Press.

Olson, R. E. (1995). "ECKANKAR: From Ancient Science of Soul Travel to New Age Religion." In T. Miller (ed.).

O'Toole, R. (1996). "Religion in Canada: Its Development and Contemporary Situation" in *Social Compass* 43:1, 119–34.

Rawlinson, A. (1993). "A History of Western Sufism." *Diskus* 1:1, 45–83.

Stark, R. (1993). "Europe's Receptivity to New Religious Movements: Round Two." *Journal for the Scientific Study of Religion* 32:4:389–97.

Tobey, A. (1976). "The Summer Solstice of the Healthy-Happy-Holy Organization." In C. Y. Glock and R. N. Bellah (eds.).

Williams, R. (1988). *Religions of Immigrants from India and Pakistan: New Threads in the American Tapestry.* Cambridge: Cambridge University Press.

Wilson, B. (1990). *The Social Dimensions of Sectarianism: Sects and New Religious Movements in Contemporary Society.* Oxford: Oxford University Press.

Wright, S. (ed.). (1995). *Armageddon in Waco.* Chicago: University of Chicago Press.

Wuthnow, R. (1988). "Religious Movements and Counter-Movements in North America." In J. Beckford (ed.). *New Religious Movements and Rapid Social Change.* Newbury Park, CA: Sage.

Introduction

John R. Hinnells

The history of the South Asian presence in Britain is quite different from that in Canada or the United States because of the history of the British empire. From the seventeenth century the British had a changing set of images of South Asia, just as South Asians did of Britain.

The story of South Asians visiting Britain dates back to the 1720s. There were at least three different groups of British who reported back and formed British opinion:

1. The officials (either of the East India Company, or later Imperial administrators) and soldiers who typically saw themselves as "bearing the White Man's burden" which required them to direct the affairs of the "natives" who were in need of fatherly care. The traders also saw the Empire as a resource for the development of British industry (Rich 1990).

2. Missionaries who not only sought to convert the natives, but also published in Britain accounts of "the heathen," which determined public opinion. From the middle of the nineteenth century some of these accounts became more informed and sensitive (Pailin 1984).

3. Adventurers and travelers who, though sharing some of the assumptions of the two previous groups, were generally not as hostile in their accounts of the natives and some of whom were pioneers in oriental studies. Many, however, retained an imperial perspective (Sharpe 1975; Firby 1988). When South Asians settled in Britain there was, therefore, a long history of the conditioning of British perceptions of the people from the subcontinent, to a far greater extent than in Canada or the United States.

The nineteenth-century traffic was not all in one direction. From the eighteenth century some Indians traveled to Britain, some princes, some as servants of returning officials. After the 1840s some individuals came to see British industry in order to develop their own businesses in India and then from the 1860s to study formally at British universities, particularly in the fields of law and medicine (Visram 1986; Hinnells 1996). They had relatively little impact on the British public, but some of them carried back a more positive impression of Britain than was often gained in British India. Despite its large servant classes, Britain did not have the same body of Black slaves that were found in the Caribbean and the United States (though there were more Black than Asian servants). In the late nineteenth and early twentieth century Indian lascars jumped ship and lived in poverty in English ports. The general public's stereotypical image of them was that they mingled with white prostitutes and thereby produced a mixed race which would literally embody the sins of both sets of parents (whether that image was legitimate is another question). In the early twentieth century they were also joined by a few peddlers. The consequence of this limited early migration was the reinforcement of the stereotypes of South Asians (and other non-European migrants) as poor, unskilled, fit only for menial manual labor (Holmes 1988).

Indian troops and funds (mostly Parsi) aided the British war effort in the First World War, and a few settled in Britain afterward, exercising the right of all Imperial subjects to travel to, and settle in Britain. But despite the war-time support of the leaders of the Indian National Congress, Britain did not change its attitude toward Independence for the peoples of the subcontinent. The consequences of the Second World War were rather different, partly because it was followed by Indian Independence, but also because more ex-soldiers from India settled in Britain, mostly people who had worked in the Medical Corps coming to work in the newly created National Health Service. Because of the huge losses of soldiers, there was a serious shortage of young male workers. The British government therefore actively recruited laborers from the Caribbean in the 1950s. Workers also came from the subcontinent, first from India, then from newly created Pakistan, mostly in the late 1950s and early 1960s. These young men were employed in heavy industry and for the low paid work that the White Anglo-Saxons did not want. Women were also employed in transport, nursing, and some service industries. The South Asians who came were from particular areas, namely the Punjab, Gujarat, and Bengal. Indeed many came from specific villages within these regions. It was not a migration of a representative sample of people from across the subcontinent or from across Indian society. Chain migration meant that certain villages lost many of their young active males, for wives, parents, and children were left behind in the family village. Those who came assumed that they would stay only for a limited period, in which time their aim was to save as much money as possible to send home and increase family honor thereby. In order to save money they were willing to undertake as much overtime as possible at work, working the unsociable hours of the night shift in the factories. White racism meant that they found it difficult to obtain accommodation and so funds were raised to buy the cheapest housing possible, inevitably in run-down inner-city areas, where Asians not only lived several to a room in dormitory-type accommodation, but even took turns sleeping in a bed as individuals worked different shifts. Money was sent to the old country regularly, and on the periodic visits back home it was important that they returned bearing generous gifts. Such visits kept alive the myth of the return to the homeland. The stay in Britain was thought to be a temporary one (Anwar 1979). The early history of the South Asian migration to Britain was, therefore, totally different from the migration of educated professionals to Canada and the United States, both because of Imperial history, and because of the sort of migrants who came.

In the late 1950s and early 1960s the White population increasingly feared that they would lose their jobs and houses, and that their country would be "swamped" so that the "purity of the island race" was under threat. Race riots, and election victories of candidates "tough on immigration" provoked government action and from 1962 a sequence of legal measures were introduced which increasingly restricted entry to Britain. By the end of the 1980s primary migration had virtually ceased and only close family members of those already settled were usually allowed entry. Only a very small number who have special qualifications are now allowed to settle, and the xenophobic fears have not disappeared in the 1990s (see Dowds and Young 1996).

But the 1960s legislation had the opposite effect of that planned by the government. As the word spread that entry would become more difficult, many of the families joined their men folk in Britain. The women soon ensured that the men ceased their bad habits of drinking alcohol and smoking. Religious issues also grew in importance. This did not happen at a uniform pace across the country. Sikh and Hindu women joined their men folk before the Muslim women did. The early Indian cultural centers, where Hindus, Sikhs, and Jains met together, gave way to more specifically religious buildings. Gurdwaras and mosques were built early on in the community histories, whereas the home base of Hinduism meant that Hindu temples were a relatively later development, although the first Hindu temple was opened in 1969 (Ballard 1994, introduction; Fryer 1984).

In the 1960s and early 70s the generally affluent and professional East African Asians felt increasingly compelled to leave Kenya, Zanzibar (after the revolution), and Tanzania, as their governments pursued policies of Africanization. The most dramatic moment of this migration came in 1972 when General Idi Amin compelled all Asians to leave Uganda, taking with them only what they could carry, and soldiers en route to the airport not uncommonly relieved the refugees of much of that (Robinson 1995). Some of them went back to the old country of India and Pakistan, but at that time the South Asian economies were not flourishing and so provided little attraction for the great majority. A few went to Canada as part of the Commonwealth, destinations encouraged by the British Government. But the great majority went to the old Imperial capital, and the center of the Commonwealth, England.

The arrival of the East African Asians had an impact both on the White Anglo-Saxon population and on the Asian communities already in Britain. The television pictures of plane loads of Asian refugees while evoking the sympathy of some, caused greater fears of many regarding the perceived threat to "the island race." The result was more and stricter legislation to restrict immigration. Just at the time that Canada and the United States were liberalizing their entry permit procedure, Britain was closing its doors. There were moves by the governments, mostly the Labour Party, to introduce race relations legislation, the aim of which was to provide some measure of security for the "colored minorities" by banning racial discrimination, first in public acts and in housing and then in employment. Later legislation was somewhat more positive in that funds were allocated to regions with high proportions of such migrants to support the social and educational services. The 1970s were, however, a time when the extreme Right-wing racist National Front had a high public profile. In the 1980s its profile declined, partly, it has been said, because the Tory government under Mrs. Thatcher dealt with race relations in a way which appeased popular hostility toward the minorities (Rich 1990; Saggar 1992; Solomos 1989).

But the East Africans also had their impact on the fellow Hindus, Muslims, Sikhs, and Parsis, as these "twice migrants," as they have been called, joined their coreligionists. Some of the East African Asians had been able to get some of their wealth out of Africa and into Britain, and so were able to move straight to the suburbs and did not have to join the South Asians in the deprived inner-city areas. Others were not as fortunate. They were compelled to settle in the inner cities and others chose to be there near their coreligionists. Further, the East African Asians were either successful entrepreneurs or professionals, unlike the earlier settlers who came direct from the subcontinent. But from the point of view of religion what was even more important was that in East Africa they had both evolved a more portable form of diaspora religion, which had given them experience of practicing their religion away from the old country, they had evolved strategies for preserving their identity in another country, skills the direct migrants had yet to develop. Also many had typically preserved more of the nineteenth-century traditions, living as they had done isolated from other religions in East Africa and without the Anglicizing influences of twentieth-century British India. In Parsi terminology, the East African Asians injected a strong measure of orthodoxy into what had been a growing liberalizing, if not reforming, tendency among their coreligionists in Britain. It took some time for the East Africans to make their presence felt, but by the 1980s various South Asian religious groups in Britain were facing demands for a reassertion of "traditional" beliefs and practices (Bhachu 1985).

There is a further distinctive feature of South Asian religious life in Britain compared with America. Since 1944, religious education has been a compulsory part of the school syllabus, and that education has been presumed to be Christian. Further, an act of corporate worship has also been required. In theory parents have the right to withdraw their children from this worship and these lessons. In practice relatively few have done so, partly because they do not want to be seen as trouble makers, and partly because it is very difficult to do so. For example, at Christmastime almost all Junior Schools mount Christmas plays, which dominate the daily timetable for many days if not weeks. The Christian indoctrination these events may involve also commonly reinforces stereotypes as any Asian child is generally given the role of the magi—bringing tribute to the infant Jesus. From the 1970s there was a move to broaden the syllabus in various education authorities and in the 1990s the government indicated to them that where there are many Asian families in an area the syllabus should take account of that fact and the major religions (identified as Judaism, Hinduism, Buddhism, Sikhism, and Islam) should be part of the syllabus. But it is still stated that the syllabus and act of worship should be "broadly Christian." Lessons about Christianity are not the only influence on young Hindus, Sikhs, and Muslims. Even when their religions are taught they are commonly being taught by people with little or no higher education in those subjects. Further, they all too often approach the subject from a typically Protestant perspective, emphasizing doctrines and texts, thus giving an image of the religion that many of the young people find does not accord with what they experience at home (Jackson and Nesbitt 1993). The same religious education program and corporate acts of "predominantly Christian" nature are not the same factors in Canada and the United States.

Until the 1990s it has always been extremely difficult to give an accurate idea of the numbers of South Asians in Britain because previously "the ethnic question" had been excluded from the census. Earlier figures are therefore necessarily estimates and even now the question is an ethnic not a religious one. It is therefore possible to say how many people there are in Britain from Pakistan, but not whether they are Muslims, Parsis, Sikhs, Christians, and so on. There has also been serious questioning over the formulation of "the ethnic question" (see especially Ballard 1997). The following figures (Table 1) would, however, command reasonably widespread acceptance as best guesses.

Table 1. Decadal Figures by Country of Origin

	1961	1971	1981	1991
India	81,400	240,730	673,704	840,255
Pakistan	24,900	127,500	295,400	476,555
Bangladesh			64,562	162,835
E. Africa		44,860	181,321	
Totals	106,300	413,155	1,215,048	1,479,645
% of total pop.	0.23%	0.85%	2.52%	3.4%

(NB. This chart conflates figures from Ballard 1994, p. 7 for 1961–1981, Coleman and Salt; 1996, p. 88 for 1991.)

(Robinson (1996: 98) estimates that there were 142,000 East African Asians in Britain in 1991.)

It is important to indicate the broad patterns into which these overall figures break down. The different groups have migrated from particular areas in the subcontinent: the Indians from North India (Gujarat, Punjab, and Bengal—with few South Indians); Pakistanis from Mirpur; and Bangladeshis from Sylhet. These South Asian communities are not spread evenly throughout Britain. Different nationalities tend to concentrate in different regions as indicated in Table 2 (based mainly on materials in the chapters of Owen and Salt in Coleman and Salt 1996; and Peach "Introduction" and Robinson, Ballard, and Ede et al. in Peach 1996).

Thus, whereas the Indian and Bangladeshi communities are concentrated in the Greater London area, though the Indians are more in the suburbs and the Bangladeshis in the inner city, the Pakistanis are in the Pennine regions, the old textile industrial areas. The West Midlands is an area of heavy industry, especially car manufacture. In these areas, therefore, the South Asian population is predominantly in manual labor. It is these three areas outside London that suffered most in the economic slump of the 1970s and early 1980s, so that the South Asian population suffered proportionately badly from the recession. The Indian community in Greater London has more professionals than the other groups and

Table 2. Regional Distribution of South Asian Communities

	INDIA	PAKISTAN	BANGLADESH
Greater London	347,091 [41.3%] (esp. Ealing)	87,738 [18.4%]	56,579 [34.7%] (esp. Tower Hamlets)
West Midlands	141,359 [16.8%] (esp. Wolverhampton)	88,268 [18.5%]	18,074 [11%]
Greater Manchester	29,741 [3.5%]	49,370 [10.3%]	11,440 [7%]
West Yorkshire	34,837 [4%]	80,540 [16.9%] (esp. Bradford)	5,978 [3.7%]

[Figures in square brackets indicate % of total British Indian/Pakistani/Bangladeshi residents in the region]

Leicester in the East Midlands is also an area with a high Indian population.

they therefore suffered less in that depression. The Bangladeshi population has a particularly high proportion of people with rural origins, and as the most recent of the migrant groups to establish family networks in Britain, is the one with least material resources, living mainly in council rather than private accommodation. They, therefore, experience more educational difficulties than, say, the Indians who have lived in Britain longer and settled in more socially desirable areas. The East African Asians live predominantly in the desirable suburbs of South East England and in Leicester. The South Asians of all groups who live away from these main "centers" tend to be professionals who have moved away because of career options.

The broad demographic picture of the communities is of a much younger population than that of the majority White population, with all groups having more young than old people. The household sizes are largest among the recent Bangladeshi groups, smallest among the earliest settled groups and among the Indians. The Pakistanis are in the middle. The household sizes decrease toward that of the White population among the second generation. Almost half of British Pakistanis were born in Britain, just under half of British Indians (41%) were born in Britain, as were 36 percent of British Bangladeshis. Ballard estimates that in the areas where South Asians are most heavily concentrated, something like one-quarter to one-third of births are to women of South Asian origin. Because the South Asian population in Britain is typically younger than that of the White Anglo Saxons, it may be expected to have a lower death rate and so it is generally assumed that the South Asian population in Britain will reach approximately 2.5 million by 2001. There are far fewer single-person households among South Asians in general than among the White population (less than 10% compared with over 25%) but extended families living in joint dwelling is more widespread, especially among Pakistani and Bangladeshi families. Cohabitation is very rare in all communities.

The nature of the population is, however, changing significantly. In a study of the labor force and other surveys, Jones has shown that the South Asian population is pursuing education to a far greater extent than the Whites are. Whereas only 10 percent of the white male population are graduates, 16 percent of young East African Asians are, and so are 15 percent of Indians. This trends looks set to continue.

Table 3. Percentage of 16–19-year-olds in education in 1989–1990

	MALES	FEMALES
Whites	36%	38%
S. Asians	60%	53%

(Jones 1993: 42; see also Ballard 1996 on the Pakistanis.)

The figures need breaking down for the South Asians. The East African Asians have the highest proportion of their young remaining in education, followed by the Indians, then the Pakistanis; and the Bangladeshis (the latest group to settle as families) have the lowest proportion remaining in education, especially among the women. But the point here is that whereas the South Asian population in Britain in the 1960s consisted mostly of young, single, male, uneducated, manual workers, predominantly from rural backgrounds, living in poor, shared housing in deprived inner-city areas, in low paid work, now a substantial and growing proportion of the younger people is well educated and are professional people, working in accountancy, law, and medicine in particular. It is, therefore, becoming more like the first generation of South Asians in Canada and the United States.

What of the religions? In round figures it is thought that the religions break down as follows: Muslims 1,200,000; Sikhs c. 450,000; Hindus 300,000; Jains 20,000; Parsis 5,000 (Knott, 1996: 761). Ballard, however, estimates there are 750,000 Muslims; 300,000 Sikhs, and 500,000 Hindus, a difference that illustrates the problems in calculating figures and illustrates why so many are campaigning for the British government to include a religious question in the 2001 census. In Britain Islam is predominantly a South Asian phenomenon, even though Turkish, Middle Eastern, and Black African immigration increases in greater proportion than that from South Asia. Similarly Britain does not have the large East or South East Asian populations found in Canada and the United States, though for historical reasons there are approximately 50,000 Hong Kong Chinese. But Buddhism is rarely mentioned in discussions of South Asians in Britain, because that is predominantly a White Anglo-Saxon phenomenon.

───────────── ACKNOWLEDGMENTS ─────────────

I am grateful to Roger Ballard and Kim Knott for their comments on an earlier draft of this chapter and for saving me from many errors. Any that remain are, of course, my own responsibility.

───────────── BIBLIOGRAPHY ─────────────

Anwar, M. (1979). *The Myth of Return.* London:

Ballard, R. (ed.) (1994). *Desh Pardesh, the South Asian Presence in Britain.* London: Hurst.

────. (1996). "The Pakistanis: Stability and Introspection." In Peach (1996), pp. 121–49.

────. (1997). "The Construction of a Conceptual Vision 'Ethnic Groups' and the 1991 UK Census." In *Ethnic and Racial Studies,* vol. 20, no. 1, January 1997.

Bhachu, P. (1985). *Twice Migrants: East African Sikh Settlers in Britain.* London: Tavistock.

Coleman, D. and Salt, J. (eds.) (1996). *Ethnicity in the 1991 Census, Vol. I, Demographic Characteristics of the Ethnic Minority Populations.* London: HMSO.

Dowds, L. and Young, K. (1996). "National Identity." In R. Jowell et al. (eds.), *British Social Attitudes: The 13th Report, Social and Community Planning Research.* Aldershot: Dartmouth Pub. Co., pp. 141–60.

Eade, J., Vamplewt., and Peach, C. (1996). "The Bangladeshis: The Encapsulated Community." In Peach (1996), pp. 150–60.

Firby, N. (1988). *European Travellers and Their Perceptions of Zoroastrians in the 17th and 18th Centuries.* Berlin: D. Reimer.

Fryer, P. (1984). *Staying Power: The History of Black People in Britain.* London: Pluto Press.

Hinnells, J. R. (1996a). *Zoroastrians in Britain.* Oxford: Clareadon Press.

────. (ed.) (1996b). *The New Handbook of Living Religions.* Oxford: Blackwell.

Holmes, C. (1988). *John Bull's Island: Immigration and British Society, 1871–1971.* Basingstoke: Macmillan.

Jackson, R. and Nesbitt, E. (1993). *Hindu Children in Britain.* Stoke on Trent: Trentham Books.

Jones, T. (1993). *Britain's Ethnic Minorities*. London: Policy Studies Institute.

Knott, K. (1996). "The Religions of South Asian Communities in Britain." In Hinnells, 1996b, pp. 756–74.

Miles, R. (1993). *Racism after "Race Relations."* London: Routledge.

Miles, R. and Phizacklea, A. (1994). *White Man's Country*. London: Pluto.

Owen, D. (1996). "Size Structure and Growth of the Ethnic Minority Populations." In Coleman and Salt (1996), pp. 80–123.

Pailin, D. (1984). *Attitudes to Other Religions: Comparative Religion in Seventeenth- and Eighteenth-Century Britain*. Manchester: Manchester University Press.

Peach, C. (ed.) (1996). *Ethnicity in the 1991 Census, Vol. II, The Ethnic Minority Populations of Great Britain*. London: HMSO.

Rich, P. B. (1990). *Race and Empire in British Politics*. Cambridge: Cambridge University Press.

Robinson, V. (1995). "The Migration of East African Asians to the UK." In Cohen, R. (ed.). *The Cambridge Survey of Migration*. Cambridge: pp. 331–36

———. (1996). "The Indians: Onward and Upward." In Peach (ed.), 1996, pp. 95–120.

Saggar, S. (1992). *Race and Politics in Britain*. London: Harvester Wheatsheaf.

Salt, J. (1996). "Immigration and Ethnic Group." In Coleman and Salt (eds.), 1996, pp. 124–50

Sharpe, E. J. (1975). *Comparative Religion: A History* (2nd ed. 1985). London: Duckworth.

Solomos, J. (1989). *Race and Racism in Contemporary Britain*. Basingstoke: Macmillan Education.

Visram, R. (1986). *Ayahs, Lascars and Princes: Indians in Britain, 1700–1947*. London: Pluto Press.

4

Hinduism in Britain

Kim Knott

I n the late summer of 1995 Hinduism was in the public eye in
Britain as never before. Thousands had attended the inaugu-
ration in north London on 20 August of the Shri Swaminarayan
Mandir, the first marble Hindu temple to be built in Europe, an
outstanding architectural feat of imported craftsmanship and materials, local voluntary labor and donations. While the Hindu community celebrated this historic moment, it also awaited earnestly the
verdict of the Secretary of State for the Environment concerning
the fate of another major Hindu institution, Bhaktivedanta Manor,
the temple and seminary belonging to the Hare Krishna movement,
International Society for Krishna Consciousness (ISKCON), at the
heart of a ten-year controversy with local government over planning
issues (Nye 1996, ISKCON 1995). Having defied an Enforcement
Notice issued by Hertsmere Council by publicly celebrating the anniversary in 1994 of Lord Krishna's birth, the festival in August
1995 was a quiet affair at the Manor. The temple president was

awaiting trial for allowing the 1994 celebration to go ahead. Hindus country-wide were waiting to hear the results of the Public Enquiry.

Both the building of the new Swaminarayan *mandir* and the campaign to save Bhaktivedanta Manor from closure to the public attracted media comment. Press and television covered both stories, with the Manor issue being revisited many times in the duration of the ten-year legal battle. Local and national political support was sought by Hindus at the heart of both projects, with leaders of the main political parties offering their congratulations on the opening of the new temple, and Members of Parliament of all persuasions being lobbied in the campaign for the retention of Bhaktivedanta Manor as a public place of worship. Additionally, both issues had significance for Hindu religious and political agendas. Although Bhaktivedanta Manor and the Shri Swaminarayan Mandir represented particular Hindu *vaishnava sampradaya*, they were both keenly aware of their role in representing "Hinduism" in Britain and in mobilizing British Hindus.[1]

The public focus on Hinduism in the late summer of 1995 did not end with coverage of these two issues, however. On 22 September, news broke that around the Hindu world icons of Ganesh were consuming milk.[2] Hindus flocked to temples to make offerings and to observe the phenomenon. "Miracle," "hallucination," "simple scientific explanation," and "politically-inspired hoax" ran the headlines, as the old debate between faith and science reemerged. This issue went to the heart of Hindu theology, to Hindu understandings of the nature of divine manifestation, particularly the meaning of the incarnation of God in the *murti* or temple icon. It was an issue about Hindu belief and ritual action; it was also a reflection of British Hindus' participation in global Hindu relationships, of extended kin and caste groups, *sampradayas* and international religiopolitical movements such as Vishwa Hindu Parishad and Rashtriya Swayamsevak Sangh (the British wing of which is the Hindu Swamam Sevak Sangh). Word spread fast by telephone, fax, and Internet from initial reports in North India. Mobilized by faith and devotion, many British Hindus responded by visiting their local temples to experience the benign blessing of Lord Ganesh for themselves. Others remained at home, skeptical of the miraculous claims.

A Brief History of Hindu Settlement and Institutional Development

These events are indicative of the dynamism of British Hindus, their diversity, their willingness to fight for Hindu causes and a

Hindu identity, and their determination to reproduce Hindu practices and institutions on British soil. These characteristics have come to the fore gradually in the forty years of Hindu community development in Britain.[3] In writing about the religions of those of South Asian origin in Britain in the early 1960s, Rashmi Desai informed his readers that, unlike Sikhs or Muslims, Hindus had no temples in Britain (1963, 93). At that time Hindus were in a minority among South Asians, those who were resident being predominantly Punjabi and male, and settled with Sikhs and Muslims from the same region of origin in urban areas where employment could be gained in industry.[4] Some Gujaratis had also begun to settle, and Desai's account illustrates well the settlement process in one northern city, Bradford, in this period. The desire of Bradford's Gujaratis to meet together and develop a cultural base issued forth in the establishment of the Bhartiya Mandal in 1957, founded to provide mutual support irrespective of caste differences. Premises were obtained in 1959, and language classes and festivals began to be held soon after.

Nearby, in the city of Leeds, Punjabi Hindus and Sikhs joined together to develop facilities, establishing a gurdwara in 1958 for worship and the practice of festivals and life-cycle rites (Knott and Kalsi 1994). This joint Punjabi venture, of which a Hindu was vice president, disintegrated in 1963 when attention to theological differences became more pronounced.[5]

By the end of the 1950s in the south of England, other groups had emerged. One, for example, brought together Maharastrians resident in London in a place of worship dedicated to Shirdi Sai Baba in a private home.[6] Another was established for Indo-Caribbean migrants, the Hindu Dharma Sabha, in south London. A third served Indian students, particularly Gujarati followers of Yogiji Maharaj of the Bochasanwasi Akshar Purushottam Sanstha. Arising from this group came the Swaminarayan Hindu Mission, London Fellowship Centre, formed and registered with the Charities Commission in 1959.

If the 1950s saw no grand Hindu temple inaugurations, they certainly saw the emergence of many small groups formed from those sharing a common ethnic background, hence a common language and culture. These were predominantly male, as it was men who had migrated initially for work. As they were joined in the early 1960s by increasing numbers of women and children, the need for further facilities developed, such as cultural and religious centers, language classes, shops, and other services. The arrival of women from all South Asian religious communities in Britain at that time was critical for the development of domestic religious practice, life-cycle rites, and religious nurture.

Probably the major change in the development of Hinduism in Britain arose with the settlement from the mid-1960s to the early 1970s of well-educated, middle-class Hindus from East Africa. Encouraged to leave Tanzania, Kenya, Malawi, and Uganda as a result of postindependence policies of Africanization, many came to Britain with experience and skills relevant to community development and the formation of religious institutions. Predominantly Gujarati by ethnic origin, the East African Hindus settled in urban centers throughout Britain, particularly in Leicester and north London. They came as whole family units, often sending a single member first to establish a base and make links with extended family members already in residence. Once settled, they began to reproduce organizations and practices familiar to them from their time in Africa.

From the mid-1960s Hindu associations, charitable trusts and devotional groups (*satsangs*) were formed in abundance. Then, in 1969, two public temples were inaugurated, one by East African migrants in Leicester, the other, the first Hare Krishna temple, opened in London by A. C. Bhaktivedanta Swami in the presence of Western devotees and local Indian Hindu guests (Coney, in this volume). In the early 1970s the first Swaminarayan *mandir* was opened by Yogiji Maharaj in Islington, London, and a Sathya Sai Centre was opened for public worship in a private home in Bradford.

The 1970s was an important time for the public face of Hinduism. Temples were opened in British cities like Leeds, Coventry, Birmingham, and west London, some by visiting Indian *swamis* from the Vishwa Hindu Parishad or other Indian Hindu movements. These *mandirs* were registered with local authorities and funded partially by local government grants. Regional media and press often covered their inaugurations, and dignitaries from local civic agencies attended. Hindu places of worship, generally in buildings converted from previous uses as schools, community centers, churches, or houses, joined with mosques, gurdwaras, synagogues, and churches as important neighborhood landmarks providing services of various kinds to their users, including regular worship, life-cycle rites and festivals, mother-tongue and English language classes, facilities for sports and cultural activities, and space for women's groups and youth meetings.

In this period interest in Hindu ideas and practices was not limited to Indian and East African settlers. New Hindu movements, often deriving from North America, were emerging and attracting young white British followers (Coney, in this volume). The media covered stories of the Beatles' interest in the Maharishi Mahesh Yogi's Transcendental Meditation (TM) and in the Hare Krishna movement (ISKCON). The "boy-guru," Maharaj Ji, attracted interest. A few years later, tales of dynamic meditation, orange clothes, sex, and big cars brought followers of Bhagwan Rajneesh to the fore. Some of these movements, notably ISKCON, the Radhasoamis (a Punjabi guru-based movement) and the Sathya Sai Baba movement, acquired a mixed white and Asian membership; others, like TM and the Rajneesh movement remained predominantly white and non-Asian in membership.

ISKCON, the Sathya Sai Baba movement, and the Swaminarayan Hindu Mission mentioned earlier are just three of the *sampradayas* that have been popular among Hindus of Indian ethnic origin in Britain. Other groups to emerge have included those focused on historical or living charismatic leaders such as Jalaram Bapa, Shirdi Sai Baba, and Morari Bapu, those deriving from well-established Indian Hindu movements such as the Pushti Marg (the Vallabhacharya movement), the Ramakrishna Mission, and the Arya Samaj, and those that have developed around caste interests such as the Valmikis. The latter, like some other movements of Punjabi origin, occupies a religious space that is influenced by both Hindu and Sikh ideas and practices (others include the Radhasoamis, Ravidasis, Nirankaris, the followers of Baba Balaknath, and the devotees of the deity Vishwakarma).[7] A proliferation of *satsangs* and *mandirs* associated with these and many other groups occurred in the late 1970s and 1980s.

Broad-based, eclectic temples also grew in number. Generally focused on Krishna, Rama, or a manifestation of Devi, but including a wide range of other Hindu deities, they served Hindus in their local areas, in some cases, like temples in Leeds and Edinburgh, seeking to appeal across ethnic and sectarian boundaries, and in others serving a specific caste or ethnic membership while not discouraging other visitors (e.g., the Gujarati Prajapati Hindu Temple in Bradford, the Sri Murugan Temple in London, founded by Tamil Hindus, and the Indo-Caribbean temple in south London). Some of these eclectic, nonsectarian temples retained a pattern of use similar to that of the majority of temples in India, with devotees visiting spasmodically according to personal need, particularly at festival times. Others became more congregational in type offering weekly gatherings for worship, generally on a Sunday.[8] Despite the growth of interest in Hindu *sampradaya* in Britain, important developments continued to occur in what was often referred to as *sanatana dharma*, the broad-based, brahmanical tradition.[9] One such example was the Dharma Jyotir Sabha, founded in 1988 in northwest London by a resident Trinidadian Hindu *pandit*, and supported by Hindus from Britain, East Africa, the Caribbean, Fiji, and Mauritius. The Sabha became identified with the tradition of textual rendition common in Indian and Caribbean Vaishnavism, with annual readings of the *Ramayana, Bhagavad-gita*, and *Bhagavat-purana*. However, the repertoire of texts grew with the *Siva-purana* being read, with Hindi and English commentary, before the festival of *Mahasivaratri* in 1997, and attracting an attendance over the seven nights of 1,200 visitors. The *Devi-purana* was also recited in 1997 during *Navaratri*, the nine-night festival to the goddess. The great majority of Hindus in Britain were unfamiliar with all but the most common Puranic stories. These public renditions gave them an opportunity to enjoy the Sanskrit and to hear the texts interpreted by a well-qualified *pandit* with a knowledge of Hindi and English and an appreciation of British Hindu concerns.

Irrespective of the type of *mandir* or the group it has served, of significance has been the role of ordinary lay Hindus in its formation and maintenance. Trained Hindu religious specialists have been small in number in Britain and generally hired from India on annual contracts by temple management committees. Such committees, comprised of men and increasingly women, have raised funds for and established temples, and have retained the right to hire and fire *pandits* according to need and popularity. Where it has proved difficult to appoint such a specialist, because of financial stringency, problems with work permits, or internal wrangling over candidates, committees have charged respected and willing individuals from within their own midst to conduct regular *puja*, buying in help from *brahmans* living nearby for important occasions such as life-cycle rites. Additionally, two *sampradayas* in Britain have had their own trained specialists: The Swaminarayan Hindu Mission has had *sadhus*, ascetics, trained in Gujarat who have conducted worship and administered their new Neasden temple, and ISKCON has trained *pujaris* (who have acquired the status of *brahman* through spiritual attainment and initiation) who have served in its temples and have been hired out to perform life-cycle rites and *yajnas*, fire offerings. ISKCON has developed diploma courses in ministerial training, deity worship, and temple management at their College of Vaishnava Studies at Bhaktivedanta Manor. This college offers the only formal training currently available in Britain for Hindu religious specialists.

Many Hindu *mandirs* in Britain, including those of ISKCON, are affiliated to the National Council of Hindu Temples, founded in the 1970s, with a membership in 1997 of around 90 temples. This represents only a small number of Britain's Hindu groups and associations, many informal, which total over 650 including national, regional, and local bodies, temples, caste associations, *bhajan mandals*, youth groups, and so on (Weller 1997). Although this figure has been calculated directly from information gathered nationally for the directory, *Religions in the UK*, other statistics for British Hindus are less reliable. No data are collected on religion in the national population census, though relevant estimations have been derived from census information on country of birth and, since 1991, ethnic origin. A calculation for 1977, of just over 300,000 Hindus, was made by Knott and Toon (1982), and estimates for the 1990s have suggested a population of around 400,000 (Weller 1997). These figures refer to nominal religious identification rather than active religious participation, the figure for which would be lower. Knott and Toon also established that the Hindu population was approximately 70 percent Gujarati and 15 percent Punjabi, with 15 percent originating from other states or countries. Perhaps of more importance in the 1990s is that, of those declared to be of Indian ethnic origin in the 1991 census (including Sikhs, Jains, Indian Christians, and Parsis), 45 percent were under 25 years old with the great majority born in Britain (Owen 1993).

Before returning to the subject of the public face of Hinduism at the end of this chapter, I will first consider the perspectives of Hindu young people and women as a means of exploring more broadly some contemporary developments and future possibilities within British Hinduism.

Young Hindus and an Agenda for the Future

As I noted above, many British Hindus are young and British-born, with little or no link with India and with English as their primary language of communication. Most have an awareness of some aspects of their families' religious practices and participation in festivals, and a knowledge of stories about Krishna, Rama, Ganesh, and the goddesses. Nurture at home is not restricted to hearing from and imitating elders, however, but is received also through video, TV, and audio cassette (Jackson and Nesbitt 1993). Films about the deities and well-known *sants* and gurus, video recordings of family weddings, *mundan-sanskar,* festivals, and visits to places of pilgrimage in India or the UK (such as the temple in Neasden or Bhaktivedanta Manor), and cassettes of devotional music are all important resources for acquiring a Hindu worldview and lifestyle (in addition to a Hindu birth). Periodicals such as *Hinduism Today*, "the Hindu family newspaper affirming the Dharma," *ISKCON World Review* and *Back to Godhead, Swaminarayan Bliss,* and *Sangh Sandesh* (produced by the Hindu Swayam Sevak Sangh); as well as ethnic newspapers (e.g., *Gujarat Samchar*); and caste group newsletters, all help to affirm Hindu and related sectarian, ethnic, and caste identities, though young people may well prefer comics, magazines, and cartoon books (including the *Amar Chitra Katha* series about the lives of the deities). Some young Hindus attend supplementary classes or religious youth groups, held often at temples or community centers, where they learn community languages, religious education, music, dance, and physical activities of various kinds. Additionally, many will have had some exposure to Hinduism in the school classroom where *Divali*, the characters of the *Ramayana,* and Mahatma Gandhi make an appearance. There may well be little relationship between Gujarati, Punjabi, or Tamil Hindu experience at home and the representation of Hinduism in school, but the affirmation of a Hindu identity produced by its place in the religious education curriculum is important. Very few will have received an education in a Hindu school, though the Swaminarayan Hindu Mission offers primary and secondary education in its private school in north London and ISKCON runs a *gurukula* for primary-age children at Bhaktivedanta Manor.

The character of Hindu children's religious socialization depends much on the commitment of other family members and the extent of their participation in Hindu institutions and movements. The work of Eleanor Nesbitt has shown that, of the young Hindus she interviewed, those who were members of *sampradayas* generally exhibited the greatest knowledge of Hindu principles, values, and dietary rules, with those who had been to *sampradaya* classes being particularly conversant with scriptural teaching and "*sampradaya*-specific terminology" (Nesbitt, forthcoming). However, many other Hindu young people also demonstrate a good knowledge of ritual practices, being able to describe common activities such as weddings, festivals, and *puja,* but also those associated with *vrats*, vows and fasts, *jagrans*, vigils, and *sanskaras*, life-cycle rites (Logan 1988, Jackson and Nesbitt 1993, Knott 1996). Children's participation in these activities, as onlookers, assistants, or key participants (e.g., in *yagnopavita*, the sacred thread ceremony, or as *goyani* or *kanjak*, female participants in the worship of the goddess), is important for the transmission of Hindu practices to a younger generation.

The reproduction of particular sectarian Hinduisms is partly facilitated by their youth provision. Hindu Swayam Sevak Sangh organizes youth activities nationwide, some of which mirror the training activities of the Indian nationalist parent organization, the RSS (*Sangh Sandesh*). Young people in the Sai Baba movement attend *bal vikas* classes and play an important role in regular Thursday worship, leading *bhajan* singing and distributing *prasada* (Bowen 1988, Jackson and Nesbitt 1993). The Swaminarayan Hindu Mission runs separate male and female groups for children and young people (*bal mandal, yukak mandal*) in which instruction in the teaching of Lord Swaminarayan, moral matters, spiritual practice, and religious etiquette is disseminated (Brear 1992, Pancholi 1993). ISKCON's youth groups offer a similar training, oriented around the *Bhagavad-gita* and *Srimad Bhagavatam* (the *Bhagavata-purana*), and the interpretation of their founder-*acharya*, A. C. Bhaktivedanta Swami Prabhupada. One of the youth groups emerging from ISKCON, Pandava Sena, was active in organizing Hindu support for the campaign to save Bhaktivedanta Manor and, on a nonsectarian ticket, in demonstrating in London about the Manor's importance for Hindu identity in Britain and the rights of British Asians (Nye 1996, forthcoming).

Although the reproduction of *sampradaya* teachings and practices is an important objective within these youth wings (many of which are run by community elders) they are not immune to change as this last example shows. Young Hindus are active agents with their own agenda, not simply the passive recipients of sect doctrine and the views and values of their elders. A passion for environmental issues, pride in a Hindu identity, innovation in fund-raising and communication, a competitive streak, and a desire for personal achievement are the marks of many youth activities within these *sampradayas*.

One broad-based movement, established and led by young Hindus, is the National Hindu Students Forum. Begun in 1991, it has chapters on many university campuses. Some branches have set up World Wide Web sites to publicize their objectives and to encourage communication between Hindu students locally and globally. The sites provide access to the sister body in North America and to other web sites on Indian and Hindu affairs.

British Hinduism in the hands of pro-active young people in these and other groups is dynamic. There is an increasing demand for English-medium instructional material, for the meaning of beliefs and practices to be explained, for new leadership opportunities, greater ethical engagement (e.g., on issues of sexuality and environmentalism) and more public responsibilities for women. The extent of the retention of vernacular practices, particularly those from folk rather than brahmanical traditions, remains to be seen. While some young people are able to recount family stories about caste traditions, the efficacy of fasts, malevolent spirits, and magical practices, few express personal belief or active interest in such matters (Jackson and Nesbitt 1993, Knott in Ballard 1994, Knott 1996). How far will such ideas withstand the modernist critique—rational and scientific—which is second nature to most young Hindus educated in Britain, or indeed their urban-educated Indian counterparts? Another important question is how far young Hindus might wish to reproduce an Indian communalist agenda in Britain? Young Hindus are certainly aware of Muslim and Sikh groups in Britain, and some members of Hindu Swayam Sevak Sangh and the National Hindu Students Forum, for example, have armed themselves verbally to withstand the proselytizing strategies of Muslim outreach organizations (such as Tablighi Jama'at and Hizb-ut Tahrir), and have sought to develop a sense of Hindu identity and an awareness of Indian religious politics. However, as temperate British Hindu and Muslim reactions to events in 1992 at the Babri Masjid in Ayodhya showed, the violence associated with a Hindu communalist agenda in India rarely manifests itself in Britain, even though revivalist rhetoric is evident periodically in the writings of movements such as the Vishwa Hindu Parishad and Hindu Swayam Sevak Sangh and their British Muslim counterparts (Burlet and Reid 1995).

Hindu Women in Britain: Perspectives and Possibilities

In order to understand fully the nature and development of Hinduism in Britain it is essential to hear separately from women. Hindu women have been involved in most aspects of community development in Britain, participating in fund-raising, the running of temples, informal *satsangs* and *sampradaya* groups, worshiping at home, nurturing children, and maintaining kinship networks. However, as in most aspects of British public life, they have generally been less in evidence than men, though no doubt active agents behind the scenes. A few women have exercised powerful roles within British Hindu temples. Vertovec (1992) describes the charismatic function of Mother Shyama in the Balham temple in south London, a woman who has been viewed as a living saint and pure, celibate devotee, composer of devotional songs, and inspiration to many Hindus locally and further afield. Nye (1995) recounts the story of an East African Asian settler, Mrs. Anand, and her role in the establishment of the *mandir* in Edinburgh. Wilkinson (1994) mentions the roving spiritual leader, Dr. Bageeshwari Devi, who has visited numerous British Hindu temples and lectured in English on matters philosophical. Additionally, there are those women who have been active on the management committees of temples in cities like Leicester and Birmingham. It is noteworthy, however, that the newspaper *Hinduism Today*, in an issue featuring women religious leaders (February 1994) was able to identify only one such woman in Britain (Mataji Nirmala Devi, see below), but many more in other diaspora locations such as North America, South Africa, and Australia.

At a local rather than national level women have been actively involved in the organization of *satsangs, bhajan mandals* (singing groups), and *mahila mandals* (women's circles), many of which take place in homes rather than in public spaces. Women's religious roles in the domestic arena extend far beyond this, however, as it generally is they who take responsibility for regular worship (*puja*), their children's religious nurture, and the organization of life-cycle rites.

In this informal, but vitally important arena, women are particularly active in practices involving goddesses, such as Ambamata, Parvati, Santoshima, and Kali. In these, no *brahman* intermediaries are required, men are rarely present, and women communicate directly with the deity of their choice, by petitioning her, representing her, or by acting as her medium or one possessed by her. Some of these activities are sanctioned by brahmanical tradition and others derive their authority from folk traditions, but in all of them women acquire or utilize power. In the practice of *vrats*, when women fast weekly, monthly, or annually to acquire a good husband or sons or to bring about good health and longevity for husbands and other family members, they exercise their power in the service of a goddess (or occasionally a god) in exchange for their desired objective. As *goyanis*, young unmarried girls or married women whose husbands are still alive, they represent a goddess such as Ambamata or her female kin in annual rituals and life-cycle rites. As a *bhui*, a woman is possessed by the goddess, with the power to give counsel and to mediate her answers to prayers and requests for help.

Many older Hindu women in Britain perform such religious practices, with younger ones learning by example and participation.

Some of the latter are critical of their efficacy or reject them as superstitious. Some reinterpret their meaning in terms of modern rationalist explanations, seeing periodic fasting as healthy, or trance behavior as therapeutic. The culture of Hindu women's relationships with the goddesses remains popular and continues to be an important expression of women's agency in religious matters.

Occasionally, a woman will acquire a public following from men as well as women, non-Hindus as well as Hindus as a result of her reputation for embodying the goddess. One such woman was Prabhadevi Chauhan, a devotee of Ambamata from a low-caste background. She held public *satsangs* at her house in Leeds in the north of England for nearly 20 years from the mid-1960s (Knott 1986a, 174; Knott in Ballard 1994, 224–26). Her charisma outweighed issues of caste and religion for those who visited her, and she offered an alternative but nonetheless traditional form of Hindu worship to that available in eclectic and sectarian temples.

Several other Hindu women have exhibited charisma in attracting a following in Britain, particularly from among a Western rather than an Asian audience. Mataji Nirmala Devi, founder and guru of Sahaja Yoga, Mother Meera (who has never visited Britain but is well-known there), and leaders of the Brahma Kumari movement are examples (Coney, in this volume). The latter, founded in North India in the 1930s, was described by Babb (1984) as a form of indigenous Indian feminism as a result of its celibate stand against the male oppression of women. It has not publicized itself as a movement for women or women's issues, but it has been significant in presenting a form of neo-Hinduism informed by an awareness of gender issues. The Swaminarayan *sampradaya* has also been interesting in this regard, its segregationalist policy embraced in order to protect women and offer them opportunities for spiritual progress with no threat from men (Pancholi 1993). Both movements have represented reformist, pro-women strategies within neo-Hinduism and both have had followings, albeit quite different, in Britain.

Not all women born Hindu have accepted that Hindu traditions and movements are capable of the reforms necessary to liberate women from what they see as the oppressive nature of both the Hindu family and brahmanical orthodoxy. In Britain, some who have come to this conclusion have occupied an alternative secular space, shared with other non-Hindu feminists, from where they have offered a critique of Hinduism and other religions. As members of groups such as Southall Black Sisters and Women Against Fundamentalism they have campaigned against issues with their roots in either brahmanical Hindu teachings, such as feticide, or the Hindu social system, such as dowry abuse or domestic violence (Sahgal and Yuval-Davis 1993). It would be wrong to suggest that it was only secular feminists who had challenged traditional teachings or customs seen as oppressive to women, however. Many Hindu women have withstood, either by public demonstration or private subversion, the pressure to conform to normative roles or to accept abuse in the name of their religion (Barton 1987, Knott 1996). Some have felt unable to continue to practice as Hindus; others have found strength in the way of *bhakti* or from following the teachings of their guru.

The Making of British Hinduism

If we add the diverse and less commonly voiced perspectives of women and young people to the varied public facets of British Hinduism, a rich and complex picture emerges. The importance of highlighting the former becomes evident if we return to the events of 1995 with which this chapter began. In two of those, the campaign to save Bhaktivedanta Manor and the opening of the Swaminarayan Mandir, the mantle of British Hinduism was donned by particular groups (*sampradaya*), and the interests of British Hindus were claimed to be served by their actions. ISKCON and the Swaminarayan Hindu Mission emerged, not for the first time, as powerful bodies claiming to represent the British Hindu constituency.[10] In the third event of 1995, many believed an Indian Hindu communalist agenda to have been the catalyst for the contagious global excitement surrounding the miracle of Ganesh. All three of these events raise the important issues of dominant ideology and political interest. Whose interpretation of Hinduism is most persuasive among British Hindus, and why? Furthermore, who represents Hinduism in Britain to a wider audience, to the State, its national and local agencies, to those in educational circles, and those in other religions? Is it possible for national representative networks like the Hindu Council of the UK, formed in 1994, or the National Council of Hindu Temples to control the public presentation of Hinduism, or are the more powerful *sampradayas* (which can quickly mobilize followers and draw on their own sectarian understandings of the history, teachings, and practices of Hinduism) able to fulfil this role more proficiently? Has there been "an iskconization of British Hinduisms" as Nye suggests (forthcoming), or has the Swaminarayan movement now claimed the principal representational role through the medium of its glorious *mandir*, attracting Hindus and non-Hindus alike? These questions, on the making and interpretation of British Hinduism, deserve a fuller treatment than can be given here. However, on the basis of the events of 1995, it is tempting to conclude that the key actors in this process have been the *sampradayas*. Before we do so, we should remember the challenging voices, often those of women or the young, who judge the adequacy of what is created and interpreted in the name of British Hinduism, rewarding it with their support or ignoring it for something different of their own making. Seen from the more intimate perspective of Hindu family life, it is in the domestic religious domain of women that Hindu teachings and practices are best nurtured. Referred to by Logan as "the heart of Hinduism," perhaps it is here rather than in its public manifestations that British Hinduism is formed?[11]

NOTES

1. A *vaishnava sampradaya* is a guru movement that focuses on the worship of Vishnu, Krishna, or Rama or one of their manifestations, for example, Lord Swaminarayan. ISKCON was started in the West in the late 1960s by a *sannyasi* from the Gaudiya Vaishnava Math in Bengal. It upholds the worship of Krishna as expounded by Chaitanya. The Swaminarayan Hindu Mission (the Gujarati name is Bochasanwasi Akshar Purushottam Sanstha) is a branch of what Williams (1984) has called "the Swaminarayan religion." The parent *sampradaya* was founded in the early nineteenth century by Sahajananda Swami, a follower of Krishna. The Sanstha seceded from the parent body and is theologically distinct, revering Lord Swaminarayan (Sahajananda Swami) and his principal disciple, Gunatitanand Swami. These are just two of the many Hindu bodies in Britain. They differ from one another and from other Hindu groups both theologically and practically. Like others, they offer their own systematic teachings on the nature of the divine, the human condition and the means to liberation. For these reasons I refer to them at times as "Hinduisms." I retain the use of "Hinduism" in the singular to indicate the full range of movements and perspectives that share a family resemblance.

2. Ganesh is the elephant-headed deity, son of Shiva and Parvati and renowned for his benevolence in granting wishes and offering protection. Ganesh is found among other widely worshiped Hindu deities in eclectic, non-*sampradaya*-based Hindu temples in Britain.

3. Hindu communities have been emerging since the late 1950s in Britain. Studies of their development have been published since 1980. A few brief overviews have been compiled (Knott 1981, Kanitkar and Jackson 1982, King 1984, Burghart 1987 [Introduction and Conclusion], Knott 1989, Thomas 1993, Baumann 1998) with most studies being regional or thematic. Hindu communities or practices in the following cities have been described: Coventry (Jackson 1981, Jackson and Nesbitt 1993), Leeds (Knott 1981, 1986a), Bradford (Bowen in Burghart 1987), Derby (Law 1991), south and west London (Vertovec 1992), Edinburgh (Nye 1995). There has been an absence of published work on Hindus in Leicester, north London, or Birmingham. Thematic studies have focused around particular caste and sect groups (e.g., see articles by Barot, Carey, and Taylor in Burghart 1987, and by Dwyer, Nesbitt, Knott, Warrier, and Vertovec in Ballard 1994, and books by Williams 1984, Knott 1986b, Bowen 1988), ritual practices and festivals (e.g., Jackson 1976, Michaelson, McDonald and Knott in Burghart 1987, Logan 1988, Firth 1997), and children and nurture (Logan 1988, Nesbitt 1991, Jackson and Nesbitt 1993). The majority of those who have researched and published work on Hinduism in Britain have been non-Hindus using a phenomenological and/or ethnographic methods of study, but important exceptions have included Rohit Barot who has researched the Swaminarayan movement (1980, in Burghart 1987) and Nilaben Pancholi who has written material for teachers and an MPhil thesis on women in the Swaminarayan movement (1993). Devotees in Hindu *sampradayas* have also produced books and articles that contribute to our knowledge of British developments (e.g., Swaminarayan Hindu Mission 1995 and *Swaminarayan Bliss*, ISKCON 1995 and *ISKCON Communications Journal*).

4. For more detailed accounts of the settlement history of South Asians in Britain see John Hinnells's "Introduction" in this volume and Ballard (1994).

5. Hindu Punjabis were requested not to perform a *mundan-sanskar*, head-shaving ceremony, on *gurdwara* premises because of the Sikh teaching on uncut hair, despite the fact that most of the Sikh committee members were themselves clean shaven.

6. Helen Kanitkar (1996), from whose paper this information is obtained, also refers to Hindu students and other visitors present in varying numbers since the end of the nineteenth century. Such individuals never constituted a community, but those who stayed on sometimes became a focus for later developments.

7. For information on such groups see Nesbitt 1991, Nesbitt in Ballard 1994, Kalsi 1992, Geaves 1997.

8. For further discussion of the issues of congregation and community among Hindus in Britain, see Knott 1986a, Vertovec 1992, and Nye 1995.

9. Although the term *sanatana dharma*, eternal tradition, is used periodically by all Hindus, regardless of allegiance, to describe the authenticity of their traditions, earlier this century it was used to identify mainstream, eclectic, brahmanical Hinduism in opposition to the Arya Samaj, a neo-Hindu movement critical of Hindu iconic worship, caste, and brahmanism.

10. As executive members of the National Council of Hindu Temples, ISKCON devotees have not infrequently represented the interests of British Hinduism in public meetings. At its Cultural Festival of India held in 1985 at Alexandra Palace in London, the Swaminarayan Hindu Mission expressed on behalf of all British Hindus their pride in their religious traditions and homeland.

11. From the title of an unpublished paper by Penny Logan, Thomas Coram Institute, University of London.

─────────── **BIBLIOGRAPHY** ───────────

Babb, L. (1984). "Indigenous Feminism in a Modern Hindu Sect." *Signs* 9:3, 399–416.

Ballard R. (ed.) (1994). *Desh Pardesh: The South Asian Presence in Britain*. London: Hurst.

Barot, R. (1980). "The Social Organization of a Swaminarayan Sect in Britain." Ph.D. thesis. London: University of London (SOAS).

Barton, R. (1987). *The Scarlet Thread: An Indian Woman Speaks (Her Story as Told to Rachel Barton)*. London: Virago.

Baumann, M. (1998). "Sustaining One's 'Little India': The Hindu Diasporas in Europe." In G. ter Haar (ed.), *Religious Communities in Diaspora*. Kampen: Kos Pharos.

Bowen, D. (1988). *The Sathya Sai Baba Community in Bradford*. Leeds: Community Religions Project, University of Leeds.

Brear, D. (1992). "Transmission of a Swaminarayan Hindu Scripture in the British East Midlands." In R. B. Williams (ed.), *A Sacred Thread: Modern Transmission of Hindu Traditions in India and Abroad* (pp. 209–27). Chambersburg, PA: Anima.

Burghart, R. (ed.) (1987). *Hinduism in Great Britain: The Perpetuation of Religion in an Alien Cultural Milieu*. London: Tavistock.

Burlet, S. and Reed, H. (1995). "Cooperation and Conflict: The South Asian Diaspora after Ayodhya." *New Community* 21:4, 587–97.

Desai, R. (1963). *Indian Immigrants in Britain*. London: Oxford University Press.

Firth, S. (1997). *Death, Dying and Bereavement in a British Hindu Community*. Kampen: Kos Pharos.

Geaves, R. (1997). "Worship of Baba Balaknath." Unpublished paper, Punjab Research Group, Coventry University.

Hindu Swayam Sevak Sangh. *Sangh Sandesh*.

Hinduism Today.

ISKCON (1995). *Shree Krishna Janamasthami*. Watford: ISKCON.

———. *ISKCON Communications Journal*.

———. *ISKCON World Review*.

———. *Back to Godhead*.

Jackson, R. (1976). "Holi in North India and in an English City: Some Adaptations and Anomalies." *New Community* 5:3, 203–10.

——— (1981). "The Shree Krishna Temple and the Gujarati Hindu Community in Coventry." In D. Bowen (ed.), *Hinduism in England* (pp. 110–17). Bradford: Bradford College.

Jackson, R. and Nesbitt, E. (1993). *Hindu Children in Britain*. Stoke-on-Trent: Trentham Books.

Kalsi, S. S. (1992). *The Evolution of a Sikh Community in Britain*. Leeds: Community Religions Project: University of Leeds.

Kanitkar, H. (1996). "The Hindu Diaspora: Britain." Unpublished paper, Centre for South Asian Studies, SOAS, London.

Kanitkar, H. and Jackson, R. (1982). *Hindus in Britain*. London: University of London (SOAS).

King, U. (1984). "A Report on Hinduism in Britain." *Community Religions Project Research Paper 2*. Leeds: University of Leeds.

Knott, K. (1981). "The Hindu Population in England: Hinduism in Leeds." *Religious Research Paper 4*. Leeds: Department of Sociology, University of Leeds.

——— (1986a). *Hinduism in Leeds*. Leeds: Community Religions Project, University of Leeds.

——— (1986b). *My Sweet Lord: The Hare Krishna Movement*. Wellingborough: The Aquarian Press.

——— (1989). "Hindu Communities in Britain." In P. Badham (ed.), *Religion, State and Society in Britain* (pp. 243–58). Lewiston/Queenston/Lampeter: Edwin Mellen Press.

——— (1996). "Hindu Women, Destiny and Stridharma." *Religion*, 26:1, 15–35.

Knott, K. and Kalsi, S. S. (1994). "The Advent of Asian Religions." In A. Mason (ed.), *Religions in Leeds* (pp. 161–79). Stroud: Alan Sutton.

Knott, K. and Toon, R. (1982). "Muslims, Sikhs and Hindus in the UK: Problems in the Estimation of Religious Statistics." *Religious Research Papers 6.* Leeds: Department of Sociology, University of Leeds.

Law, J. (1991). "The Religious Beliefs and Practices of Hindus in Derby." *Community Religions Project Research Paper 8.* Leeds: University of Leeds.

Logan, P. (1988). "Practising Religion: British Hindu Children and the Navaratri Festival." *British Journal of Religious Education,* 10:3, 160–69.

Nesbitt, E. (1991). *My Dad's Hindu, My Mum's Side Are Sikhs: Issues in Religious Identity.* Charlbury: National Foundation for Arts Education.

———. (forthcoming). "The Contribution of Nurture in a Sampradaya to Young British Hindus' Understanding of Their Tradition." In J. Hinnells and W. Menski (eds.), *From Generation to Generation: Religious Reconstruction in the South Asian Diaspora.* London: Kegan Paul.

Nye, M. (1995). *A Place for Our Gods: The Construction of a Edinburgh Hindu Temple Community.* London: Curzon.

——— (1996). "Hare Krishna and Sanatan Dharma in Britain: The Campaign for Bhaktivedanta Manor." *Journal of Contemporary Religion,* 11:1, 37–56.

——— (forthcoming). "The Iskconization of British Hinduisms." In J. Hinnells and W. Menski (eds.), *From Generation to Generation; Religious Reconstruction in the South Asian Diaspora.* London: Kegan Paul.

Owen, D. (1993). *1991 Statistical Paper No. 5: Country of Birth, Settlement Patterns* and *1991 Statistical Paper No. 2: Ethnic Minorities in GB, Age and Gender Structure.* University of Warwick: Centre for Research in Ethnic Relations (National Ethnic Minority Data Archive).

Pancholi, N. (1993). "The Role and Contribution of Women in the Swaminarayan Hindu Sampradaya." MPhil thesis. Leeds: University of Leeds.

Sahgal, G. and Yuval-Davis, N. (eds.) (1993). *Refusing Holy Orders: Women and Fundamentalism in Britain.* London: Virago.

Swaminarayan Hindu Mission. (1995). *Mandir Mahotsav: Shri Swaminarayan Mandir, Neasden, London.* London: Swaminarayan Hindu Mission.

———. *Swaminarayan Bliss.*

Thomas, T. (1993). "Hindu Dharma in Dispersion." In G. Parsons (ed.), *The Growth of Religious Diversity: Britain from 1945* (pp. 175–204). London: Routledge.

Vertovec, S. (1992). "Community and Congregation in London Hindu Temples: Divergent Trends." *New Community,* 18:2, 251–64.

Virat Hindu Sammelan. (1989). *Virat Hindu Sammelan Souvenir.*

Weller, P. (ed.) (1997). *Religions in the UK*, 2nd ed. Derby: University of Derby/Interfaith Network (UK).

Wilkinson, S. (1994). "Young British Hindu Women's Interpretations of the Images of Womanhood in Hinduism." Ph.D. thesis. Leeds: University of Leeds.

Williams, R. B. (1984). *A New Face of Hinduism: The Swaminarayan Religion*. Cambridge: Cambridge University Press.

5

Muslims in Britain

Ethnic Minorities, Community, or Ummah?

Jørgen S. Nielsen

O f all the countries of western Europe it is probably true to say that Britain was the first to see the collection of information and material about its Muslim communities. The reasons for this are comparatively obvious, having to do with the earlier settlement of the communities as we shall see below. But it is probably equally justified to suggest that scholarly research, as distinct from collection of data, on Islam in Britain did not really take off earlier than in the rest of the region. This is doubtlessly due to responses to events in the Muslim world and the consequent higher profile and visibility of Islam. But it probably has at least as much to do with circumstances in the research community and its environment; financial pressures have forced anthropologists to consider doing field studies in local communities rather than in more exotic places. Finally, current developments relating to Muslims in Britain are the product partly of their particular histories and their interaction with the British social and political environment, often and increasingly influenced by the process of observation (including scholarly), but also and increasingly significantly by international developments.

The history of the immigration and settlement of Muslims into Britain has been surveyed elsewhere in this volume. This chapter will of necessity have to reiterate briefly the characteristics of the Muslim communities, and the particular issues that have contributed to determining their internal development and their relationships with their environment. Subsequent to that, however, I shall attempt to consider issues and aspects that to me appear to be important both for an understanding of the current situation but also as preparation for possible continuing developments relating to British Islam into the future. While so doing I shall occasionally draw comparisons with other European situations in the belief that they are both of intrinsic interest to the topic of this book and of actual and potential impact on the British situation.

Islam Arrives

Yemenis and Somalis were the first communities of Muslim background to arrive in Britain, having been recruited through Aden after the opening of the Suez Canal in 1869 (Halliday 1992). Otherwise, until the immigration stop of 1962, the immigration of people of Muslim background was part of the general process of immigration, although small groups had made themselves noticed as Muslims in the period between the two world wars. This was when the Yemenis and Somalis who had originally settled in the ports began to establish themselves in inland industrial centers. It was also during this period that Muslims of more aristocratic backgrounds laid some of the early institutional foundations for Islam in London, specifically around the mosque in Woking and the Islamic Cultural Centre in Regent's Park (Nielsen 1995, chapters 1 and 4).

The immigration stop of 1962, like the one a decade later in the rest of western Europe, not only led to a reunion of families, it also had the effect of bringing Islam consciously into the equation. This can be shown by reference to the growth in numbers of mosques. In 1963, the Registrar-General had only registered 13 mosques, a figure that had been relatively stable for a number of years. From

1966 the number started increasing at a steady rate to 81 in 1974 and then at an even faster rate to 314 in 1985 and 452 in 1990 (Nielsen 1995, 45). Informed observers suggest that the actual figure is probably more than double.

One of the earliest scholarly studies of a Muslim community in Britain says of early Bangladeshi male migrants that they experienced an almost complete cessation of religious activity: it is surmised that their families back home "prayed for them." But when the family came, so did the religion (Barton 1982, 12f). A later community study suggests that the migration of wives and fiancées was, at least in part, rationalized in religious terms. They had come to "save" their menfolk from moral corruption and to bring them back to their cultural and family roots (Shaw 1988, 46ff).

This process of the relocation of religious life was not merely an act of piety out of a sense of nostalgia. It was moved along by many quite practical necessities and the tensions that these imposed on traditional ways of life. Once the families arrived, the pressures on the men grew. The financial pressures are the most obvious. It was more expensive to keep a family in Britain than it was to keep it in the home village, and the rest of the extended family at home was still expecting some support. But there were also new kinds of pressures. It was expected that, as the male head of the family, he had responsibility for relating between the family and the host country institutions necessary to the family's welfare: schools, health services, social security, and so on. Often he would find himself on his own in this, simply because the network of relatives that at home had helped provide contacts and influence either no longer existed or was ineffective in relation to the institutions of the new society. The man also found that he was being required to provide social and psychological support to his wife, a role that traditionally had been in the hands of the network of female relatives.

While men had their problems that were challenging traditional roles and perceptions, women were also having to face new circumstances. Until not long ago, the female sector of society in the countries of origin was invisible to the outside observer who tended to bring European male spectacles through which to observe. A new generation of women anthropologists in the countries of origin and the experience of people working with the ethnic minority communities have encouraged at least the beginnings of a major change of perceptions. It is clear that generalizations about the effect of migration on the life of women are very difficult. On the one hand, there is evidence that during the first phase of migration, the wives in the absence of their men acquired a good deal of autonomy. They had to handle all the family affairs, including the disposition of money sent home (Engelbrektsson 1978, 186f). This kind of development seems not to be unusual in places, like parts of Turkey or generally urbanized areas, where there was already a move toward an emphasis on the nuclear family household. On the other hand, there is equally evidence that, especially in South Asia, the extended family retained the traditional hierarchy of collective responsibility and control not only in the country of origin but also, at least to some extent, in the country of settlement (Shaw 1988, 85–110).

At the risk of overgeneralization it may be possible to make two suggestions as to the effect of migration on women. First, the fact that the vast majority of immigrants have come from village backgrounds means that the rate of illiteracy, or at least minimal literacy, was very high. They often had little experience of coping with urban life and the bureaucratic state apart from their extended family networks. In Britain this meant that they had to depend on others to obtain services in educational, health, and social welfare. Those others have tended to be their husbands, who have often been inadequate as suggested earlier or have interpreted their wives' needs through their own perceptions of priorities. Or those others have been functionaries of the host system—social workers, teachers, doctors, and so forth—who have not been able to interpret the women's needs because of ignorance or prejudice.

Many of the decisions of daily life that both women and men had to face were ones that had been associated with deeply ingrained cultural and religious values and expectations, above all in the fields of women's health and children's education. In the home environment, it was unusual for it to be necessary to explicate these values as a rationale for customary practices. In the new environment, the customary practices were often not possible, as the new institutions and their values and expectations thwarted or undermined them. So they had to be defended in terms that both sides could understand. Often this was almost impossible, and in the extremes the outcome could be expressed in terms of mental illness. Of the various layers of rationalization in defense of custom, religion increasingly came to be seen as one that could serve a multiple purpose. Islam was the rationale that was individually most satisfactory as well as finding the widest support among the minority community as a whole. Given the generally secular idioms of the host institutions, it was ironically a religious defense that was discovered to have the most positive resonance; indeed, appeal to religion could in fact motivate the support of individuals in the host institutions. This was most clearly the case in education, but it also worked in hospitals and in local community situations.

The family reunited was thus the route as well as the cause and the locus for the immigration of Islam to Britain. The fact that the environment into which Islam moved was a generally secularized post-Christian one helped to determine the shape that Islam took in its initial stages. In the countries of origin, little effort had to be made by most people to ensure access to facilities for the performance of explicitly Islamic acts of piety. Ordinary everyday necessities were in consonance with people's expectations in areas such as food, clothing, housing patterns, and human relations. A mosque was usually available, provided by a variety of different sources but often maintained by the village collectively, as was basic Islamic instruction for the children.

The Reconstruction of Islam

In the British urban setting, however, people individually had to make efforts to obtain every minor detail of these customary expectations. As communities grew, so the reconstruction of tradition became easier even as it tended to further emphasize its distinction from the environment. But the provision of religiocultural services still needed efforts beyond the traditional. It was therefore natural that initiative toward the organization of Islam in Britain should have come from movements that had already established themselves in the countries of origin for particular religious and political purposes in forms that marked them out from the "background noise" of general everyday practical piety.

With the South Asian Muslim communities, therefore, came the organized Islam of South Asia (Robinson 1988). In terms of research most attention has been devoted to the network of organizations related to the Jamaat-i-Islami: The Islamic Foundation, the UK Islamic Mission, and the Muslim Educational Trust, plus more recent youth organizations (most recently Geaves 1996). There is little doubt that this network has been the most successful in establishing a public profile and in attaining an influence generally rather above that justified by its support among Muslims in Britain. Much more widespread are the various networks of personal followings of "holy men," *pirs*, some comparatively local in character and others linked into major international Sufi networks, often generally subsumed under the heading Brelwi although not always correctly. With a smaller but very active and organized following are the Deobandis with a number of mosques and several "colleges."

This first phase of Muslim organization took place primarily with the purpose of providing the facilities that the Muslim community needed to reconstruct its religiocommunal life in the new context. Centrally this meant places of worship. For the first several decades these were converted properties: warehouses, private homes, shops. By the 1980s a few purpose-built mosques had been constructed and plans were being laid for dozens more. But by this time the functions of the mosques had expanded significantly. From an early stage, mosques were places for Islamic instruction as well as places of worship. Instruction was traditional in content and method and the teachers were untrained volunteers, usually led by an imam imported from the village of origin. Institutions associated with the larger countrywide organizations, in particular those in the Deobandi and the Jamaat-i-Islami related networks, tended to have better-organized structures, both in terms of curriculum and of teachers.

As has been the case in regard to the Muslim world generally, outside observers had for long assumed that the Sufi traditions were in terminal decline (Trimingham 1971). In Britain, for a long time after the arrival, it was as if Sufi networks were invisible, and it was a rare researcher who recognized their significance as did Ally in his account of the early Yemeni immigration (Ally 1981). Only from the mid-1980s was attention turned seriously in that direction. Such renewed visibility of Sufism may be attributed to the requirement that if they wanted to have access to public funds they needed to have an associational form that the public funder could recognize. Thus Sufi orders, arriving and living as informal networks, began to take on formal and therefore more visible structures during the late 1980s.

In due course the larger mosques have developed other activities as well. Some have facilities for preparing the dead for burial, a few even have their own mortuaries. Many have at least rudimentary space for public meetings and basic libraries. As the economic climate changed during the 1980s and unemployment grew, some of the larger mosques began to liaise with local government offices and official agencies to provide employment training and advice. At the same time a decline in the number of local government funded voluntary associations servicing the ethnic minorities provided the space for Muslim organizations to play a more prominent role (Nielsen 1994).

For a long time relations between Muslim organizations and the state were limited to the occasional polite and symbolic meeting on occasions such as those arranged by the Union of Muslim Organizations (UMO) to mark Muslim festivals, when a government figure would be guest of honor. The generally idiosyncratic way in which churches relate to the state did not lend itself to a public recognition of the kind that was granted in Belgium in 1974 and in Austria in 1979.

A New Generation

So far I have concentrated on the immigrant generation and the direct effects of the first generation of settlement. But as I have already indicated, there is a growing proportion of young people who have been born and brought up in Britain. A further number arrived in Britain while they were still in preschool age. This makes for an increasing number who have been brought up in homes and communities dominated by parental cultures and the pressures of living these cultures in a strange environment, and in schools totally part of the host environment. In Britain we have in recent years seen more and more of this British generation coming out of education, setting up their own homes and bringing up their own families. This first generation of indigenous ethnic minority has often been described as being "between two cultures." It is tempting to see why. On the one hand they are being socialized in a close environment dominated by the parental culture, reinforced by the institutions set up by the community, such as mosques and Qur'an schools, local groceries, and so on. Surveys in Britain have shown how attached especially Muslim children are to aspects of their parents' way of life, including a widespread acceptance of traditional arranged marriages and gender roles (Anwar 1981). On the other hand they have been and are being educated in a European system of education with its emphasis, at least in theory, on the development of the autonomous critical individual—a concept that both in theory and practice challenges both their parents' expectations of respect for authority and the wider community's expectation of adherence to religious authority and communal solidarity.

The picture is rather more complex than the idea of "between two cultures" might suggest. First, of course, it is not possible simply to talk of two cultures. As Gerd Baumann points out (1996, chapter 2) cultures are complex, multiple, mobile, and with porous borders. Second, there is no "standard reaction." There are certainly those who become rootless, and can cope with neither parents' or general British expectations and feel rejected by both. This is evidenced especially in growing juvenile delinquency, a phenomenon that is beginning to appear even among the hitherto most law-abiding in Britain, namely the Muslims from South Asia.

But there are also those not insignificant numbers of young people who are living in and with both cultures, who are able to operate successfully in both, and who as they grow up and start their own families are beginning to create a positive functional synthesis of both. They tend to be the better educated who have the conscious intellectual tools to undertake the analysis of their situation necessary to develop visible choices. The fact that they are educated also means they are likely to be in reasonably paid employment and housing and therefore have the space for maneuver, which others under material pressures do not have. It is likely to be people from this group who will provide the leadership and role models for the next generation of the Muslim community.

A smaller group, also often among the better educated, appear to have opted for integration in the culture and context of the host society—although assimilation is not usually possible for simple reasons of skin color encountering racist attitudes. In Britain, as also in France, numbers of young people have committed themselves to the domestic political processes, although still only at the local level. For long this tended to find expression in association with groups and movements that had adopted an analysis of society of a Marxist nature, rejecting the particular cultural and ethnic backgrounds of their parents, identifying themselves instead as "black" on the lines classically depicted by Castles and Koszak (1973). While the category "black" is still used by many secularized youth activists, its ideological overtones has weakened substantially in recent years, probably in the main due to the general retreat of Marxist discourse in the broad left of the political spectrum.

The "Rushdie affair" is also likely to have been a significant contributory factor to this decline of interest in a racial categorization among young Muslims. They may very well have agreed with the facts and experiences of rejection and racism underlying this option, but they have increasingly rejected the consequent identification and political program. It was at the end of the 1980s that young people of Muslim background ceased being a collection of individuals only but also developed a demographic character. The 5–15-year-olds of the 1981 Census, then the largest 10-year age group among Pakistanis and Bangladeshis, were in their teens and early 20s by 1989. They were experiencing the disappointed expectations of people who had been promised equality of opportunity both by their leaders and by the educational system, however flawed the latter may have been in practice. Running up against discrimination and unemployment, the Rushdie affair became a rallying cry that activated thousands of young people who had hitherto had little or no connection to Islamic religious institutions. The fact that the vast majority were UK citizens by birth or through their parents' naturalization or registration increased the sense of frustration. Here only France, of the countries of western Europe, had anything like a similar situation where the children of immigrants were growing up with citizenship. It was probably no coincidence that France had its own *cause célèbre* later in the same year of 1989 in the "head scarves affair," when five young Muslim girls challenged the laicist educational system by turning up for school wearing head scarves (*Hommes et migrations* 1990).

At the same time, one has to recognize that these three suggested tendencies do not include the majority of the young. There are no reliable surveys. My own impression is that the majority, in fact, are still generally satisfied finding security within their parents' cultural domain, while making the necessary minimal adaptations to be able to function in the surrounding economic arena. In light of the widespread British and European reluctance to accept the ethnic minorities as full and equal partners in a multicultural society, one can readily understand their own reluctance to commit themselves to their British context to the extent of cutting off the roots on which they continue to depend.

In recent years higher and further education have become of fast growing importance. Many such young people have been through these tertiary levels, the vast majority looking for preparation for professional careers. But a growing number have also been looking to colleges and universities for the resources to help them understand and develop their self-awareness as Muslims. Already in the early 1980s small numbers of Muslims were doing degrees in Arabic so that they could explore the Islamic sources properly. Anecdotal evidence from university departments in the 1990s suggest that in some places they may now be the majority of students on Arabic and Islamic studies programs. Information from the School of Oriental and African Studies in London, for example, suggests that undergraduate programs in Arabic, Urdu, and Bengali are particularly popular with young women living at home within commuting distance. In Birmingham, a teacher training program specifically designed for religious studies with Islam as a major component was developed in the Selly Oak Colleges and taught at Westhill College, one of the colleges of that federation. With one or two exceptions, all the students on that program have been Muslims, mostly young women.

The primary and secondary school religious education (RE) programs, which these young people are being trained to teach, have often been *causes célèbres* in education and community politics, especially in England. The 1944 Education Act's provisions for school worship and religious education, and its delegation to local government of the responsibility for managing this, had been predicated on "religion" meaning essentially Christian. The space for plurality had been granted on the assumption of various Christian denominations plus a small Jewish community. From the early 1970s new educational theories and the recognition that there were now other religions in the country led to new "multi-faith" RE syllabuses being developed together with the necessary changes to teacher training (Nielsen 1989). From the mid-1980s there was something of a backlash against educational practices generally subsumed under the heading "multicultural," which coincided with a growing self-confidence among the organized Muslim leadership. These two trends came uncomfortably together in various local clashes on educational policy which, in the case of Bradford, could be argued to have led directly into the campaign against Salman Rushdie in 1989 (Lewis 1994). Subsequently there have been growing Muslim demands for their own schools to receive public funding on a par with the many Roman Catholic and Church of England schools, as well as a number of instances where local agreements have been made with Muslim parents in individual schools.

On the background of growing Muslim self-confidence and the political reverberations of the Rushdie affair, Muslim organizations have come to be taken more seriously by central government. The UK Action Committee on Islamic Affairs (UKACIA) has become a regular interlocutor with government departments and politicians. The Department of the Environment, which includes the remit for local government, has set up an Inner Cities Religious Council that includes Muslim representatives. Other national institutions have also extended such practical, as distinct from legal, recognition. In 1993 Prince Charles gave a positive speech about "Islam and the West" in Oxford, in which he welcomed the Muslim presence in Britain (Prince Charles 1993), and he reiterated this positive attitude in another speech in 1996 (*BMMS* December 1996, 1f). He also established his own advisory committee on Islam (*BMMS* January 1997). The Archbishop of Canterbury has also invited to a number of meetings of Muslim leaders as well as undertaking a high-profile meeting with Shaykh Al-Azhar in Cairo, a visit that was returned when the Shaykh visited Britain in May 1997.

Is There a Muslim Community?

Through the first part of this chapter I have regularly, but tentatively, talked of Muslims and Muslim communities. Naturally this begs questions, most centrally whether one can justify talking of a community in this context—beyond the rather vague sense that journalists and others use it. But it also raises the question of what might be meant by Muslim. These are questions not only raised within the scholarly community but also among Muslims themselves. In his recent study of Southall, Gerd Baumann (1996) clearly shows the mobility and flexibility of the concept of community. Some scholars have put the question in even more provocative terms: Do not observers by talking of the Muslim community actually participate in the creation of the phenomenon that they are claiming to describe (Rex and Modood 1964)?

Often, when participants talk of themselves as being part of a Muslim community, representing the Muslim community, or speaking for the Muslim community, they are engaged not in description but in a normative claim. The claim may, by its very repetition, bring about the creation of the phenomenon claimed. However, despite such claims, it is difficult as yet to justify talking of *the* Muslim community in Britain. The two events that in recent years could most have been expected to show the existence of the Muslim community were the Rushdie affair in 1989 and the Gulf War in 1990–1991. But while the campaign against *The Satanic Verses* did mobilize significant numbers across the country and led to the creation of new Muslim structures, particularly the UKACIA, the majority were not roused. Indeed, significant portions were either against the campaign or isolated themselves quietly from it. Such divisions were clearer during the Gulf War, when the protests against Western involvement in Desert Shield and Desert Storm were supported only by about one-third of Muslims, with another third supporting Western involvement. It is arguable that every time someone has tried to organize the "Muslim community" into common action or a common stance, the community has been further split.

It may be more justified to identify a Muslim community at a local level. Numbers of local studies over the last decade have shown a degree of internal social cohesion among populations presented as Muslim—or is that only because the researcher has explicitly asked the question? But precisely at this level, it is also recognized that individuals and groups of individuals engage in the kind of manipulation of multiple identities that makes it very difficult, as Baumann stresses, to talk of *the* community. Often "community leaders" will present themselves as speaking for the Muslim community, and on other occasions the very same people will suddenly appear as representatives of the Pakistani community or the Kashmiri community. But looking at this local level highlights the problem, for each locality presents a different picture—sometimes a very different one. Two cities that are often used by researchers as a base are Bradford and Birmingham, the former with a generally homogenous Muslim community, certainly in terms of ethnic origins and social and material circumstances, the latter with a community of great diversity in terms of ethnic, religious, and political components. A few miles from Bradford, the Muslims in Keighley present yet another picture (Vertovec).

It seems that there may be at least some truth in the suggestion that it is the outside observer's claim to be observing a Muslim community that creates a Muslim community. The political fall-out of the Rushdie affair included recognition by the political structures that religious identity could not be ignored. The Department of the Environment, responsible for local government, set up an Inner Cities Religions Council. Local authorities established formal and informal processes to negotiate with the religious communities, especially the Muslims. Bradford City Council had started this process already in the mid-1980s in an attempt to control a difficult educational situation; it is probably no coincidence that it was in Bradford that the Rushdie affair first hit the headlines (Lewis 1994). People chose to relate to a particular group under a specific identity label like Muslim for the sake of solving a particular political or social issue. Thus activated, the people concerned are encouraged to act according to that label for other purposes as well. So claims to be a Muslim community, the work of outside observers, and political reactions to specific events interact with each other to develop something called "the Muslim community." This is only one collective identity among several, and each is mobilized in different situations according to what the various parties consider to be the most likely to be effective.

However, this does not entitle one to dismiss the whole process as completely manipulative—quite apart from the consideration that however imaginary the identity may initially have been, the process gives it a social and political reality. There is a real process taking place that has to do with Muslims identifying with Islam. This process has dominated the scene for the last decade and is likely to increase in its impact over the coming decade. It can be linked to two superficially distinct processes that nonetheless interact. On the one hand is the maturing of the first generation of British Muslims, and on the other is the self-assertion of Islam in the wider world.

Toward a British Islam?

Ethnic minorities of Muslim background in Britain are ethnically, culturally, and linguistically mixed in a way that is much less the case for Sikhs or Hindus or, in other parts of Europe, for Armenians or Syrian Orthodox Christians. Certainly in village to city migration in the Arab world or Pakistan there is an element of cultural migration as there may be of ethnic or linguistic migration. But in these circumstances, it is the ethnic, cultural, or linguistic identity that is challenged in the first instance. The environment remains Muslim in expression. In fact, this migration also contributes to provoking significant change: it is often identified as one of the main reasons why urban immigrant areas in the Middle East are the most fertile ground for radical Islamist movements. In Europe the environment is not Muslim and may often be anti-Muslim. In this situation defense of identity is more easily expressed in terms of Islam, especially in matters relating to family life. But at the same time the wide mix of Muslim backgrounds forces on the minority the necessity of defending their "Muslimness." It becomes increasingly difficult to defend particular cultural practices as Islamic, when the Muslim neighbor is defending very different practices on the same basis. The mix in Britain, in other words, forces Muslims to determine what is centrally Islamic and what is a culturally relative expression of Islam. The latter can then be discarded or modified while the former can be strengthened. The young people are increasingly at the forefront of this process. Their education in and familiarity with the British environment have given them the tools to engage in such an analysis. The process is taking place all over the country in numbers of small and large groups, some formal and many informal. One expression of this process can be seen in the hitherto most successful of new Muslim newspapers, the weekly *Q-News*.

The analysis is often likely to put the young people at odds both with their parents and with the older generation of community leaders, both of whom are often solidly rooted in the particular cultural traditions of their origins. The Muslim religious leadership in Britain, in all its diversity, is admitted to lack serious education in Islamic studies (Raza 1991) and, unlike the situation in North America, there is only a very small professional and educated middle class in the immigrant generation.

A significant dimension of this process is the increasingly active role being assumed by young Muslim women. Over the years there have been women of the immigrant generation who have contributed to Muslim organizational life. They have been mostly professionals, especially doctors and academics. But their numbers have been small and they have understood how to make an impact, often against heavy odds, within traditionally male-dominated structures of various South Asian styles. The younger women grown up in Britain and successful in education are increasingly breaking with this pattern. However, there is no common course being followed. While they have shared vested interests in changing gender roles, they have differing starting points. Those from middle class and professional families, especially of East African origin and often of various Shi'ite adherences, tend to find more encouragement from their social environment, while those from families of South Asian village background usually have to struggle against tough, even violent opposition. And in cities where there are large comparatively homogeneous communities, the social pressures can be mobilized by the community to much greater effect to keep young women in line.

As a result young women during the 1980s tended toward interethnic radical feminist and antiracist groups, risking a serious break with their families. Following growing interethnic tensions in the mid-1980s and the "Rushdie affair" in 1989, the mobilization of young Muslims as Muslims also raised Islamic consciousness among young Muslim women. But reading the sources for themselves has led them to a situation where they in ever-growing numbers are being heard to make the point that the Qur'an and Sunnah provide for a status for women that Muslim society has consistently flouted. In the mid-1990s it is most often young Muslim women who are protesting against forced marriages, restrictions on women being educated and having careers, and a subservient status in the home.

Muslim women's groups have proliferated, and links have been established to Muslim women activists in other parts of Europe and the Muslim world generally.

The deepest challenge that these issues impose on young Muslims, of both sexes, is where to look for guidance: Where is religious authority to be found? The cultural ties of their parents and the lack of Islamic education of the bulk of the religious leadership tend to disqualify both groups. Together the two seek to defend their position using the available tools of social and political persuasion and pressure. But these are of only limited efficacy outside the social environment in which they were developed: techniques of social control developed in Kashmiri villages have only limited effect in an inner city district of Bradford. Some of these young people are beginning to lay the foundations of a new religious leadership. A few who have graduated from the traditional Islamic training systems of the Deobandi *dar al-'ulum* in places like Dewsbury have gone on to get degrees in Islamic studies from Al-Azhar University in Cairo. They have then returned to do degrees in law or other career-oriented subjects thus getting both Islamic training and a source of income. The numbers are very small but growing. Together with those doing Arabic and Islamic studies at British universities, are these the core of the Muslim religious leadership a generation hence?

This process also raises question marks against locations of religious authority. While the organizations and movements that have entered Britain with the immigrant communities retain a strong position—this is particularly true of some of the tendencies within the Brelvi groups (Werbner 1988)—many of them have only weak links with institutions of religious learning and authority outside their own region of origin. The new cadre of young people are beginning to construct their own direct links with other centers of authority. These are mostly in the Arab world but there are also links being developed with the Malay world and in some instances to the Turkish-speaking world. It is still much too early to assess the nature and impact of such new links. Their construction is motivated by a search for credible Islamic scholarship which can speak to the situation of young Muslims in Britain, and this is as much a search for resources of knowledge—and funding—as it is for authoritative guidance, and the latter does not necessarily follow the former.

Part of this process is obviously the identification of what is centrally Islamic, and this sooner or later directs Muslims back into the mainstream of Islamic thought, in two ways. In the process of trying to identify what it means to be Muslim, the debate is almost inevitably brought back to questions that have exercised Muslims since the very beginning of their history. These were the questions of belief, ethics, and social and political action that were at the center of the early splits into various religious tendencies from soon after the death of the Prophet in 632 C.E. until well into the 'Abbasid period in the eighth to tenth centuries. Here were the debates that formed Kharijites, Shi'ites, and among the Sunnis Mu'tazilites, Ash'arites, and the various other theological and legal schools. By the very fact of edging into this debate young Muslims in Britain are finding themselves being reconnected to the ongoing tradition of the Muslim *ummah*, the Community.

But the Community they are reconnecting to is one that is itself at the international level undergoing its own reidentification after generations of following the initiatives of outsiders. Personally, I think it is difficult to underestimate the potential impact of these dimensions in the years to come. More and more, young British Muslims are identifying themselves with the wider Muslim world; it has been remarkable how much more they have been moved by the plight of Muslims in Bosnia and Palestine in the mid-1990s than they were over a decade ago by events in Lebanon, and especially the Sabra and Shatila massacres. As they are doing so, they are also listening more intensely to what is going on there. They are beginning to learn Arabic, still in small numbers but increasing, and not just as the ritual but un-understood sounds of the Qur'an but as a Muslim *lingua franca*, ironically second to English. Certain Sufi networks are playing a distinct role here in linking people together across the traditional ethnic and regional divides, as is the Tablighi-jamaat movement. Islam on the Internet is an as yet unassessed force. This growing linkage between Muslims in Britain and the wider Muslim world may yet contribute to producing a British Muslim community in a way that the countless claims of "community leaders" and academic observers have not succeeded so far in doing.

BIBLIOGRAPHY

Ally, M. M. (1981). "History of Muslims in Britain." Unpublished MA thesis, University of Birmingham.

Anwar, M. (1981). *Young Muslims in a Multicultural Society*. Leicester: The Islamic Foundation.

Barton, S. (1982). "The Bengali Muslims of Bradford." *Research Papers: Muslims in Europe*, 13 (March 1982).

Baumann, G. (1996). *Contesting Cultures*. Cambridge: Cambridge University Press.

BMMS. British Muslims Monthly Survey. Birmingham: Centre for the Study of Islam and Christian-Muslim Relations.

Castles, S. and Koszak, G. (1973). *Immigrant Workers and Class Structure in Western Europe*. London: Oxford University Press.

Engelbrektsson, U.-B. (1978). *The Force of Tradition*. Gothenburg: University of Gothenburg.

Geaves, R. (1996). *Sectarian Influences within Islam in Britain*. Leeds: University of Leeds, Community Religions Project.

Halliday, F. (1992). *Arabs in Exile: Yemeni Migrants in Urban Britain*. London: I. B. Tauris.

Hommes et migrations (1990). Laicité-Diversité: I. L'Ecole, la laicité à l'épreuve; II. Intégration et droit à la difference; III. Islams en France, Islam de France. Special number, 1129–30, February.

Lewis, P. (1994). *Islamic Britain*. London: I. B. Tauris.

Nielsen, J. S. (1994). "Islam, musulmani e governo britannico locale e centrale: fluidita strutturale." In J. Waardenburg et al. (eds.), *I musulmani nella societa europea* (pp. 143–56). Turin: Fondazione Giovanni Agnelli.

———. (1989). "Muslims in English Schools." *Journal: Institute of Muslim Minority Affairs* 10:223–45.

———. (1995). *Muslims in Western Europe*, 2nd ed. Edinburgh: Edinburgh University Press.

Prince Charles (1993). *Islam and the West*. Oxford: Oxford Centre for Islamic Studies.

Raza, M. (1991). *Islam in Britain: Past, Present and Future*. London: Volcano Press.

Rex, J. and Modood, T. (1994). Muslim Identity: Real or Imagined? *CSIC Papers: Europe*, 12 (November 1994).

Robinson, F. (1988). *Varieties of South Asian Islam*. Coventry: University of Warwick, Centre for Research in Ethnic Relations.

Shaw, A. (1988). *A Pakistani Community in Britain*. Oxford: Blackwell.

Trimingham, J. S. (1971). *The Sufi Orders in Islam*. Oxford: Oxford University Press.

Vertovec, S. (n.d.). *Local Contexts and the Development of Muslim Communities in Britain: Observations in Keighley, West Yorkshire*. Coventry: University of Warwick, Centre for Research in Ethnic Relations.

Werbner, P. (1988), " 'Sealing the Koran': Offering and Sacrifice among Pakistani Labour Migrants." *Cultural Dynamics* 1:77–97.

6

The Growth and Changing Character of the Sikh Presence in Britain

Roger Ballard

L ike the Sikh presence in Canada and the United States, the historical roots of Britain's Sikh population are considerably deeper than is commonly appreciated, but no less specific in character. Thus while it was largely Jat Sikhs who established a pioneering toehold in California and British Columbia at around the turn of the century, the founders of the Sikh settlement in Britain had rather different origins: most belonged to the Bhatra caste, whose traditional occupation was as hawkers and peddlers. Just how they first made their way to Britain is still shrouded in mystery, but by the late 1920s small groups of Bhatra pioneers, few of which were more than half a dozen strong, could be found in many of Britain's seaports, where they had begun to make a living by selling clothes and other household goods from door to door. Although success demanded great feats of memory and a considerable amount of interpersonal skill, for most peddlers sold on credit although they spoke very little English, the niche proved profitable. Before long, their kinsmen in Punjab began to set out for Britain to take advantage of this newly identified seam of opportunities.

The Bhatras' monopoly of this niche did not last for long, however. As news of their success began to filter to other Sikh communities, others—many of whom were Jats from farming families in the Jullundur Doab—began to follow in their footsteps. While the Jats had no prior experience of peddling, their high levels of entrepreneurial commitment, together with a willingness to borrow from and to build on the Bhatras' long-established skills more than made up for that deficiency. They, too, began to prosper, so when the Second World War broke out in 1939, several hundred Sikhs were making a living in Britain as peddlers. All were men, mostly aged between 20 and 40; I would estimate that around half were Bhatras and the remainder mostly Jat.

The onset of hostilities inevitably brought many changes, some of which were negative, but others much more positive. Thus although travel back and forth to the Punjab came to a halt for the duration, a wide range of new opportunities of which the pioneers were quick to take advantage also opened up. Some continued to make a living as peddlers, but with an extra twist. They took advantage of their contacts with other parts of the Punjabi diaspora to become door-to-door distributors of nylon stockings, which although freely available in the United States were much sought after in Britain. To make the most of this they arranged for Punjabi seamen (most of whom were Mirpuri Muslims) working as stokers on trans-Atlantic convoys to buy nylons and other similarly sought-after goods in bulk in New York, which they then sold on very profitably to their delighted British customers. By no means all stayed on in the peddling trade, however. Following the introduction of conscription many industrial enterprises ran acutely short of labor, giving the pioneers an opportunity to move into areas of waged employment from which they had hitherto been excluded. To be sure the jobs on offer were invariably those that were hard, dirty, and dangerous, but if one was prepared to work long hours of overtime, they could be reasonably well paid. Many former peddlers found the prospect of earning regular wages attractive, especially since their income could be supplemented by door-to-door selling during their time off.

While wartime brought wider opportunities, and even comparative prosperity for the most entrepreneurial peddlers, the reverse was true in its immediate aftermath. As demobilized soldiers clamored to return to work, those who had filled the gaps in the employment market during their absence found themselves forced to one side once again. Some of the early pioneers managed to protect their newly acquired gains, but most found themselves pressed back out to the margins once again. Nevertheless, the Sikh pioneers did at least have a fall-back. While those who had had enough took the opportunity to return to Punjab with their accumulated profits, most simply returned to doorstep selling. This was not without its advantages in the medium term. Standards of living began to rise again, but all manner of household goods were hard to obtain. As their (mostly working-class) customers grew less poverty-stricken, peddlers' profits began to increase, and many began to swap their suitcases for stalls in local markets. To this day few local markets anywhere in Britain lack a Sikh stall-holder, and the most successful among them have gone on to yet better things, first as wholesalers, and later still—in the case of the most successful— into large-scale clothing manufacture.

Mass Migration

While these early pioneers played a crucial role in the development of the local Sikh presence, since they provided a bridgehead through which much larger numbers of settlers made their way to Britain during the subsequent phase of mass migration, that inflow was in fact precipitated by another major change in circumstances: the acute demand for additional industrial labor that erupted during the course of Britain's postwar economic boom. But for a few temporary hiccups, the boom lasted from the early 1950s right through to the end of the 1970s, and throughout this period a wide range of industrial units in outer London, in the metal-manufacturing centers of the West Midlands, and in the textile towns in the Pennine region ran acutely short of manpower, and found that the only way in which these deficiencies could be filled was by hiring migrant labor. Migrant workers—and especially those who were visibly of non-European origin—were stood right at the bottom of the ladder, and were only given access to jobs that indigenous workers preferred to avoid. Nevertheless wage rates even for these jobs were still sufficiently attractive to draw in a steadily growing inflow of migrant workers from Britain's former Imperial possessions.

Nevertheless, these inflows were far from random. Those best placed to take advantage of the new opportunities were by definition those who were aware of their location and existence, and who had access to the contacts and connections that would help them find their way through the otherwise obstacle-strewn course of migration and settlement. Given the presence of the early pioneers Punjabi Sikhs were particularly well placed in this respect, so as news of the new opportunities flowed back through kinship networks to the pioneers' villages of origin, an ever-increasing number of adventurous young Sikhs took the opportunity to take a passage to England. Besides enabling them to explore the wider world, there was also an excellent prospect of their being able to earn and save money with unprecedented speed.

However, just like the early pioneers, few envisaged that they would stay in Britain for long, and still less that it might become their permanent home. On the contrary the universal expectation—at least at the outset—was that they would return with their accumulated savings after a few years, when they would be in a position to buy more farmland, to invest in agricultural machinery, or to build a new house for themselves and their extended families. This was not, then, a flight from absolute poverty. Sikh emigration, even from rural areas, was an entrepreneurial activity, and its participants were overwhelmingly drawn from moderately well off families of peasant stock. As such their central objective was usually to catch up with, and better still to overtake, those of their kin who were better off than they were themselves.

Nor was migration an individual matter: instead it took the form of a well organized (although informal) process of chain migration, in which kinship reciprocities, supplemented by ties of friendship and of clientage, played a central role. Thus apart from a small number of well-educated city-dwellers who set off on a more individualistic basis, the vast majority of settlers found their way to Britain by taking advantage of the bridgeheads which had already been established by their predecessors. It was through them that they heard about the opportunities available, and to them that they also turned for immediate assistance in finding accommodation and a job when they first arrived in Britain. Nor did the process stop there. Having established themselves in their new environment, most settlers promptly offered similar assistance to their own kinsmen and acquaintances. So it was that although the migratory process was ultimately driven by labor shortages in Britain together with the inequality in living standards between the two arenas, at a more personal level chain migration led to the establishment of a series of well-worn corridors down which ever increasing numbers of young Sikh men made their way from villages in the central and eastern parts of the Jullundur Doab to jobs in mills and factories in cities such as Southall, Birmingham, Wolverhampton, Huddersfield, and Gravesend. In so doing chain migration not only facilitated their access to the British employment market, but also ensured that fellow-kinsmen often tended to assemble in the same place. Hence it provided settlers with ready-made foundations for the construction of new communities.

Immigration Control and Family Reunion

Just how large the inflow might have become had immigration remained uncontrolled is a matter of speculation. But that was not to be. During the course of the 1950s popular concern about the inflow of non-European migrant workers—who were not just recruited from Punjab, but also from many other parts of Britain's former Empire—became steadily more intense, particularly within those sections of the indigenous working class with whom the newcomers were competing (or at least perceived to be competing) for scarce resources. By the early 1960s this had become a major electoral issue, with the result that ever more stringent restrictions were imposed on Commonwealth Citizens' rights of entry. Even so the Sikhs, like many of their South Asian compatriots, displayed considerable ingenuity in evading these restrictions. Thus when new regulations required that all potential immigrants must show that they had a job to go to, established settlers simply asked their employers—many of whom were still keen to recruit extra hands—to issue the necessary employment vouchers, further facilitating the very process that the new rules were intended to restrict. Less than three years after its introduction the voucher system was abandoned as a failure. Since the mid-1960s halting the entry of "primary migrants" (adult males) became the central plank of government policy, and has remained so ever since.

Nevertheless Britain's Sikh population has continued to grow rapidly, not least because settlers who had already established themselves in Britain began—as was their right—to reunite their families. Until the late 1950s very few had done so: since the early pioneers invariably saw themselves as sojourners rather than settlers, their aim was to rejoin their families in Punjab at the earliest possible opportunity. But as time passed so their perspectives began to change. The longer they stayed overseas, the more they began to feel the pains of separation. As local settlements grew steadily larger and more complex as a result of chain migration, the prospect of rebuilding a Punjabi moral order in the midst of what had hitherto been regarded as a wholly alien environment slowly began to seem more realistic. As this occurred the personal attitudes began to undergo a sea change. Until then they had regarded Britain as little more than a social and cultural no-man's land in which they had little alternative but to put all their norms of civilized behavior into temporary abeyance, and where almost all forms of gratification would have to be deferred. But as the scale of local settlements grew steadily larger, they found that all the resources needed to reconstruct a more familiar moral, social, cultural, and religious order were beginning to crystallize around them. As this occurred all their previous fears about the moral dangers to which their wives and children would be exposed were they to join them in Britain began to fall away, so much so that during the course of the 1960s family reunion became commonplace.

It was as a result of all this that the volume of migration from Punjab to Britain reached a peak toward the end of the 1960s. Not only were long established settlers in the midst of reuniting their families, but so too were those young men who had found some way of avoiding or evading increasingly tight immigration controls. Few were in a position to do so immediately, since it invariably took at least a year before they could save enough to repay the cost of getting themselves into Britain, let alone to buy and furnish a house, and to purchase airline tickets for their wives and children. Immigration controls therefore took some considerable time to bite in the Sikh case, but they eventually had their desired effect. Once the process of family reunion was complete, as was so by the mid-1970s, the volume of immigration declined sharply, and has stayed at a low level ever since.

What is clear, however, is that during the course of little more than a decade the Sikh settlement in Britain underwent a far-reaching change in character. Not only did it increase dramatically in size, but as a result of family reunion, it provided a ready base for community reconstruction. Yet would this be one community or many? With that in mind we must pay some careful attention to the migrants' social origins. On the face of it they shared many commonalities. Overwhelmingly of rural origin, few had any significant command of spoken English when they first arrived, and fewer still possessed any immediately marketable educational, technical, or professional qualifications. Even so the settlers were anything but a homogeneous population in their own eyes. for despite their common commitment to the Sikh faith, they were also deeply divided by caste. Thus while the Bhatras still occupied a position of numerical dominance in many seaports, as indeed they do to this day, by the time that mass migration was complete the center of gravity of Britain's Sikh population had shifted to a range of inland industrial cities, where the settlers were overwhelmingly drawn from villages in the central and eastern parts of the Jullundur Doab. Hence in cities such as Southall, Birmingham, Wolverhampton, and Huddersfield the Jats (peasant farmers) now form a clear majority, although they are also accompanied by smaller local communities of Ramgarhias (Craftsmen), Ramdasias (Leather workers), Jhirs (Water carriers), and Valmikis (Sweepers).

That caste disjunctions of this kind may still remain important often comes as a surprise to outsiders. On the one hand Sikh spokesmen regularly suggest that their tradition is deeply hostile to caste principles, and on the other hand it is often assumed that these hereditary occupational distinctions would immediately become irrelevant in a British context. Yet despite the apparent plausibility of these arguments, it would be a great mistake to assume that caste disjunctions must therefore be absent among British Sikhs. Far from it. The occupational basis of caste may indeed have been eroded, but even so British Sikhs remain almost as committed to the rules of endogamy as they ever were, with the result that all kinship networks are necessarily caste specific. Given that chain migration funneled newcomers into particular localities along channels of kinship, and that kinship reciprocities played such a key role in subsequent processes of ethnic consolidation, virtually all the most important interpersonal networks that Sikh settlers have generated among themselves are strongly caste-specific. That is not all. As these disjunctions have been further reinforced by the growth of intercaste rivalry, most groups have also sought to build up their own distinctive pattern of both cultural adaptation and upward social mobility, but most Gurudwaras in Britain are now effectively controlled by members of a single caste. Despite the radical change of context, caste is still almost as important a source of social differentiation among British Sikh settlers as it was (and is) in rural Punjab.

The East African Connection

While the majority of British Sikhs arrived as direct migrants from Punjab, somewhere between one in five and one in ten families would identify themselves as East Africans. They, too, exhibit a specific pattern of caste affiliation, since virtually all are Ramgarhias (Craftsmen) by caste, even though their ancestral roots can be traced to the same set of villages in the Jullundur Doab as their direct migrant peers. Nevertheless they have a distinct history of migration, which can be traced back to the East African Railways' need to recruit skilled technicians to build and operate the new line into the interior that was constructed during the early years of the century. Those recruited from the Punjab were overwhelmingly Ramgarhia by caste, and once they had established themselves they, too, set off a process of chain migration. As a result Ramgarhias began to move into an ever wider range of technical, clerical, and professional occupations in East Africa, and thus to take up a position midway between the European colonial elite and their African subjects. However, Independence rendered that position increasingly untenable. Many families were forced to flee, often leaving the greater part of their financial assets behind them. The experience was traumatic, of course, but once they had got over the initial shock, most of these "twice migrants" (Bhachu 1985) found it easier to adapt to life in Britain than their direct migrant peers. Almost all arrived with reasonable fluency in English, and their children found it easier to adjust since they had previously attended English-medium schools and sat British public examinations. Moreover their experience as a semimarginalized minority in East Africa meant that they were already well aware of the benefits to be gained from developing alternative institutional arrangements of their own, and that the adoption of a strategy of ethnic consolidation was wholly compatible with a strong commitment to collective educational and professional advancement.

Thus despite the initial trauma of expulsion, East African Sikhs soon began to reconstitute their kinship networks and community structures, while also making the most of their technical, professional, and organizational skills, so much so that they soon became by far the most affluent component of Britain's Sikh population. In these circumstances families with East African connections are invariably keen to identify themselves as such, not least because this also allows them to identify themselves as an elite as compared to the "uneducated" (and of course largely non-Ramgarhia) majority. Yet despite being better educated, better qualified, and considerably more affluent than their direct migrant counterparts, such that they also tend to enjoy a much more Westernized lifestyle in material terms, it would be a mistake to assume that this is also true of all aspects of their behavior, for at the same time the East

Africans tend to be much more religiously active, and hence far more likely to sustain the external symbols of their faith. Hence while the majority of Jats—who normally regard themselves as the elite of Sikh society—have cut their hair and abandoned their turbans, a much higher proportion of East African Ramgarhias have chosen not to follow their example.

Ethnic Consolidation and Upward Mobility

Nevertheless, the broad pattern of upward social mobility of which the East Africans are such exemplars is by no means unique. Despite the many obstacles they have encountered, Sikhs of all castes, direct- as well as twice-migrant, and especially their British-born offspring have by now achieved a striking degree of material success. By dint of frugal living and a great deal of hard work (in the early days many worked 12-hour shifts six or even seven days a week) almost all have achieved a moderate degree of prosperity, while some, and especially those who started their own businesses, have succeeded beyond their wildest dreams. Virtually all Sikh families have long since abandoned the inner-city terraced houses where they initially settled, and now live in much more comfortable suburban properties. Many older people, and especially those of rural origins, remain in blue-collar occupations, but by now most of their offspring have moved on into a wide range of professional and semiprofessional jobs. To be sure the degree of mobility varies a great deal from family to family, but even so the lifestyles now enjoyed by the vast majority of British Sikhs can only be described as a comfortable and broadly middle class.

Yet despite these achievements, Sikh settlers and their offspring have not been following a path of comprehensive social and cultural assimilation, for almost all have made a great effort to sustain a sense of moral distinctiveness, particularly in personal and domestic contexts. Indeed as a series of ethnographic studies of specific local communities very clearly demonstrates, the social, cultural, and religious dimensions of the Sikh heritage are still in very good shape in contemporary Britain. Thus in addition to my own work (Ballard 1977, 1994) in Leeds, Aurora (1967) offers us a graphic account of the early phase of settlement in Southall, while James (1979) and Helweg (1986) provide some particularly rich descriptions of life within Jat Sikh settlements in Huddersfield and Gravesend respectively. By contrast Bhachu (1985, 1988) has explored the way in which East African (and hence Ramgarhia) Sikhs have reestablished themselves in South London, and in so doing shows how young women have carved out an increasingly autonomous role for themselves within (rather than outside) their families, while both Nesbitt (1994) and Juergensmeyer (1982) provide some graphic insights into developments within the often overlooked, and certainly routinely marginalized Valmiki and Ravidasia communities. Last but not least Baumann (1996) has adopted a very different perspective in order to explore the interconnections which have sprung up between young people whom all the previously cited studies would regard as being affiliated to quite separate ethnoreligious communities.

Such is the richness of these ethnographic reports that there is now no shortage of material from which to construct an overview of the processes of change and adaptation that have taken place during the course of Sikh settlement in Britain, and especially of the way in which the members of each of its many components have drawn on the resources of their own distinctive heritage as they set out on a process of ethnic consolidation. But even though each such group has consequently constructed what can perhaps best be described as an ethnic colony around itself, such arenas are anything but hermetically sealed. Quite the contrary. In the course of earning a living, let alone through their participation in a wide range of extra-domestic activities, all British Sikhs—and especially those who are locally born and bred—are by definition active participants in the wider social, cultural, and behavioral order, and by now feel thoroughly at home with its styles and conventions. With this in mind it is worth remembering that public appearances can be most deceptive. Just because someone has the capacity to present themselves in a comprehensively anglicized way does not preclude the possibility that they may deploy radically different styles of speech and behavior when they enter another social arena.

While ethnic colonies are as much conceptual as physical spaces, the reason they have emerged should be obvious enough. Settlers had little alternative but to look to each other for mutual support if they were to survive, and hence it was only to be expected that arenas within which interactions were based on their own familiar linguistic cultural and linguistic premises would soon emerge. But with the best part of 50 years of history behind them, the outcomes of these processes have become increasingly elaborate. In addition to such everyday matters as the conventions which underpin patterns of dress, cuisine, and personal hygiene, ethnic consolidation has also facilitated the vigorous reconstitution of the patterns of reciprocity that underpin extended family structures, together with the dynamics of hierarchy, hegemony, and interpersonal competition to which they give rise. That was not all. Once extended kinship networks had been reactivated, the stage was also set for the ever more elaborate celebration of a wide range of domestic rituals, and most especially those associated with marriage and fertility. Dowries have become more complex and expensive, guests are invited by the hundred, and after having been sumptuously feasted are likely to find themselves being entertained by a highly professional Bhangra group.

To cut a long story very short, it is now quite clear that British Sikhs are making themselves at home in their new surroundings largely on their own terms, and that their strategies of cultural reconstruction have been particularly successful in the relative privacy of their personal and domestic domains, and that the driving force behind these processes is grounded in much more than a sentimental commitment to "tradition" or "identity," since they have also provided their users with an extremely effective means of resisting, circumventing, and where appropriate, challenging the forces of racial and ethnic exclusionism they so often encounter. Ethnic consolidation has therefore helped British Sikhs of all ages and generations to sustain a strong sense of confidence in their own capacity to succeed, and on that basis to develop a wide range of ethnically specific strategies—from chain migration onward—by means of which to achieve their goals.

Yet if ethnic mobilization has been the key to Sikh success, no less than it has for every other component of Britain's South Asian population, it is equally clear that this has not been based on the straightforward reproduction of so-called traditional practice. On the one hand that vision of "tradition" is itself a fiction, social and cultural conventions in Punjab itself are subject to constant change, but the pace and complexity of these changes have become even more rapid in diasporic contexts. British Sikh lifestyles are therefore in no sense a mere carbon copy of some earlier "tradition": instead they are the outcome of an active process of creativity, in which inspiration drawn from the settlers' own social, religious, and cultural heritage has been supplemented by those drawn from many other sources. Nor have these processes given rise to a single uniform outcome: differential strategies of adaptation devised around differences of caste, class, sect, gender, and age have ensured that there is no one way of being a British Sikh. So it is that although Sikhs in Britain take a great deal of pride in their distinctive heritage, Sikh behavior is anything but uniform. Given their familiarity with an ever-widening variety of cultural codes, they have also become adept at switching between them as and when appropriate.

The Process of Religious Reconstruction

Despite their considerable skills as cultural navigators, two spheres of activity are worth identifying as having a particularly strong Sikh—and indeed Punjabi—character: first the networks of kinship reciprocity to which I have already paid a good deal of attention, and second the arena of collective (and in that sense public) religious practice.

At an institutional level the Sikh tradition in Britain is currently in very good shape: virtually every British city now contains at least one Gurudwara, and wherever the local Sikh population includes more than a couple of hundred families, caste and sectarian conflicts have invariably ensured that several rival institutions have emerged. Nevertheless few of the early sojourners would ever have predicted such an outcome, since the reconstruction of formal religious practice was in no way part of their agenda. It is easy to see why: during the initial phase of settlement they lacked the time, energy, and financial resources even to think of doing so. Even so it would be a mistake to assume that they were wholly irreligious, and in this respect Joginder Shamsher's collection of Punjabi industrial workers' oral literature offers a wonderfully evocative insight into the way in which they used the mystical dimensions of their heritage as a source of solace in an otherwise barren environment. Poetry figures prominently in the collection, and its general mood is evoked with particular clarity by Surjit Hans when he laments:

> *The parrot of my life*
>   *is trapped in the pain of separation every day*
> *Dying every day, being born every day*
>   *if he falls ill, he can bear the pain in his body*
> *But how can he banish the pain in his soul?*
>   *in this country no-one wants to hear my words*
> *To what physician can I tell my pain?* (Shamsher 1989: 6–7)

Poetry is of course one of Punjab's most popular art forms, and one of its great advantages is that it can be articulated in the absence of any institutional base: hence the material that Shamsher has recorded was originally recited when industrial workers gathered for a drink of beer in the pub. Moreover such modes of expression transcended formal religious boundaries: Hans's words are as much inspired by the *kafis* of Bulleh Shah as the *sloks* of Guru Nanak.

Yet despite the ecumenical character of these early initiatives, once local settlements began to increase in size the more formal dimensions of religious practice slowly began to be reconstructed. At first these amounted to little more than small groups of religiously minded men meeting together to recite their morning and evening prayers, and perhaps to further entertain themselves by singing *bhajans*. But as time passed these informal gatherings gradually began to increase in size, so much so that it became possible to contemplate raising the money to buy a terraced house, perhaps even a derelict church or church hall, for use as a permanent base for such activities.

This led to a further transformation in the character of local settlements. While the object of such exercises may have been to establish an arena within which formal religious practice could be reconstituted, a great deal of effort was required before that goal could be achieved. *Sewa*, the voluntary contribution of money, materials, and labor for the collective good of the local community was the traditional means of doing so, and the moral pressure to make such a contribution was so great that even those who had hitherto shown no interest in the revival of religious practice felt they were honor-bound to do so. This had yet further consequences: besides bringing all Sikhs in the surrounding area together in a collective enterprise, its completion further strengthened the nascent community's solidarity and vitality. Local Gurudwaras were much more than merely religious institutions. Once in operation they provided a forum within which settlers at long last could pursue their own agendas on their own terms, and where the external world could be held comprehensively, if only temporarily, at bay. Hence in addition to offering spiritual inspiration and solace, a weekly visit to the Gurudwara each Sunday provided everyone with an opportunity to relax with friendly company in familiar surroundings, to share news from home, to exchange information about job opportunities, and to check out on new arrivals. The institution of the *langar* was also swiftly revived, so that after the formal *diwan* all participants could also sit down and share a meal.

That the newly constituted Gurudwaras immediately became centers of social as well as religious activity was in no way incongruent with Sikh ideals: the *sangat* had always been expected to serve such a dual purpose. But for just that reason the construction of Gurudwaras was also of great symbolic significance, for the emergence of local *sangat*s immediately suggested that it was possible to reconstruct a Sikh *dharm*—a Sikh social and moral order—even in the midst of what had hitherto been regarded as a wholly inhospitable environment. Against that background it is most significant that family reunion soon became increasingly commonplace: besides further reinforcing the reconstitution of moral conformity, it also yet further transformed the character of activities in the Gurudwara itself. Perhaps the most significant change of all was that the full range of domestic life-crisis rituals—especially those associated with childbirth and marriage—could now be locally celebrated.

At first doing so presented all sorts of practical difficulties, such that many rituals had to be carried out on a do-it-yourself basis, but the gaps soon began to be filled. Shops selling such items as jewelry, wedding sarees, aigrettes, and invitation cards began to open. The huge cauldrons needed to prepare curries for large numbers of guests were imported from India, while groups of *gyani*s (preachers) and *ragi*s (singers) began to tour the country, offering their services as ritual officiants. As a result Britain soon became an arena within which the all-important value of *izzat* (honor) could be competed for, and given the central role this plays in every family's sense of self-worth, no one could afford to be left behind. Mutual rivalries became steadily more intense, such that marriages, like most other domestic rituals, began to be celebrated in an ever more elaborate way—a process that continues to this day. Nor have these revivalistic processes been confined to the religious arena of the Gurudwara. Most Sikh parents also made great efforts to ensure that their children were familiar with Punjabi behavioral norms, and to ensure that they conformed to them as comprehensively as possible, at least in domestic contexts.

Even so the actual outcome of these processes is a good deal more complex than is commonly appreciated. While settlers certainly sought to reconstruct both the patterns of belief and worship and the family and kinship structures on which they had relied prior to their departure, and while they may well believe that they have successfully achieved that goal, closer inspection invariably reveals that local Sikh practices are by no means wholly congruent with those on which they are ostensibly modeled. While some of these changes are little more than necessary adaptations introduced in response to differing material circumstances, others, and especially those pressed forward by the younger generation of British Sikhs, offer some much more far-reaching challenges to long-established social and cultural conventions, most particularly with respect to issues of age and gender inequality. How far and in what form current structures will survive these challenges is still an open question. Few British-born Sikhs are sufficiently fluent in Punjabi to follow proceedings in the Gurudwara with any great degree of understanding, let alone to articulate any kind of critical perspective on them. However, kinship reciprocities are in better shape. While stresses and strains abound, the broad patterns of loyalty, responsibility, and obligation in which they are grounded have as yet not been called into serious question.

Diversity and Diversification

Yet despite the strength of the resulting processes of ethnic consolidation, it should not be assumed that all Sikhs resident in a given locality will, of necessity, have coalesced into a single coherent community. Quite the contrary. Despite their strong commitment to the principle of unity, as the years have passed differences of caste and sect have become steadily more salient, so much so that it is usually far more appropriate to talk of local Sikh communities in the plural rather than in the singular. Some moves in the opposite direction have occurred, of course, notably in the aftermath of the assault on the Golden Temple in 1984, but even the sense of outraged unity that those traumatic events precipitated did not last long. Within a year or two the Sikh tradition's notoriously fissiparous tendencies reasserted themselves once again. It is worth exploring why.

As Kalsi (1994) has shown in his admirably detailed account of sectarian developments amongst Sikh settlers in Leeds, such disjunctions were for the most part successfully overridden during the early stages of settlement. While the construction of the city's first Gurudwara was still in train, there were few arguments about just who could legitimately be involved in its management, or about the precise forms of ritual practice that would be acceptable within it. Unity was all, so much so that the inclusion of Hindu Brahmin in its first management committee was not regarded as contradictory. Such open-mindedness did not last for long, however. Although no entry restrictions have been imposed in this or any other Gurudwara, expectations about who might be elected to the management committee, and even more so about who might conduct the formal rituals that take place during the course of the *diwan* have grown steadily more restrictive. Access to such activities is now very often limited not just to those who have maintained the external symbols of the *Khalsa,* but to those who have become fully initiated *amritdaris.*

Nevertheless Kalsi's account provides a useful reminder that these changes are by no means straightforwardly coterminous with an increase in religious orthodoxy, if only because that condition cannot be defined with any precision. While a support for religious revivalism has certainly been growing steadily among Sikh settlers, just as it is among their Hindu and Muslim counterparts, it is by no means a unitary phenomenon. The reasons are quite straightforward. Given that charismatic spiritual teachers—each of whom invariably develops his own distinctive theological perspective—invariably play a leading role in sparking off such movements, heterogeneity is intrinsic to the process of revivalism itself, and inevitably leads to the growth of sectarian differentiation. So it is that even though they may all find inspiration in the teachings of Guru Nanak and his successors, Leeds Sikhs—and especially those with strong religious commitment—are deeply divided in sectarian terms. Some are affiliated to well-known movements such as the Namdharis, Nirankaris, Ravidasis, and Radhasoamis, others to smaller and much less well known movements founded by teachers based in rural Doaba, while the teachings of the recently deceased but East-African born Baba Puran Singh have found a great deal of favor among local Ramgarhias.

Similar developments have occurred within every Sikh settlement in Britain, and have had a powerful, if paradoxical, impact on patterns of religious practice. Although revivalism has thereby been promoted, for such movements invariably urge their followers to be more punctilious in fulfilling their religious duties, they also tend to precipitate vigorous disputes about the precise details of what this should entail. Thus while few charismatic teachers fail to urge their followers to allow their hair and beard to grow, re-adopt the turban if they have ceased to wear it, and to avoid meat and alcohol, each nevertheless tends to present his own specific slant on matters of fine detail, thus providing fertile grounds for endless quarrels. Even if the teachers themselves may make considerable efforts to avoid becoming caught up in such mundane matters, that is certainly not true of their devotees. If, as is often the case, they take the view that those who ignore the advice of their much-respected Guru are deliberately slighting his capacity for spiritual insight, explosive disputes can easily be precipitated, especially if they are also congruent with caste divisions. Indeed virtually every major Gurudwara in Britain has periodically been wracked by such disputes. Sometimes they can be resolved by negotiation, but very often one or the other group splits off on its own account to established its own separate Gurudwara. Hence the Sikh tradition in Britain may be thriving, but in steadily less uniform ways.

Conclusion

On the basis of this brief survey, four points stand out with particular clarity. First, there are no indications that British Sikhs are losing their sense of distinctiveness. While turban-wearing appears to be growing steadily less frequent among all groups except the East African Ramgarhias, the great majority nevertheless remain deeply enmeshed in their families and kinship networks. Second, Sikhs form a less comprehensively united community than outsiders commonly suppose. Since the principal resource around which ethnic colonies have been reconstructed are popular rural traditions, disjunctions of caste, class, sect, clan, gender, and age have all reemerged in Britain, despite a radical change in the character of the local environment. Third, while these popular and demotic aspects of the Sikh heritage are having a far-reaching impact on trajectories of adaptation, these outcomes should be regarded as an intrinsically *British* phenomenon, since they are the product of a comprehensive reworking, and indeed reinvention, of what went before. Fourth—although there has hardly been space to touch on the issue in this Chapter—these processes need to be understood as part of a much wider pattern of globalization. As expert migrants of long standing, Sikhs have hitherto used their kinship links to establish a worldwide network of communications, but this is now being further supplemented by direct communication through the Internet. The local developments described in this chapter are therefore both a part of, and feed into, some much more global processes.

———————————— **BIBLIOGRAPHY** ————————————

Aurora, G. S. (1967). *The New Frontiersmen*. Bombay: Popular Prakashan.
Ballard, R. and Ballard, C. (1977). "The Sikhs." In Watson, J. (ed.), *Between Two Cultures: Migrants and Minorities in Britain*. Oxford: Basil Blackwell.

Ballard, R. (ed.) (1994). *Desh Pardesh: The South Asian Presence in Britain.* London: Hurst and Co.

Baumann, G. (1996). *Contesting Culture: Discourses of Identity in Multi-ethnic London.* Cambridge: Cambridge University Press.

Bhachu, P. (1985). *Twice Migrants: East African Sikh Settlers in Britain.* London: Tavistock.

———. (1988). "Apni Marzi Kardi." In Bhachu, P. and Westwood, S. (eds.), *Enterprising Women.* London: Routledge.

Helweg, A. (1986). *Sikhs in England.* Delhi: Oxford University Press.

James, A. (1974). *Sikh Children in Britain.* London: Oxford University Press.

Juergensmeyer, M. (1982). *Religion as Social Vision.* Berkeley: University of California Press.

Kalsi, S. S. (1992). *The Evolution of a Sikh Community in Britain.* Leeds University: Community Religions Project.

Nesbitt, E. (1994). "Valmikis in Coventry: The Revival and Reconstruction of a Community." In Ballard 1994.

Shamsher, J. (1989). *The Overtime People.* Jalandar: ABS Publications.

PART II

South Asians in Canada

Introduction

Harold Coward

C anada is the cultural, social, and political product of immigrants who have entered this part of the North American continent since the exploitation of fish and fur-bearing animals in the sixteenth century gave way to the colonization of land in the seventeenth century. Throughout the entire seventeenth, eighteenth, and nineteenth centuries and for most of the twentieth century, the vast majority of immigrants were drawn from the United Kingdom and France. During the first half of the twentieth century, significant numbers of immigrants began to arrive from other parts of Europe, notably from Germany, Scandinavia, and the Ukraine. As late as 1950, 50 percent of Canada's population claimed British heritage, and 31 percent French. Canadians of non-European origins such as the Chinese who were descendants of laborers on the Canadian National Railway, or the Sikhs who had established a community in Vancouver by 1905, remained until recently a small minority in terms of both ethnic background and religion.

Over the last 25 years, however, there have been increasing numbers of immigrants from South Asian countries. The pace at which South Asian immigrants were arriving was accelerated in 1986 when sweeping changes were made to the legislation that governs immigration into Canada. Prior to 1986, Canada had favored immigrants of European background who came to their new country with very few material assets, but great hopes for achieving economic security after their arrival. After 1986, it became very difficult for this class of Europeans—often referred to as "economic refugees" to gain acceptance into Canada. The new legislation gave preference to two other categories of applicants: (1) political refugees who normally arrive with few skills and even fewer assets, and (2) wealthy entrepreneurs or investors, notably, immigrants from the Middle East and South Asia who have at their disposal financial resources well beyond those the majority of Canadians within the host community can ever hope to acquire. Among the South Asian Sikh and Hindu immigrant communities, for example, this has resulted in a higher than average participation by its members in the professions, which translates into higher income and greater security (D'Costa, 1993: 181–95).

Of the 420,000 South Asians in Canada, 135,000 are Sikhs, 120,000 are Hindus, 90,000 are Muslims, 55,000 are Christians, 3,000 are Buddhists, 70 are Jews, and the remaining 4,000 number among them the Jains and Parsis. Among the religious traditions introduced into Canada by South Asian immigrants are Hinduism, Buddhism, Sikhism, Jainism, Chinese Popular Religion, and Islam. These individuals have settled mainly in Ontario (131,000), British Columbia (104,000), Alberta (40,000), and Quebec (30,000), with the remainder spread across the other provinces and a few even locating themselves in the far north (the Yukon and North West Territories). Most who have not settled in one of the three main ports of entry—Montreal, Toronto, and Vancouver—live in Calgary, Edmonton, Winnipeg, or Ottawa.

South Asian immigrants in both the refugee and investor categories have had a significant impact on the country's social, economic, and political institutions in the post-1986 period, as well as on the development of religious, ethnic, and racial relationships within Canada. This trend is most evident in Canada's three main ports of entry—Montreal, Toronto, and Vancouver. In Montreal, members of the Muslim and Hindu religious traditions constitute a significant part of both the English- and French-speaking communities. In Toronto, where those of non-European/non-Judeo-Christian background now constitute more than half of the population, immigrant religions have established a highly visible presence. During the last decade, more than 80 percent of new immigrants who arrived in Vancouver were from the religious communities of South Asia.

By the time of the 1991 census, there were approximately 420,000 South Asians in Canada. This is about one-half the South Asian population of the United States and between one-third and a quarter of that of the United Kingdom. While South Asians constituted about 0.4 percent of the American population, and about 3 percent of the United Kingdom's population, they represented 1.4 percent of the Canadian population.

The response to this new wave of immigrants on the part of the host community has been mixed. Some welcome the investors and their development funds while others resent their ability both to control local economies and to affect the housing market through the large-scale purchase of land. The response to refugees has also been mixed, as humanitarian and compassionate concerns are weighed against the perceived drain on Canada's beleaguered social security system. In the past, Canadians of European Judeo-Christian heritage have shown enthusiastic support for ethnic events such as folk fairs, craft exhibits, and dance performances. They have also applauded the trooping of flags of the countries of origin of immigrants in Canada Day celebrations. Yet, as the proportion of visible minorities in Canada rapidly expands, the presence of such groups appears to be generating a growing anxiety among host Canadians. This anxiety has already expressed itself on occasion in a status-preservationist backlash to which members of misunderstood and misrepresented religious, ethnic, and racial minorities often fall victim.

Despite the anxiety generated by the South Asian immigrants in Canada, by virtue of their distinctive dress, food, culture, and religion, they have become a very productive, high-profile, and permanent part of Canada's multicultural mosaic. They have developed the reputation of being hard-working, self-sufficient immigrants, many of whom are well-educated professionals or successful businesspeople. Their temples, gurdwaras, mosques, and community centers have added a rich diversity to the architecture of Canadian cities. South Asian classical music and dance have become established as a part of Canada's cultural life. South Asian authors such as Michael Ondaatje (winner of the 1992 Booker Prize for his novel, *The English Patient*) and Rohinton Mistry (winner of the 1991 Governor General's award for his novel *Such a Long Journey*) are ranked among the best of Canada's creative writers.

While their reception by other Canadians has not always been a warm one, South Asian immigrants do have certain advantages in adjusting to life in Canada. Unlike other groups such as the Chinese, South Asians usually arrive with some knowledge of English. They also tend to come from other Commonwealth countries where the legal and political institutions bear a marked similarity to their Canadian counterparts. This has enabled them to adapt quickly and successfully to life in Canada through a syncretism of familiar political institutions and traditional religious ones.

Overall, it remains to be determined whether Samuel Huntington's forecast of "A Clash of Civilizations?" is in evidence here (*Foreign Affairs*, vol. 2, no. 3 [Summer 1993]: 22–49), or if Canadian society is responding with determination to accommodate the new religious communities created by its South Asian immigrants. In order to more clearly identify both the potential sources of conflict and the potential for peaceful and productive accommodation, we must develop a better knowledge and understanding of the new Hindu, Muslim, and Sikh communities themselves.

BIBLIOGRAPHY

D'Costa, R. (1993). "Socio-Demographic Characteristics of the Population of South Asian Origins in Canada." In M. Israel and N. K. Wagle (eds.), *Ethnicity, Identity, Migration: The South Asian Context.* Toronto: Centre for South Asian Studies, pp. 181–95.

7

Hinduism in Canada

Harold Coward

Hindus, generally, have been positively received in Canada. This has been helped by the fact that the first major group of Hindus came to Canada as part of the large influx of South Asian professionals who arrived in Canada as independent immigrants in the 1960s. Canada was short of qualified professors in the rapidly expanding universities of the day and had vacancies in other professional areas such as teaching, engineering, and medicine. Well-qualified Hindus filled many such positions and were gratefully received into Canadian life for the contribution they made. The fact that many in this first large group of Hindus were educated, upper-middle-class persons who spoke English fluently enabled them to fit into Canadian society fairly smoothly and to be generally appreciated by the host culture. Later groups of Hindu immigrants were not always received with as positive a reception.

In this chapter we will examine: (1) migration history and the current situation; (2) the changing experience of Hindu worship

152   *Harold Coward*

and ritual; (3) strategies of adaptation in sacred language and education; (4) higher education; (5) public policy issues; (6) women; and (7) relations with the "old country."

Migration History and Current Situation of Hindus in Canada

Canadian Hindus have a variety of ethnic backgrounds and histories in their coming to Canada. The earliest Hindus were Punjabis. A small group of mainly males from farming backgrounds, they came to Canada to make some money with which they could return home and buy farmland. They arrived along with the first wave of Sikh migration to Canada reaching the coast of British Columbia between 1900 and 1908. As the numbers of South Asians swelled to some 5,000 (mostly Sikhs) by 1908, they—together with the Chinese and Japanese immigrants to southwestern British Columbia—began to be perceived as a threat by the relatively small Anglo-Saxon population of the lower mainland. Up to this point they had been accorded full British citizenship, including the right to vote. But the British Columbia legislature in 1908 removed that privilege denying Hindus and all South Asians municipal and federal voting rights and excluding them from serving as school trustees, on juries, in public service, holding jobs resulting from public works contracts, purchasing Crown timber, or practicing the professions of law and pharmacy. Through the "continuous journey" legislation of 1908, the federal government effectively banned further South Asian immigration by requiring South Asians to purchase a ticket for a through passage to Canada from one's country of origin. Since no shipping company covered both the India–Hong Kong and the Hong Kong–Canada legs of the trip, the purchase of a continuous ticket was impossible, effectively cutting off immigration to Canada (Buchignani and Indra 1985). Although in the 1920s a few wives and children were allowed in to join husbands already living in Canada, the South Asian community remained basically static until the 1950s. The whole South Asian community was constantly referred to as "Hindus" by the Canadian public of the day, even though they were mostly Sikhs.

The first large group of Hindus came directly from Uttar Pradesh and surrounding regions in northern India. They were Hindi speakers who were largely urban middle class in background. They came as part of the large group of South Asian professionals who arrived in Canada as independent immigrants in the 1960s. During this same period some Tamil Hindus from the Madras area came to Canada as teachers. Bengali Hindus began to arrive during the 1970s. Also during the 1960s and 1970s Hindus arrived in Canada from former British colonies that were achieving independence and discriminated against South Asians. Thus, substantial numbers of Hindus and Muslims arrived in Canada from East Africa, South Africa, Fiji, Mauritius, Guyana, and Trinidad. While Hindus from East Africa tended to be professionals and businesspeople, those arriving from the other areas were mainly blue-collar workers (Buchignani and Indra, 1985 212–47). In Canada, Hindus spread themselves across the country settling mainly in larger cities. According to the 1991 Census, the major concentrations of Hindus are as follows: Toronto 90,140; Vancouver 14,880; Montreal 13,775; Edmonton 5,815; Ottawa 4,780; Calgary 4,155; Winnipeg 3,105; Kitchener 2,815; and Hamilton 2,800. The age breakdown of Hindus in the major cities of Toronto, Montreal, and Vancouver is given in Table 1. In all three cities the bulk of the population is in the under 15 years and in the 25–44 years categories. Thus it is very likely that the Hindu population will grow significantly through childbirth, with continued immigration as an extra addition. From the religious perspective, this demographic pattern raises the prob-

Table 1. Concentrations of Hindus in Major Canadian Cities

	Total Population	Less than 15 Years	15–24 Years	25–44 Years	45–64 Years	65 Years And Over
Toronto						
Hindu	90,100	21,625	13,925	37,925	13,625	3,040
Males	47,480	10,780	7,320	20,565	7,350	1,460
Females	42,665	10,840	6,605	17,360	6,275	1,580
Montreal						
Hindu	13,775	3,540	1,900	6,030	1,925	375
Males	7,410	1,825	925	3,425	1,055	175
Females	6,370	1,715	980	2,610	870	195
Vancouver						
Hindu	14,800	4,055	2,215	5,485	2,440	680
Males	7,365	2,010	1,020	2,695	1,290	345
Females	7,515	2,045	1,195	2,790	1,145	335

Source: Statistics Canada, *Religions in Canada,* 1993, Table 2.

lem of how to effectively pass on the tradition in the midst of a majority secular and materialistic culture. A typical pattern seems to be that the children of the immigrant parents frequently attempt to distance themselves from the Hindu traditions that are so different from their peers in the secular host community. Young people of the third generation, however, are often much more interested in identifying and rediscovering their own religious tradition. As families become established and prosper, many seek to bring their aging parents to Canada to join them and re-create, to some degree at least, the traditional Hindu extended family.

The Changing Experience of Hindu Worship and Ritual

Unlike Sikhs, Hindus do not have a unified set of beliefs and practices that are shared by all believers. Nor is their religion as heavily focused on a community temple with weekly congregational worship. Hindu religious practice is more individual in nature and centered at home in the family. This was especially the case with regard to orthodox Hindu practice in India. A Canadian Hindu immigrant from a South Indian Brahmin family describes life at home in India as living from ritual to ritual:

> The household had priests . . . dedicated to (it). They would come and remind us that your birthday is on so-and-so date or there is a particular constellation appearing in this time of year or there is an eclipse here or you have to perform certain ceremonies for departed souls in your family. We'd fix a time and he would come and do it. From birth I was very attracted to rituals, so every day I used to spend about three to four hours watching and listening to them. We started, my sister and I, at about 4:30 A.M. In the prayer hall we had pictures of the various deities and we used to take a wet cloth and clean each one. I would make a lot of sandal paste and then we used to anoint these pictures. . . . the priest was there so we used to sit . . . till about 6:30. (Goa et al. 1984, 97).

Others talk of chanting Hindu scriptures (*Veda, Upanisad,* and *Gita*) with a father early in the morning so that the texts were easily learned by heart at a young age. The women would make daily offerings of food to the gods, bless the images with holy water, and set aside a portion from the table for wandering holy men and for the family cow. A grandmother would pay homage to the image of her *guru* tucked away in her bedroom. The family might relate to the deity of a particular temple and would join everyone else in the village or town for seasonal or festival *pujas*. What happened to this richly textured religious life when the Hindu immigrants arrived in Canada?

Being used to having religious ritual focused on the home, Canadian immigrant Hindus at first felt no pressure for a public place of worship. However, by 1970 Hindus extended their individual worship to include group prayer services held in people's homes—especially if a visiting teacher from India was passing through. Such meetings, however, often remained ethnic-specific. In the 1970s secular issues surrounding marriage and death in Canada led Hindu groups to begin to think of erecting temples. In Canada, unlike India, marriage or death rites were public occasions, and a Hindu community without a temple had nowhere to celebrate them. This need drew diverse groups of Hindus together in the larger centers, and buildings were constructed. One of the first was the Vishva Hindu Parishad of Vancouver, which in 1974 "opened a multi-use temple with a generalized program of worship as well as opportunities for specific Hindu religious and ethnic groups to use its facilities" (Buchignani and Indra 1985, 190). As Hugh Johnston observes, "The members of the Vishva Hindu Parishad, who have been raised in many local Indian traditions, have made practical compromises to create a religious community in Canada; and they have created a place of worship that is as much a church or gurdwara as it is a temple" (Johnston 1988, 11). Worship is congregational, Sundays, 12:00 noon to 1:00 P.M., with people arriving and leaving on time in Protestant fashion, unless there is food in the kitchen below provided by a family, Sikh style.

Permanent multi-use facilities now also exist in Calgary, Edmonton, and Toronto. In other locations, Hindus depend on temporary arrangements such as renting the halls of Christian churches for their religious celebrations. Unlike the Sikhs, for whom the fundraising to build a gurdwara meant an appeal to a single ethnic community, Hindus have had to span many different ethnic and religious groupings in order to raise the required funds. This has often been a difficult task, requiring diplomacy. Once a temple is established, its use is allocated by time to the various Hindu groups. General prayer services and religious lectures designed to serve all usually occur on Sundays. Individual families book the temple for marriages, funerals, and other special occasions. As Buchignani observes, "This multi-use concept is a brilliant solution to the difficulties posed by divergent Hindu practice and belief" (Buchignani and Indra 1985, 190). It has helped draw Hindus together so that Hinduism has an organizational basis on which to be recognized as a formal religion within Canada. Toward this end the Vishva Hindu Parishad of Vancouver in 1983 organized a national conference to develop the constitution for a Hindu Council of Canada (Buchignani and Indra 1985, 190). The Vishva Hindu Parishad has also been active in Hindu student associations in Canadian universities. Not all Hindus have been satisfied with this unifying approach. In Toronto, where Hindu numbers are sufficiently large to make such a development possible, various ethnic groupings have established their own institutional organizations and obtained their own buildings.

Milton Israel reports that there are now more than 50 Hindu temples and organizations in Ontario, most in the Toronto area. The oldest Hindu temple there, the Prarthana Samaj, was established in 1967 when a former church was purchased. Immigrants from Guyana and Trinidad under the leadership of Dr. Bhupendra Doobray, a cardiovascular surgeon who also served as priest, purchased a building on Young Street in 1981 that became their temple—the Vishnu Mandir. A new temple was built in 1984, which attracted India-born Hindus in large numbers, enabling a full-time priest to be brought from India. Sunday services attracted 250 people and continued to grow, necessitating the tearing down of the newly built temple to construct a larger one that opened in 1990. It draws 600 to 700 people to a Sunday service that is followed, Sikh style, by a congregational meal sponsored by a family. Temple staff numbers six priests from India and one from Guyana, Dr. Doobray, who preaches the sermon. The service proceeds in Sanskrit, Hindi, and English. A variety of images are present in the temple and the front altar holds statues to the gods Durga, Hanuman, Ganesh, and Rama, with discussion underway regarding the possible inclusion of the Buddha and Lord Mahavira of the Jains. The eclectic nature of this very successful Hindu temple is evident. However, some of the original Guyanese members have broken away and established their own ethnic temple. The large congregation is now planning to build a senior citizen home and a cultural center (Israel 1994, 52–54). While extremely successful, the Vishnu Mandir temple continually debates how far it can accommodate to include a wide variety of Hindus with their various ethnic backgrounds and images, and yet keep the involvement of the traditionalists. Other temples, such as that of the breakaway Guyanese group, have no desire to reach out to other Hindus, but concentrate on maintaining the traditional approach to worship of their ethnic community.

This is also the practice of the Ganesh temple established by Tamil immigrants from South India, South Africa, Singapore, Malaysia, and refugees from Sri Lanka. The emphasis of this group is on the purity of the building and its rituals from a Tamil perspective—such as the festival to Lord Murugan, the patron God of the Tamils. Building of the Ganesh temple complex (it also contains a senior citizen facility, living apartments for priests, a wedding hall, and a cafeteria) began in 1984 and is still continuing. Rather than adapting to a Canadian congregational style, as the Vishnu Temple has done, the Ganesh temple attempts to faithfully re-create South Indian Hindu worship in Canada—as the Sri Venkatesawara Temple has done in Pittsburgh. Around the large hall are 14 altars where *murtis* or images of individual gods such as Ganesh, Shiva, Durga, and Murugan are installed, each with "their own space where individual worshipers may come and pray, alone or with the mediation of a priest" (Israel 1994, 57). Thus several activities involving different worshipers, priests, and gods may be going on simultaneously reproducing the general cacophony of sound typical of a South Indian temple. Unlike the Vishnu temple, Sunday is not a special day at the Ganesh temple. Festival days, however, are special and then 10,000 to 15,000 people may attend (Israel 1994, 58).

A third example of the variety of Hindu practice in the Toronto area is provided by the Arya Samajis. Followers of Dayananda Saraswati, they reject the use of images in worship and instead focus on a simple Vedic fire ritual which any member of the Samaj can perform. They also reject caste. Arya Samaj followers came to Canada mainly from East Africa and the Caribbean as well as from India. In Toronto there are two Arya Samaj communities that are part of a North American network with congregations in more than 70 cities including London, Windsor, Calgary, and others in Canada. Ethnic differences separate the two Toronto groups. One is made up of mainly Hindi speakers from East Africa or India and conducts worship in Hindi. The other is made up of immigrants from the Caribbean who do not know Hindi and conduct their services in English. Both groups, however, chant the Vedas in Sanskrit. The first group owns its own house and land while the second group rents church halls for its Sunday services. While ethnic and language differences continue to separate the two groups, a campaign to raise funds for the building of a Vedic Cultural Centre on the property of the first group may yet succeed in uniting them (Israel 1994, 60).

The Toronto area, with its large concentration of close to 100,000 Hindus, offers a magnification of the patterns that exist in more or less developed form in other Canadian cities. While a multi-use temple with Canadian Protestant-style congregational worship may be satisfactory in communities with smaller numbers of Hindus, ethnic and sectarian differences seem to manifest themselves once the population of Hindus becomes large enough to support such divisions. Ethnic languages play a major role in such separations, and it is an open question as to how successful these first generation communities will be in passing their languages on to their children.

Another aspect of Hindu religion that was present in India, and which has assumed increased importance in religious practice in Canada, is the role of the guru. Scholars have concluded that the enlightened guru is the dynamic sacred center of Hinduism—that the guru's interpretation of scripture, tradition, and experience is more sacred than the sacred texts or rituals themselves. In India renaissance gurus such as Dayananda, Vivekananda, and Aurobindo played a central role in the continuity and change of Hinduism in response to new challenges. Is this also true for Hindu families that have taken up residence in Canada? A Canadian field study suggests that the answer is "yes" (Goa, Coward, and Neufeldt 1984). In addition to attending the temple, serious Hindu families carry on traditional patterns of daily devotions in their homes. One room is set aside for worship and an altar with images installed. In addition to the deities one would find in the temple, photos or images of an individual's or family's guru often occupy center stage on the altar. It dominates the altar, receiving prayers, and focusing the *mantra* given to the family members during initiation by the *guru*. These devotional acts, accompanied by the offering of holy water and fruit, all to the statue of the *guru*, have replaced the traditional cycle of worship associated with the *Panch Devta* or five deities. The role of the guru has been to restructure traditional *puja* and ritual of village India to meet the challenge of modern life both in India and Canada. Almost all informants reported that a guru dramatically shifted the ritual practice of the household, especially in Canada. The guru restructured the ritual so that it would work in Canada—to free one from the rat-race of Canadian life and give one a spiritual basis.

The ritual pattern associated with death has also undergone change to accommodate to Canadian life. Unlike in India, death in Canada usually occurs in a hospital. Following initial arrangements with a funeral director, a priest or lay priest is contacted.[1] Family and friends gather around the body at a funeral home with the necessary facilities for cremation. Following a welcome and eulogy, the priest conducts the ritual for the deceased. An invocation to Lord Vishnu may be offered followed by a *mantra* from the *Upanisad*, "From the Unreal lead me to the Real; from Darkness lead me to the Wisdom Light; from Death lead me to Immortality. Oh Peace, Peace, Peace" (*Brhadaranyaka Upanisad* 1, 3, 28). The ritual actions associated with the funeral have accommodated to Canadian practice. In India or Africa the body would have been carried to a pyre, covered with *ghee* or clarified butter and a mixture of spices called *samagrese*; "fed" with water and rice balls; and offered gifts as a sign of devotion and thanksgiving. By contrast, in Canada *ghee* is placed on the body, a drop of water in the mouth, and flowers are offered and the body placed in a casket. Funeral home facilities do not allow for the *Havan*, with its rhythm of *mantras* and offerings to Agni (fire), the god who bears the dead to the eternal realm. The *mantra* alone remains. The physical contact with offerings, the ritual linking of the *Havan* and the funeral pyre with the eternal is now expressed through a mere token gesture. The pyre is now a high-technology furnace making the *ghee* irrelevant as an aspect of ignition and conflagration. The natural symbolism of *ghee*, with all its surrounding imagery from hearth and table to pyre (see Douglas 1978), is broken and, with it, the immediacy of symbolic connections "showing" the integration of the deceased with the divine.

After the funeral service, the body is pushed on a trolley to the cremation furnace, usually accompanied by family and friends. There it is raised mechanically and placed into the furnace. The traditional practice and symbolism in the old country is quite different. The body would be personally shouldered by a circle of intimate friends. It would be deliberately placed on the pyre, and the preparations visibly made. The eldest son would come forward, take the fire from Agni's *Havan*, and ignite the pyre while all were present. The final integration of the dead person's body/soul with the cosmos was engaged with conscious intent and full family participation.

The Canadian restructuring of the Hindu funeral to accommodate funeral directors, the law, and the technology associated with cremation has made the experience much more abstract and removed from the mourners than was the case in India. While the theological ideas informing the meaning of the ritual remain the same, the symbolic participation of the bereaved in the physical experience of cremation is to a large extent broken. No longer is the physical burning of the bare body by fire (Agni) actually seen. Now everything is abstracted and hidden. A casket rather than a body is what is seen—all of which disappears from sight to burn inside a closed furnace where the flame of Agni cannot be seen and experienced. The eldest son does not physically light the fire.

The danger in all of this is that the theological meaning of the *mantras* of the funeral service may lose their intimate connection with the physical events of death and cremation in the devotee's experience. When the body and the fire are not seen, it takes an act of imagination to connect what is happening inside the closed casket and high-tech furnace with the reintegration of the person's body/soul with the divine cosmos through the bright fire of the god Agni. The ritual loses some of its immediate symbolic power to interpret death as moving from the transience of the body to the unity of all creation in the Divine. By accommodating to modern North American funeral practice, Hindu rituals surrounding death are experiencing some of the same loss of power and meaning that has afflicted the Christian funeral service during the past few generations.

Strategies of Adaptation in Sacred Language and Education

Restructuring is also evident in the Canadian Hindu experience of the learning and practice of sacred language and text in daily life. We have already mentioned that in Canada there has been a shift away from traditional practice and toward practice prescribed by a *guru*. Whereas in India sacred language and text were learned easily at a young age, and served to structure one's perceptual and cognitive experience throughout life, in Canada, by contrast, little of this happens in the natural way that it did in India. In India, especially in upper-class families, sacred language and text were learned passively. From an early age one heard it over and over again as part of daily activity until the texts and *mantras* were internalized and became part of one's consciousness. The parents and grandparents taught children through daily household worship. In addition, the surrounding culture was suffused with the same texts and chants so that the learning took place, as it were, by osmosis. A good description of this process was offered by one respondent:

My father was a great scholar in Sanskrit and right from the age of four or five he used to let us get up very early in the morning and teach us all these scriptures *Upanisads* and *Vedas*, and all the religious chants. He would make us repeat it a number of times, almost by rote. We didn't know the meaning of any of those things at that time.

We had a number of occasions when we would chant them outside the house too. Suppose you go to a temple where there is a *puja* taking place and they usually chant these *mantras* too. If you have already got them by heart at home, you feel free to join with the rest of the people there . . . you simply become part of the proceedings and have a place for yourself. If you know what you are doing and can join in and do it as well as they do, you are accepted straightaway, nobody even questions who you are or what you are, you just go into the *sanctum sanctorum*.[2]

By this traditional pattern in India, passages from the *Vedas*, *Upanisads*, the *Bhagavad Gita*, *Ramayana*, and so on were first committed to memory by oral repetition at home and in the community. Through repeated rehearsal they became the underlying structuring pattern of one's mature consciousness. Learned by heart in one's youth, the remainder of adult life and especially old age would be spent in studying the meaning of these texts for life. Ritual chants such as the *Gayatri* were learned in the same way and assumed the same function in consciousness.

In Canada everything has changed. No longer do the children rise at five in the morning to chant Sanskrit texts with parents and grandparents. In many instances, even if the children did rise at that hour they would not find the adults doing their chanting. Some adults confess that they now do their morning chanting while running for the bus or while walking or driving to work. Gone is the more leisurely pace of India. In Canada it is replaced by the Protestant work ethic. Within the home it is hard to find a time either in the morning or evening when the whole family can gather for worship. Sometimes Saturday is set aside for family devotional practice. Often the absence of grandparents or other members of the extended family further reduces the power of the family to transmit the sacred tradition. Outside the family, Hindus live as a minority group in a secular, materialistic culture and so the contextual reinforcement of family practice, experienced in India, is simply absent in Canada.

In the face of these difficulties a new practice, introduced by gurus, is appearing. It responds to the complexities and time problems of Canadians by simplifying home worship into a pattern which, in essence, consists in chanting a guru's name or *mantra* 108 times, 2 or 3 times a day (Goa, Coward, and Neufeldt 1984, 103). Whereas in India practice involved both traditional Sanskrit texts chanted in rituals *and* observances relating to a guru, in Canada much of this is collapsed into one simple flexible and efficient practice—chanting the guru's name or *mantra*. This has several distinct advantages: (1) It is easy and quick to learn—as opposed to the years of practice needed to memorize Sanskrit chants in India; (2) the sacred language is retained—the guru's name or *mantra* is still in Sanskrit but can be easily memorized and chanted even though the person knows no Sanskrit; (3) the time and place of the chanting can be adjusted to suit whatever lifestyle one adopts in Canada—for example, when in public on a subway, train, plane, or in one's office, it can be done silently making regular spiritual practice possible in the constant change and fast pace of Canadian life; (4) it can be learned easily at any age; and (5) it fulfils the same spiritual role of keeping the mind controlled and focused on the divine as the traditional home rituals—the guru, through name and *mantra* opens the channel to the divine just as the learning of sacred texts and their ritual practice did in traditional approaches.

While the *guru mantra* may prove effective for Hindus living in Canada, it does raise questions. The very simplicity of the approach and the "blind faith in the guru" that is required, may well produce a Hinduism with more dependence on a priestly group (i.e., the gurus) than was the case in India. If Hindus no longer learn their scripture and ritual in childhood, the possibility of home religious practice independent of the guru may be largely lost. And without the foundation of daily worship at home, temple worship may rapidly become a shallow shell of what it once was. The important function of sacred language and text shaping one's consciousness from early youth and providing the mental structures through which all of life is perceived and given meaning may be lost. This will leave new generations open to experiencing their Hindu religion in a very nominal fashion—as a source of rituals for key moments of life like naming, marriage, and death, but little else. Just as many Canadian Christians are basically secular people, so also a secular Hinduism may develop in second- and third-generation immigrants.

Dependence on a *guru*, however, may be one way of attempting to continue daily worship in the modern Canadian context. While many families go to great effort to set aside one room of the house as the worship room and devoted mothers make a sincere effort to teach the full *puja* tradition to their children, the pace of Canadian life and the pressures of the surrounding secular society inevitably seem to result in simplifications of the *guru*-type. One respondent comments, "my mother, even in Windsor, Ontario, where we made our home, had one room dedicated for prayer, just as I have here in Calgary, and we continued all the rituals. Today I have reduced rituals very much because in 1976 our entire family got a *guru* who initiated us into the *mantra*."[3] While the *guru* urged the family to continue with their traditional practice and to chant the *mantra* given by the *guru* as well, the simplicity and ease of doing the latter meant that it rapidly came to predominate. More and more time was spent with the *guru's mantra* and less with the traditional rituals. The *guru mantra* practice being more flexible in that it could be done anywhere, and demanding no ritual materials, seemed better suited to modern Canadian life. It gave one a way of "unwinding" from job pressures and helped one to see through new problems clearly. Thus for many Hindus in Canada the changed life situation is met by a shift in ritual practice. From the full ritual life in India done in a prayer room in the home (involving the cleaning, anointing, garlanding, and worshiping of various deities and a full range of annual and special ceremonies requiring priests), Hindu practice in Canada has been simplified for many to a *guru mantra* chant that can be done anywhere, anytime, and does not require a priest. For many Hindu Canadians the *guru* has become important not only in helping them to adjust to a new life situation, but also in fulfilling the function of ritual—replacing observances that had been important in the homes of parents in India, or first-generation mothers in Canada.

While the *guru* has always been a part of traditional Hinduism in India, especially as an instrument for philosophical, religious, and social change (Miller 1976–1977, 533), in Canada the role of the *guru* seems to be expanding. For many, the *guru* now becomes the heart of Hinduism, or Hinduism personified, allowing Hindus in Canada to feel that they are still Hindu in spite of the fact that they no longer engage in the full traditional patterns. Even if they were inclined to a full-scale ritual life requiring the services of specialists, in most Canadian cities and towns such specialists are simply not available on a regular basis, and the time constraints and complexity of Canadian life also do not allow it. All of this has produced a new heightened significance for the *guru*. In India, to be Hindu may well have involved having a *guru and* engaging in traditional family and community rituals including scripture recitation in Sanskrit. In Canada, to be Hindu, for many, means simply to have a *guru*. This now may become almost the exclusive point of identification, a single ritual that provides a sacred center and a sense of belonging. The *guru* is not merely the connecting link to Hinduism: he or she becomes the sum and substance of it—the ritual, the *mantra*, and the scripture all in one. It also makes the tradition easy to pass on to children, as only the *guru*'s name or *mantra* needs to be learned. There is no need to go through the difficulties of learning a sacred language, such as Sanskrit, and the vast array of Hindu scripture and commentary.

As noted earlier, however, the danger is that such a simplified practice may prove too shallow for those wanting to experience the philosophical, aesthetic, and religious richness of the full Hindu tradition. This has led some to put much effort into the establishment of temples and/or cultural centers where languages can be taught along with music and dance. Classical Indian dance is taught in most centers by semiprofessional teachers. The Canadian South Asian community is now large enough to attract professional artists from India on tour. In most cities the cultural calendar is quite lively. In large cities like Toronto, there are also Indian language television programs. But everywhere, in large or small centers, videos and cassette tapes are playing a big role in making Hindu culture and religion easily available in the midst of the secular, materialistic, Canadian milieu. Of course the taste of the individual family dominates. On entering a home one may be greeted by a barrage of Hindi films and film music (no less materialistic than their Hollywood counterparts), by the meditative sounds of Ravi Sankar playing a classical raga on the Sitar, the family's *guru* giving a lecture or leading the singing of *puja*, or by the sight of the whole family (all ages) engrossed in one of the TV episodes of the Mahabharata. Technology is effectively bringing India into Canadian Hindu homes.

Higher Education

Enrichment is also added at the university level. The formation of the Shastri Indo Canadian Institute in 1968, with most Canadian universities as members, has done a great deal to foster intellectual exchange between India and Canada. This was especially so in Religious Studies Departments where books from India on Hinduism (as well as Jainism and Buddhism) were placed in the libraries using Indian government rupee funding. The primary scriptural texts in Sanskrit were purchased along with translations. This library resource supported the teaching of Sanskrit language and Hinduism to Canadian students interested in Indian religion as well as to the children of Hindu immigrants who wished to formally study their own religious tradition. The Shastri Institute brought Visiting Professors from India to speak in Canadian classes and offered research fellowships for Canadian faculty and graduate students wishing to study in India. All of this intellectual activity is important in itself, but it also allowed the immigrant Hindu community to see its religious ideals strongly represented in Canadian higher education. Indeed the Hindu community has worked to further highlight its presence within the university. In the mid-1980s Canadian Hindus took advantage of a federal government matching program to establish a Chair of Hindu Studies at Concordia University in Montreal. This Chair and its first incumbent, Dr. Krishna Sivaraman, have helped to give Hindu studies in Canada a high profile. The opportunity to study Hinduism in depth (including its sacred language Sanskrit; its texts, philosophy, history, and ritual) exists at the universities of McGill, Concordia, McMaster, Toronto, Manitoba, Calgary, and British Columbia. At McGill, McMaster, Toronto, and Calgary, B.A., M.A., and Ph.D. programs can be completed. This is important for the Canadian Hindu community in two ways. First, it ensures that many university-educated Canadians receive good teaching about Hinduism. Second, it enables intelligent intellectually minded young people of the Hindu immigrant community to pursue the study of their own tradition to the highest level of knowledge. To this extent the "banks of the Ganges" are present in Canada. As a professor of Hinduism for some 23 years in Canadian universities, I can think back to many students from Canadian Hindu families who first took Hinduism courses because of a sincere side interest or because they assumed it would be an easy A (it wasn't), and became so engaged in the study that they switched majors and some went on to win fellowships and complete Ph.D.s. I think of one student now completing her Ph.D. with a feminist thesis on women heroes in the *Mahabharata*. An undergraduate English major when she first enrolled in my Hinduism course, she quickly became so fascinated with studying her own tradition that she switched into Religious Studies and learned Sanskrit. Born into a serious but not pious family, she studied Indian classical dance with a local teacher while in high school and university. Apparently following the expected course of an upper class Hindu daughter, her life at university both pleased and challenged her family. Although pleased with her sincere commitment to studying Sanskrit and Hindu scriptures, her family found their plans for an arranged marriage thwarted when she fell in love with and married a Canadian Anglo-Saxon male student whom she met in my Hinduism class. Her family have since come to accept this Canadian interfaith marriage and their new grandson on whom they dote. Their daughter's feminist scholarly analysis of Hindu scripture may prove to be a harder challenge for them to accept. Not only has the Indian immigrant community brought Hinduism to Canada, the intellectual study and development of that tradition is now flourishing here—and in some areas providing the lead for world Hindu scholarship.

Over my 23 years of dealing with Hindu university students, I have noticed a difference between the males and females. While the boys show little difficulty in adjusting to Canadian life, with the girls the situation is often more difficult. Mothers sometimes expect their daughters to follow in the footsteps they trod growing up in India: no dating, staying within the extended family, and an arranged marriage. Mothers who have stayed at home to look after the family have often accommodated less to Canadian society than the children who have been at school, or the husband who has been out at his job. This can result in severe tension in the family, especially between mother and daughter.

Public Policy Issues

The tensions within families induced as a result of attempting to live Hindu religion and culture in Canada have parallels at the level of public policy. Pluralism in the form of multiculturalism is an established part of Canada's public policy (The Canadian Multiculturalism Act, 1990). As citizens of a liberal democratic country, Canadians of European Judeo-Christian heritage have traditionally shown enthusiastic support for religious ethnic events such as interfaith days, folk fairs, crafts exhibits, and dance performances. Yet as Canada's diversity grows and the size of its immigrant communities expand, tensions arise over such matters as immigration patterns and religious issues like the wearing of turbans in the Royal Canadian Mounted Police and Islamic dress in schools. While Canadian Hindus do not find themselves in the public eye to the same extent as South Asian Sikhs or Muslims, Hindu voices have been strongly present in the lively Canadian debate over multiculturalism. A senior editorial writer of Canada's national newspaper, *The Globe and Mail*, is a Hindu. And the Canadian Hindu author, Neil Bissoondath, has written a nonfiction best-seller, *Selling Illusions: The Cult of Multiculturalism in Canada* (1994), attacking Canada's public policy. "Multiculturalism," says Bissoondath, "with all of its festivals and its celebrations, had done— and can do—nothing to foster a factual and clear-minded vision of our neighbors. Depending on stereotype, ensuring that ethnic groups will preserve their distinctiveness in a gentle and insidious form of cultural apartheid, multiculturalism has done little more than lead an already divided country down the path to further social divisiveness" (77). Following the publication of his book, Bissoondath was taken to task in a front-page *Globe and Mail* story by Sheila Finestone, then Canada's Minister of Multiculturalism. In response to her claim that he was threatening the fabric of Canadian society, Bissoondath argued that the official encouragement of ethnic and religious diversity as multiculturalism may be threatening a core Canadian way of life—the old Canadian way of life that originally attracted him to Canada in the first place and that he characterizes as "a cohesive, effective society enlivened by cultural variety: reasonable diversity within vigorous unity" (224). He cites another Canadian Hindu writer, Bharati Mukherjee, in support of his analysis. In Mukherjee's view, Hindu and other immigrants leave their old countries and come to Canada to be Canadians—not to be labeled as a religious ethnic or a member of a multicultural community. "Whether or not I preserve my cultural background is my personal choice; whether or not an ethnic group preserves its cultural background is the group's choice. The state has no business in either" (220). Both Bissoondath and Mukherjee instead direct attention to the manifestations of racism in Canadian society. Clearly, Hindu voices are strongly engaged in Canada's policy debate over multiculturalism.

Another public policy area that has brought a focus on Hinduism is Health Care Ethics. Canada's recent Royal Commission on New Reproductive Technologies (Coward 1993) raised questions about the view of Hindu ethics on such issues as time of ensoulment, prenatal diagnosis for genetic disorders, abortion, artificial insemination, in vitro fertilization (IVF), sex selection, and the use of aborted fetal tissue for research. The Commission wished to be sensitive to the views of each religion in Canada in drawing up its recommended Canadian guidelines. The Commissioners recognized that religious opinion constitutes a major source of ethical view-points, even among generations no longer actively practicing the religious faith of their parents or grandparents. Although very much a minority religion in Canada, the views of Hindu ethics on these difficult questions relating to the New Reproductive Technologies were included in the Commission's documentation and policy analysis (454–58). This proved especially helpful to the Commissioners in their dealing with the use, by some Canadian South Asians, of sex selection technologies to ensure the birth of sons (usually in U.S. clinics).

Yet another area of public policy that can be problematic for Hindus in Canada is the way self-identity is conceptualized and enshrined in Canadian law. Typical of a modern liberal democracy, Canada in its Constitution assumes that the self is the autonomous, isolated, individual. However, for many South Asian Hindus self-identity is more collective than individual. Rather than the "I-self" that typifies most North American life, Hindu experience is much more the collective "we-self" of the extended family. This difference has important implications for situations involving issues of consent in health care ethics. While the Canadian health care system and Western medical ethics teaching assumes that the ethical agent is the autonomous individual, in South Asian Hindu culture it is frequently the collective "we-self" of the extended family that functions as the decision maker in matters of consent. This difference, which Hindus share with immigrants from many other traditional cultures and religions, is just now being recognized by medical ethics scholars and health care professionals (Coward 1999).

Women

Women in first-generation families frequently take the responsibility for maintaining the family altar in the home and passing on the daily home worship traditions to the children. Girls as well as boys are encouraged to continue into postsecondary education with the result that many become professionals employed outside the home. Thus the role of mothers in maintaining home worship may well change in second-generation families; however, this has yet to be thoroughly studied. The pattern of marriage in the second and third generation also seems to be changing with the desire of mothers to have their daughters follow the arranged marriage tradition receiving considerable resistance from their Canadian-born daughters. Canadian-born Hindu women who continue into university frequently evidence a desire to engage in a critical feminist reading of the textual sources and history of their tradition. In this they are not different from many of their contemporaries in India. With regard to issues of self-identity, Hindu women in Canada—be they young or old—continue to manifest a strong collective self-identity and sensitivity to all the family duties and responsibilities that brings. Older women, mothers of first-generation immigrants who later come from the old country are sometimes lacking in English language ability. If everyone else in the family goes out to work, they may find themselves in a lonely and alien situation. A current major research project (The Metropolis Project on Immigration and Integration of Immigrants in Canadian Cities) is engaging in ethnology studies to examine the experience of such women in Canadian South Asian immigrant communities.

Relations with the "Old Country"

Close ties are usually maintained between Hindu South Asians in Canada and India. There are frequent visits "home" to see members of the extended family. Money is sometimes sent to help those still in India. India is still a favored place for the finding of partners in arranged marriages. Some first-generation immigrants plan to retire in India. Touring gurus, professional musicians, and dancers now make regular circuits across Canada and receive strong support from the Hindu communities. Such visits play an important role in the passing on of religion and culture to succeeding generations. They also attract participation from members of the host culture. Officers of the Indian High Commission and its regional Consulates make frequent visits to the South Asian communities thereby helping to maintain cultural and political links with the "old country." In the educational domain, the Shastri Indo-Canadian Institute has provided fellowships enabling many Canadian South Asian Hindu students to return to the "old country" to study language, history, religion, or culture. South Asian faculty members in Canadian universities have been awarded sabbatical fellowships to do research in India—often coinciding with arranged marriages of their children in India. The Shastri Institute's Visiting Scholar program has brought some of Hindu India's finest scholars to travel across Canada speaking both to university students and to community groups. In all of these ways, Hindus in Canada have nurtured and maintained close connections with the "old country."

170 *Harold Coward*

─────────────────NOTES─────────────────

1. The following description is drawn from participant observation in Hindu funerals in Edmonton and Calgary in 1982, first reported in Goa, Coward, and Neufeldt (1984).

2. Interview with C. G. Balachrandran, Calgary, Alberta, March 18, 1982.

3. Interview with Srinivas Doraiswamy, Calgary, Alberta, 18 March 1982.

─────────────────BIBLIOGRAPHY─────────────────

Bibby, R. W. (1993). *Unknown Gods: The Ongoing Story of Religion in Canada*. Toronto: Stoddart Publishing Co.

Bissoondath, N. (1994). *Selling Illusions: The Cult of Multiculturalism in Canada*. Toronto: Penguin Books.

Buchignani, Norman. (1977). "A Review of the Historical and Sociological Literature on East Indians in Canada." *Canadian Ethnic Studies* 1.

Buchignani, N., Indra, D. M., and Srivastava, R. (1985). *Continuous Journey: A Social History of South Asians in Canada*. Toronto: McClelland and Stewart.

Canada. (1990). Department of Multiculturalism and Citizenship. *The Canadian Multiculturalism Act: A Guide for Canadians*. Ottawa: Queen's Printer.

───. (1990). *The Canadian Multiculturalism Act: A Guide for Canadians*. Ottawa: Queen's Printer, 1990.

Canada. (1993). Department of Vital Statistics. *Religion in Canada: The Nation*. Ottawa: Queen's Printer.

Coward, Harold G. (1999). "Individual and Collective Identity in Ethical Decision Making." In *Visions of a New Earth: Population, Consumption and Ecology*. E. Coward and D. Maguire, eds. Albany: State University of New York Press.

───. (1993). "World Religions and New Reproductive Technologies." In *Social Values and Attitudes Surrounding New Reproductive Technologies*. Vol. 2, Research Studies, Royal Commission on New Reproductive Technologies. Ottawa: Canada Publishing.

───. (1991) (published in 1993). "Multiculturalism and Religious Freedom." *Religious Studies and Theology* 11:2, 50–56.

───. (1989). "Can Religions Live Together in Today's World? Intolerance and Tolerance in Religious Pluralism." In *Pluralism, Tolerance and*

Dialogue, M. Darrol Bryant, ed., pp. 1–19. Waterloo: University of Waterloo Press.

———, with J. Lipner and K. Young. (1989). *Hindu Ethics: Purity, Abortion and Euthanasia*. Albany: State University of New York Press.

———, ed., with C. Bagley and J. Friesen. (1988). *The Evolution of Multiculturalism*. Calgary: Institute for the Humanities.

———, with D. Goa. (1987). "Religious Experience in South Asian Diaspora in Canada." In *South Asian Diaspora in Canada: Six Essays*, 73–86, M. Israel, ed. Toronto: The Multicultural History Society of Ontario.

———. (1985). *Pluralism: Challenge to World Religions*. Maryknoll, New York: Orbis Books.

———, ed. with L. S. Kawamura. (1978). *Religion and Ethnicity*. Waterloo: Wilfrid Laurier University Press.

Devries, J. (1987). *The Integration of Ethno-Cultural Communities into Canadian Society: A Selected Bibliography*. Ottawa: Published by the Center for Research on Ethnic Minorities, Department of Sociology and Anthropology, Carleton University by Policy and Research Sector, Multiculturalism and Citizenship Canada.

Dusenbury, V. A. (1981). "Canadian Ideology and Public Policy: The Impact on Vancouver Sikh Ethnic and Religious Adaptation." *Canadian Ethnic Studies* 13:3.

Fenton, J. Y. (1995). *South Asian Religions in the Americas: An Annotated Bibliography of Immigrant Religious Traditions*. Westport, CT: Greenwood Press.

Goa, D., with H. Coward and R. Neufeldt. (1984). "Hindus in Alberta: A Study of Religious Continuity and Change." *Canadian Ethnic Studies* 16: 65–88.

Gupta, T. D. (1994). "Political Economy of Gender, Race and Class: Looking at South Asian Immigrant Women in Canada." *Canadian Ethnic Studies* 26:1, 59–73.

Israel, M. (1994). *In the Further Soil: A Social History of the Indo-Canadians in Ontario*. Toronto: The Organization for the Promotion of Indian Culture.

Jensen, J. M. (1988). *Passage from India: Asian Indian Immigrants in North America*. New Haven: Yale University Press.

Johnston, H. J. M. (1988). "The Development of the Punjabi Community in Vancouver since 1901." *Canadian Ethnic Studies* 22:2, 1–19.

Ledoux, M. (1990). *Multicultural Canada: A Graphic Overview*. Policy and Research, Multiculturalism Sector, Multiculturalism and Citizenship Canada. Ottawa: Queen's Printer.

Miller, D. (1976–1977). "The Guru as the Centre of Sacredness." *Studies in Religion* 6: 527–33.

O'Connell, J. T. (1992). "Sikh Studies in North America: A Field Guide." In *Studying the Sikhs: Issues for North America*, 113–28, J. S. Hawley and G. S. Mann, eds. Albany: State University of New York Press.
———, ed. with R. K. Ray. (1985). *Bengali Immigrants: A Community in Transition*. Toronto: Rabindranath Tagore Lectureship Foundation.
Richardson, E. A. (1985). *East Comes West: Asian Religions and Cultures in North America*. New York: The Pilgrim Press.
Royal Canadian Mounted Police (1992). Multicultural Liaison Branch, RCMP Personnel Directorate. *RCMP Principles and Commitment to Diversity*. Ottawa: Queen's Printer.
Sekar, R. (22–23 August 1997). "'Authenticity by Accident': Organizing, Decision Making and the Construction of a Diasporic Hindu Temple in the Nation's Capital." Paper read at the International Conference on the Hindu Diaspora. Montreal.
Srinivas, K. M., with S. K. Kaul. (1987). *Indo-Canadians in Saskatchewan: The Early Settlers*. Regina: India Canada Association of Saskatchewan.
Williams, R. B. (1988). *Religions of Immigrants from India and Pakistan*. Cambridge University Press.

8

The Muslims of Canada

Sheila McDonough

Immigration

The first mosque in Canada was built in Edmonton in 1938 by Muslims mainly of Syrian trader background. Following the Second World War, the number of Muslims in Canada increased, particularly because of the communal violence resulting from the severity of the partition events when India and Pakistan came into being. Most of the South Asian Muslim immigrants to Canada in the 1950s, 60s, and early 70s had advanced academic degrees, and many of them found work in the universities, the civil service, and the professions. Most of them were from the Urdu-speaking areas, Hyderabad, Uttar Pradesh, and the Punjab. A considerable number came as students and remained to build families in Canada.

More recently Bangladeshis also have been coming, particularly after the conflict associated with the founding of Bangladesh in the early seventies. In addition, changes in immigration law

173

have meant a greater immigration of family members of all these groups. Another refugee group came from East Africa. The expulsion of Asians from Uganda resulted in a large immigration of Muslims from East Africa to Canada. Most of these were Ismailis. The largest Ismaili community in North America and Europe is in Canada, about 40,000. Ithna Ashariyya Shi'a and Sunnis were also among the East African immigrants. They, too, were mainly well educated, and many have become prosperous in the business and professional communities.

Immigrants from the Caribbean have been coming steadily to Canada for many years. Many Canadian Muslims, particularly in the greater Toronto area, are from Trinidad or Guyana. Often people in the Caribbean, descendants of indentured laborers brought from South Asia at the end of the nineteenth century, do not know what part of India they came from, but they do know whether they are Hindus or Muslims. There were mosques in all the Caribbean villages where South Asian Muslims lived. These Caribbean Muslim immigrants to Canada are much more at home with North American culture in most cases than are the first-generation immigrants from South Asia.

About half of the Muslims in Canada now are of South Asian origin. The largest Muslim population is in the greater Toronto area. Quebec has encouraged the French-speaking Muslim immigrants to settle in that province. A rough estimate of the number of Muslims in Canada in 1997 is approximately 400,000.

Cumulative Tradition

The cumulative tradition that Asian Muslims have brought to Canada has been marked by the loss of political power suffered by the collapse of the Mughal Empire in India after the failed revolt of 1857.[1] The responses of South Asian Muslims to that loss of power have mainly run in three different streams. One approach was to found a Muslim university in India, Aligarh, in order to try to incorporate into Muslim understanding all the new knowledge coming from the West.[2] A second approach, associated particularly with the founding in India of the *madrasa* at Deoband, has been to produce new generations of traditional religious leaders whose education has not changed from the medieval patterns of training.[3] A third approach has been that of Maulana Mawdudi, variously described as an integrist, fundamentalist, Islamist, separatist, or neotraditionalist. His approach is to work for a separate political entity in which Muslims could evolve their own form of effective modernism cut off from domination by other forms of modern life.[4]

Many of the highly educated Muslims who came to Canada had been trained in the Aligarh tradition and were interested in relating Muslim principles to modern life. Those from the Deoband stream were mainly the ulama who have been brought in to serve as the imams of the new Canadian mosques. The third stream, the followers of Mawdudi, also produced many highly educated persons, often engineers and scientists, who saw themselves as the vanguard of the Islamic revolution that Mawdudi had predicted would ultimately become the main force in the modern world.

The emphases of these three different schools of Muslim thought have largely shaped how different Canadian Muslims from South Asia have understood their situation in their new country. Any one Canadian mosque might well have representatives of all three points of view among its members. These schools of thought have also been evolving themselves, since nothing is static. The followers of Mawdudi in South Asia and North America have been developing new insights and points of view as time has passed. Not all the mosques have imams trained in the Deoband perspective. Sometimes mosques with large South Asian populations have imams from Egypt or Lebanon or East, South, or West Africa.

The sufi tradition is also part of the South Asian Muslim heritage. Sufism has declined over the last century in much the same ways as various forms of organized devotional and monastic discipline have declined in the other major traditions recently. However, the Sufi background has also led to the formation of new activities among branches of the traditional religious orders, such as the Naqshbandis, to new forms of "New Age" personal mysticism, and also to new kinds of Muslim missionary organizations. It was the Sufi orders who were one of the main forces in the Middle Ages for the spread of Islam to new parts of the world.[5] One new modern form of missionary organization, the Tablighi Jamaat, emerged out of a traditional Sufi center in Delhi, and has become a huge worldwide organization of Muslims who are committed to strict personal religious discipline, and to working to bring other Muslims back to such discipline.[6]

Current Situation, 1996

A booklet entitled *Muslim Guide to Canada* published by the Canadian office of the Muslim World Mission lists 60 Sunni mosques in every major Canadian city from Halifax to Vancouver.[7] There are also Ithna Ashariyya Shi'a Mosques in Toronto and Montreal, and Ismaili Jamaat Khanas in every major Canadian city. The first priority of the Muslims from all communities has been the building of mosques and Islamic centers as bases from which Muslim community life can be stimulated and helped.

In addition to the mosque communities, some Muslims have established larger organizations that hold conferences, produce journals and books, run bookstores and summer camps, and provide speakers. The Islamic Society of North America (ISNA) and the Islamic Circle of North America (ICNA) are among the most active of these organizations.[8] Muslims from Canada have been active in both groups since they were founded. In both cases, North America is divided into sections, one of which is Canada.

ICNA was established in Montreal in 1968 by a Pakistani engineer. He set up a circle (*halaqa*) of Muslims in the city to study Qur'an and Hadith together. The intention was to further understanding of the Qur'an by holding open discussions; members would take turns preparing comments on particular texts of the Qur'an.[9] From this beginning, ICNA was established formally in 1971. It is intended to be a grassroots organization, nonethnic and nonsectarian. It stresses that only democratic legal and peaceful means will be used to promote Islamic values. Its aim is to provide intellectual and moral training to build Islamic character and conduct, and to educate publish opinion to achieve its goal.

The Canadian president of ICNA in 1996, Shahabuddin Ahmed, is a retired engineer with an Indian background who has lived most of his professional life in Canada. He now devotes his activities to furthering ICNA's activities. ICNA workers hold *da'wa* (missionary) meetings, organize *da'wa* field trips, distribute Islamic literature, and arrange *da'wa* booths at public places. One ICNA publication is published in a Canadian edition of 20,000 copies a month. It is distributed in mosques across the country.

The ISNA branch in Canada has been active since the early 1970s promoting the building of mosques and Muslim schools. They have held many conferences. There are full-time schools for Muslims in a number of Canadian cities as well as weekend schools in most Islamic centers throughout the country. Both ICNA and ISNA originally had active members who came from the Jamaat Islami stream of Muslim thought established by Maulana Mawdudi, but they have developed their own priorities and values in the North American context.

ICNA has prepared a document for the use of ICNA members, which is called a personal planning and evaluation guide.[10] Members are to write down their goals for this world, and for the life hereafter. The ICNA information pamphlets on Islam stress that orientation to the life hereafter is of primary importance. Once the goals are articulated, the members are to keep records of their personal devotional and charitable activities, to indicate precisely how they use their time and money, and how they could improve. Members are to participate in NeighborNets, small groups of no more than eight, who gather every week to improve their knowledge, develop brotherhood, and do *da'wa*. They are also expected to take part in training camps, and *da'wa* field trips.

The Tablighi Jamaat is also active in Canada. There is usually at least one mosque in every city which is particularly hospitable to the travelling Tablighi missionaries. Many Canadian Muslims go to the large annual Tablighi conferences in the United States, which are attended by thousands of people. The Tablighi emphasis in Canada, as elsewhere, is on reform of Muslim devotional practice. Anyone who joins this movement is expected to attend regular discussion groups on Qur'an and Hadith and to participate in visiting other Muslims and inviting them to reform their practice. Members travel quite a lot, staying in mosques and generally living as cheaply as they can.

Ritual and Devotional Practices

Sunni Muslim devotional practices are centered around the basic pillars of Islam, namely five times a day prayer, bearing witness to the unity of God, charity, the annual month of fasting, and pilgrimage to Mecca once in a lifetime if possible. Friday at noon is the time when it is recommended for Muslims to take part in prayer in the mosque if possible, because a sermon is given on this occasion.

All the mosques and Islamic centers have prayer halls in which the five time a day prayers are regularly offered by anyone who wishes to attend. The arrangements for women who wish to pray differ from situations in which they merely stand behind the men, to places where there is a curtain or some other form of division to separate them from the men. Annual ritual festivals include the *EId* celebrations after the month of fasting, and celebrations of the Ascension of the Prophet, *Miraj*. In Toronto in 1996, the *EId* celebrations were held in the huge new stadium where the

Toronto Blue Jays play hockey. It is estimated that over 20,000
attended.

One example of a large and effective Muslim community is that
of the Taric Mosque in Toronto. They produce a newsletter which
lists new converts, gives names of members who have died, offers
congratulations on new births, and mentions members who have
just graduated from University.[11] The newsletter includes a children's
corner with a quiz on Islamic material, a marriage bureau, announcements about a community yard sale, an annual picnic and
fish-fry, a family night, an autumn boat cruise, an annual walk-a-
thon, and an international bazaar and food fest.

Once new converts join, their names and needs go into the
computer, and the community tries to help whatever needs they
may have. The mosque offers food coupons for hungry people that
can be exchanged in local grocery stores. Many Toronto imams are
in consultation with local social service agencies, and sometimes
serve as translators and helpers for whatever difficulties Muslims
may be experiencing.

Presently, a controversial practice among Sunnis in Canada is
the celebration of the Prophet Muhammad's birthday, *Milad an
Nabi*. In the summer of 1996, three conferences were held in
Vancouver, Toronto, and Montreal. The verses on the poster adver-
tising these conferences expressed the following sentiments about
devotion to the Prophet Muhammad:

He attained the pinnacle of greatness with his perfection.
He dispelled darkness with his beauty
Excellent are all his qualities
Shower blessings on him and his family.

The controversy is between those of the reformist and puritani-
cal traditions who consider that adherence to the message of scripture rather than devotion to the person of the Prophet should be
the core of Islamic commitment. In South Asia, these two approaches
were associated with the *madrasas* of Deoband and Barelwi respectively.[12] The tradition of devotion to the person of the Prophet is a
medieval Islamic practice that is being revived in a new form. The
emphasis is on personal spiritual growth rather than on more social, economic, and political attitudes to Islamic responsibilities. In
the Montreal conference, the Barelwi arguments were explicitly
put in terms of acceptance of practices, *bid'a*, which were not necessarily those of the first Muslim community. The point argued by
the Barelwis is that good innovation can occur.

The ritual practices of the Shi'a include regular prayers with ritual remembrances of various Shi'a martyrs. This latter form of worship involves services at the mosques that focus on recitation of the virtues of the historical Shi'a martyrs and prayers related to them. In this way, the long history of Shi'a martyrs remains close to the minds of the people. The Shi'a understand themselves as upholders of the original form of Islamic devotion and piety that was suppressed after the death of the Caliph Ali in 662 C.E.

In a recent newsletter of a Shi'a Mosque in Toronto, the concern for educating the children has been eloquently expressed.

The Madrasah today known as "East End Madressah" has grown into a strong beautiful tree. The number of students has grown to approximately 374. The roots of this tree are of course the 64 teachers of the Madressah . . . The flowers of this lovely tree are our students who are the lucky ones to receive the educated efforts of all the staff of the Madressah. Insha Allah, as they grow, people will be able to smell the fragrance of Islam from them.[11]

One cultural aspect of South Asian Muslim life is a long tradition of beautiful religious poetry, memorized and integrated into the daily thoughts of the people. As this quotation indicates, the poetic habit of mind is still capable of self-expression in the new milieu. The Sunni Muslims have similarly tended their educational gardens with the hope of fragrant blossoms.

The Ismaili Jamaat Khana rituals are not open to the public. As with the Ithna Ashariyya Shi'a, these Muslims also remember their martyrs and practice devotional hymn singing. In addition to these practices, the Canadian Ismaili communities have sponsored large annual public meetings open to everyone to celebrate the *Milad an Nabi*. On this occasion, representatives from other Muslim groups are invited. The intention is to strengthen mutual respect between Muslim communities based on their common loyalty to, and reverence for, the Prophet Muhammad.

Sufi groups are relatively small in Canadian cities but are increasing in membership. Their practices include regular services of remembrance of God [*dhikr*] and recitation of the names of God. Some Sufi groups like the Naqhsbandis are actively seeking to convert North Americans. Many New Age book stores include books by Sufi poets. The form of psychological analysis of personality characteristics known as the Enneagram has become one of the

streams of thought used by persons interested in non-Western forms
of self-understanding. The Enneagram is said to have come from
medieval Sufi practice.

Strategies of Adaptation

Mosques take on new forms and new roles in the Canadian context.
As religious institutions, they are required by Canadian law to
have governing boards that take responsibility for financial matters, and membership that elects the governing boards. The governing boards select the imams and take responsibility for them.
The imams are normally responsible for preaching the Friday sermon, and for directing the religious education activities. Usually at
least one mosque in a city is licensed for marriages and funerals,
and the imams carry these responsibilities also.

Many of the imams are gradually adapting to new roles as they
are expected to deal with children raised in the Canadian context,
and to function as pastoral counselors. One imam told me he was
summoned to the hospital when one of the members of his mosque
had an automobile accident, and was expected to counsel the family and help with all the legal and other problems. Another said the
experience of being regularly phoned in the middle of the night by
persons from his community with personal problems of family
conflicts was a new experience for him. The traditional training at
the *madrasas* like Deoband does not explicitly prepare imams for
most of these new counseling responsibilities; most of them are
learning on the job as best they can.

The mosques serve their traditional functions as places where
the regular prayers are offered. In addition, however, in the new
Canadian context, they often also serve as cultural centers where
Muslims meet other Muslims. In most cases, mosque members come
from many different countries, from Afghanistan and Algeria to
Zambia. Therefore, the experience of taking part in mosque activities also strengthens the fellow feeling of membership in a world
wide Muslim community rather than in a strictly ethnically defined
group.

In addition, considerable effort has been spent attempting to
establish full-time Muslim schools. ISNA in particular has served
to stimulate and to advise on these activities. Usually the schools
begin with primary classes and gradually evolve. One Montreal
Muslim school now has classes all the way to the end of secondary

education. The curriculum follows provincial guidelines, as education is a provincial responsibility in Canada.

ICNA has encouraged the use of new technologies. In every city there is a toll free *da'wa* hotline, and a Muslim alert network. The idea is to be ready to respond to media on issues concerning Muslims. Muslims in several Canadian cities have held meetings with media representatives. One branch of ICNA is *Sound Vision,* which is developing video cassettes for the use of children. This material resembles *Sesame Street* with the use of puppets and lightly humorous stories. The children are encouraged to learn Islamic values through laughter and amusing incidents. *Sound Vision* has also developed multimedia material for learning to read and to recite the Qur'an in Arabic on one's personal computer in what might be termed a user-friendly manner.[13]

Women

The South Asian Muslim immigrants of the 1960s and 70s included many women with university backgrounds. Many of them also entered the professions and the business world. A large number of these immigrant families have prospered with both husband and wife holding good jobs. In most cases, their children also have received a good education and are entering the job market, girls as well as boys. There are, of course, exceptions, particularly in terms of later immigrants, and there are instances of Muslim women who remain in the home and do not relate much to the wider society. There is, therefore, a wide spectrum of different attitudes, experiences, and expectations among Canadian Muslim women.

There is a national organization called the Canadian Council of Muslim Women. The brochure of this organization is notably professional, beginning, as most professional documents do these days, with a vision statement that reads as follows:

> To strive for Canadian Muslim Women's equality, equity and empowerment. These goals are Canadian and Islamic values, and we, as Muslim women, envision our identity within the context of the principles of Islam and the laws of Canada. We value our roles and responsibilities in the family and in the community. We believe in the interdependency of each member, so that there is a balance between the needs and the responsibilities of individuals.[14]

This approach might be seen as an instance of the adaptation of the Aligarh stream of South Asian Muslim attitudes to the Canadian environment. The emphasis on retaining basic Muslim principles while accepting Canadian law follows the Aligarh idea of separating principles from the adaptation of those principles to specific situations. The Aligarh school taught that principles such as justice were worked out differently in varying social and historical contexts.

This brochure indicates an address for a web page and also gives an Internet address. The web page provides all sorts of services. The technology makes the communication between women more effective. The national conferences set objectives and local chapters work to carry out the aims. The Ottawa chapter of the group is writing a handbook on Canadian laws and policies. The Edmonton chapter held a launch in the provincial legislative building focused on South Africa. Two Montreal graduate students are being sponsored to prepare a sociological study of the use of the *hijab* among Muslim women. Other activities include the preparation of pamphlets in Farsi, Arabic, Punjabi, and other languages on wife abuse.

A speech quoted in this brochure refers to the centuries of silence of women, particularly Muslim women. The author, Zohra Husaini from Alberta, says that the Prophet fought for the equality and dignity and justice for all humanity, but that the hold of patriarchy was too strong, and that women began to lose the rights they had been given. In her words: "Most of us have forgotten or probably never knew or were never told what the Prophet intended for us women. But it is possible to educate ourselves about this and I claim that it is up to us to continue where he left off. We can do it."[15]

Another women's activity is the South Asian Women's Centre in Montreal. This organization emerged out of a group of Muslim, Hindu, Sikh, Christian, and Buddhist women immigrants from South Asia in 1981.[16] They began informally by talking about their perceived problems, but now they are an effective agency that gets provincial government recognition. They serve to help with any difficulties South Asian women or men bring to them; they offer courses on topics that are desired, such as domestic skills. They also serve to assist other social work agencies who refer to them persons with language problems that make communication difficult. One Muslim woman who works there functions in four South Asian languages, and has to deal with problems in all of them.

The wearing of the *hijab* has been increasing among Muslim women in Canada over the last ten years. In the Muslim schools, the *hijab* is required. In Quebec there have been several incidents that have received wide coverage in the French press. In 1994, in a Catholic school in Quebec, a student was asked to remove the *hijab*. Subsequent press coverage led to wide discussion in the province on radio talk shows. Muslims felt that some journalists in the French press were actively waging an anti-Islamic campaign. The Quebec Muslims have been organizing themselves to combat this negative stereotyping.[17]

An organization of Christian women, Protestant and Catholic, *Le Réseau Ecuménique des Femmes du Québec* held a one day meeting in 1995 with Islamic women in which five Muslim women, veiled and unveiled, participated. The meeting was held in the Mother House of the CND, *Congrégation de Notre Dame*, one of the major teaching orders of nuns in Quebec. Subsequently, the Quebec Human Rights Commission issued a report on the *hijab* issue. The Quebec Human Rights Commission understands that it has a mandate under the Quebec Charter of Rights and Freedoms to investigate cases in which citizens appeal to the charter for protection of their rights, and also to promote the Charter.

In the case of the school forbidding the use of the veil, both sides had appealed to the Human Rights Commission. Although the decisions of the Commission do not have the force of law, they do tend to set the tone for what is to be considered acceptable. In this case, the members of the Commission stated that they had to consider the entire issue of religious diversity and the conflict of values as these issues were surfacing in what used to be a Quebec dominated by a Roman Catholic majority. The decision of the Commission reads as follows:

> It must be acknowledged that the veil is sometimes an instrumental part of a set of practices aimed at maintaining the subjugation of women, and that in some more extremist societies, women are actually forced to wear the veil. For example, we cannot but condemn in the strongest possible terms the terrorism to which some Algerian women are subjected. . . . A major part of the public debate of recent months has been concerned with the interpretation of the Koran itself. . . . We do not feel it is up to us to take a position on this particular question, which we believe should be considered first and

foremost within the Muslim community itself. In our view, it would be insulting to the girls and women who wear the veil to suppose that their choice is not an enlightened one . . . In general terms, therefore, the veil should be seen as licit, to be prohibited or regulated only if it can be proved that public order or the equality of the sexes is threatened.[18]

Responses to Public Policy

Public policy in Canada both provincially and federally has been that of multiculturalism, namely to encourage the understanding that many different cultures make up the Canadian mosaic, and that all should be respected as long as they are law-abiding. Various national and provincial Muslim associations have received government support for conferences and other activities.

The main national Muslim organization, the Council of the Muslim Community of Canada, was founded in 1973 after extensive consultations among Muslims across Canada. The past presidents have come from six different Canadian cities. The CMCC's brochure states that the Council has been instrumental in founding several key organizations including the Canadian Council of Muslim Women, Families Meeting Families, International Development and Refugee Foundation, Muslim Youth Camping, Islamic Schools Federation of Ontario, National Christian-Muslim Liaison Committee, Muslim Elders Network, and Vision TV. At present the priorities are the Muslim Elders and Muslim-Christian Liaison.[19]

The method of the Council is to attempt to raise consciousness at the local level on issues like the problems of elders, and then leave the local groups to implement their own ways of dealing with the perceived problems. The national Council tends to function as a catalyst. Vision TV is a distinctively Canadian attempt to handle religious broadcasting: it is the only cable channel specifically for programs on religious matters. Any group can pay to provide their own broadcast on this channel, as long as the program is not abusive of other communities. One of the main Muslim programs, *Islam in Focus*, is broadcast at noon on Saturdays from the Islamic Centre in Scarborough, Ontario.

The title *Islam in Focus* was the title of a book originally published by the Rashid Mosque in Edmonton (the first mosque in the country).[20] The author of the book, Hammudah Abd al-Ati, had come to Institute of Islamic Studies at McGill, which had just been founded under the leadership of Wilfred Cantwell Smith in the early 1950s. Abd al-Ati had come to McGill from the Azhar University in Egypt as one of the first Muslim students of the McGill Institute. His book has been republished several times and is often given as a present to new converts. The emphasis is on the personal training in moral virtues required by the Islamic tradition.

The strategies adopted by different Muslim groups depend on the underlying assumptions of the particular groups about the nature of the wider Canadian society. These assumptions derive from the earlier responses in the nineteenth-century and early twentieth-century Indian context to the processes of modernization. The current coordinator of the CMCC, an Indian Muslim, was an active member of the Edmonton mosque when Abd al-Ati was the imam there. The CMCC perspective is that of cooperating, wherever possible, with the wider society because it is assumed that Muslims should absorb modern education and live at peace in a pluralist society.

The message of *Islam in Focus* was that Muslims should focus on personal religious discipline, and on the building of sound institutions. They were encouraged to develop techniques for encountering antagonism with dignity. This is generally the approach that has characterized much of the development of Muslim life in Canada over the last 40 years.

The more extremist position, which comes in the first place from the integrists, Mawlana Mawdudi in South Asia and Sayyid Qutb in the Arab world, is to perceive all the modern world as equivalent to *jahiliya*, paganism, and to urge the Muslims to remain uncontaminated by pagan attitudes and practices. It is not easy to measure how these ideas about paganism work out in practice, but they are reflected in many sermons and other forms of literature. One measure might be discerned in Muslim readiness to enter into dialogue with persons from other religious traditions. Some will do this, and others will not; there is a spectrum of diverse attitudes among Muslims toward the wider society. The CMCC has encouraged dialogue.

Relations to the "Old Country"

South Asia is still considered the major source for religious leadership since many of the imams are brought to Canada from the South Asian *madrasas*. This is not always entirely satisfactory since the South Asia training tends not to equip these leaders for many of the demands placed on them to educate young Canadian Muslims and to serve as pastoral counselors. Nevertheless, the *madrasa* training provides a continuity of experience and perspective that is valued by many of the Canadian Muslims.

The responses to mosque life vary among young Muslims as in other communities. One distinctive response is to undertake an interest in development work in South Asia. The Ismailis explicitly encourage this; young Muslims are invited to participate in Ismaili-sponsored projects, including an annual walk in most of the large cities to raise money for development projects in South Asia.[21] The Sunni organizations like ICNA and ISNA also raise money for refugee and relief causes, and publicize through their journals stories of Muslim needs in developing countries. In this way, Canadian Muslim young people are encouraged to take an interest in development, refugee, and relief projects.

Tensions over incidents like the Rushdie Affair, the Kashmir struggles, and the destruction of the Babri Mosque cause turmoil within the Muslim community in Canada as elsewhere. The Muslim publications usually feature articles about suffering in other parts of the Muslim world, as among Bosnian Muslims, and encourage Muslims to identity with the difficulties of their coreligionists everywhere.[22]

The decision of the government of Pakistan under Zulfiqar Ali Bhutto to condemn the Ahmadi community as non-Muslim has had serious repercussions on members of that community in Canada as in other parts of the world.[23] There are Ahmadi centers in all major Canadian cities, including a very large center in Toronto. In Montreal, the Ahmadi Centre is an attractive building in the French section of the city that serves as a retreat center for many different groups. The persecution of the Ahmadis in Pakistan and elsewhere has led them to separate themselves off from other Muslims, and to strengthen the intensity of their commitment.

South Asians and Higher Education

Canadian Muslims coming from university backgrounds normally encourage higher education for their children. University education is available for most young Canadians from a middle-class background; young Muslims are often very committed and serious students. One sees Muslims, often recognizable because of the *hijab*, present on university campuses. Many of them are particularly committed to goals in engineering and medicine. The coming generations of Canadian Muslims will certainly include many highly educated persons.

Religious Studies is a discipline taught in most Canadian universities, and this normally includes courses in Islam. Many young Canadian Muslims take these courses. The Institute of Islamic Studies at McGill, established in the early 1950s, has provided a number of professors for Canadian universities and junior colleges. The emphasis at McGill has been on training, which included training by Muslim teachers, and on the presence of many Muslim students.[24] Anyone trained there has had a good exposure to Muslim presence as well as to contemporary scholarship on Islamic issues.

The only notable recent case of criticism by local Muslims of a Muslim scholar working in the university milieu took place in the Shi'a Mosque in Toronto in the summer of 1996. The scholar in question, Abdel Aziz Sachedina, was trained at the University of Toronto and took part in the affairs of that mosque for many years. He presently teaches at the University of Virginia in the United States. His book about messianism raised some issues about how the community understands the history of Shi'a Imams.[25] His writings were being criticized in Shi'a communities in other parts of the world. The Toronto mosque decided to air the issue by holding a meeting in which Sachedina could reply to his critics. The newsletter of the mosque indicates that the meeting was held, and that, after the issues were debated, the persons present at the meeting decided to put the matter behind them. In effect, it was agreed to respect and tolerate differences of opinion on matters rising from the academic study of religion.

New Muslim Voices

A recent short film was broadcast on the national TV news channel in early October 1996. Entitled *BBQ Muslims*, the film was a satirical presentation of a situation in which there was an explosion in a suburban backyard barbecue stove, and the local Muslims were immediately arrested. The program included an interview with the producer-director, a young Canadian Muslim woman wearing a blue *hijab*. She said the way to communicate with Canadians is through the use of a Canadian sense of humor.[26] The satire was evidently intended to mock the American panic after the Oklahoma bombing about the Muslim terrorists. For her generation, the negative stereotyping of Muslims is still the main perceived threat to the peace of mind of the Canadian Muslim community.

188   *Sheila McDonough*

---------------------------- NOTES ----------------------------

1. Mujeeb, M. (1967). *The Indian Muslims*. Montreal: McGill University Press.

2. Malik, H. (1980). *Sir Sayyid Ahmed Khan and Modernization in India and Pakistan*. New York: Columbia University Press.

3. Faruqi, Z. (1963). *The Deoband School and the Demand for Pakistan*. New York: Asia Publishing House.

4. Nasr, V. (1996). *Mawdudi and the Making of Islamic Revivalism*. Oxford and New York: Oxford University Press.

5. Mujeeb, M. *The Indian Muslims*, p. 167.

6. al-Haq, A. (1972) *The Faith Movement of Maulana Ilyas*. London: Allen and Unwin.

7. *Muslim Guide to Canada*, 1313 A.H. The West Mall, Ste. 1018, Etobicoke, ON, M9C 5K8. Canada. Other books are Yousif, A. (1993), *The Muslims of Canada A Question of Identity*, Toronto: Legas; and Huseini, Z. (1990), *Muslims in the Canadian Mosaic*, Edmonton: Muslim Research Foundation. Further information can be found in *The Muslim Directory of Greater Toronto and Surrounding Area* (1994), published by Madinah Masjid, Toronto. On the Ismailis in Canada, one source is Dossa, Parin A. (1986). *Dissertation Abstracts International: The Humanities and Social Sciences*, 47 (4), 1383-A. Another source is Israel, M., (1987). *South Asian Diaspora in Canada*. Toronto: Multi-Cultural History of Ontario.

8. For a history of ISNA, see Ahmed, G. (1991). "Muslim Organizations in the United States." In Y. Haddad, ed., *The Muslims of America*. New York: Oxford University Press.

9. Interview with Shahabuddin Ahmed, July, 1996.

10. *My Days in the Path of Allah, A Personal Planning and Evaluation Guide for Members of ICNA*, ICNA Canada, 100 McLevin Ave., Scarborough, ON, MIB 2V5, Canada.

11. *Taric Community News*, P.O. Box 66, Station U, Toronto, ON M82 ITO.

12. Lewis, P. (1994). *Islamic Britain*, London: I. B. Tauris, pp. 81–101.

13. *Sound Vision*, ICNA Canada, 100 McLevin Ave., Scarborough, ON, MIB 2V5.

14. *National Newsletter Spring 1996 Canadian Council of Muslim Women*, 2400 Dundas St. W. ste 513, Mississauga, ON. L5K 2R8.

15. *National Newsletter Spring 1996 Canadian Council of Muslim Women.*

16. Chew, D. (1992). "The Search for Legitimacy: The Montreal South Asian Women's Centre." In the *Bulletin of the Committee on Women in Asian Studies*: Roundtable on South Asian Women. Washington, D.C.

17. *Le Forum Musulman Canadien*, C.P. 1652 Succ. St. Laurent, Montreal, QC, H41 4L2.

18. *Religious Pluralism in Quebec: A Social and Ethical Challenge*, February 1995. Commission des droits de la personne du Quebec, pp. 17, 18.

19. *Working Together*, brochure of CMCC, 100 McLevin Ave., ste. 204a, Scarborough, ON, M1B 5K8.

20. Abd al-Ati, H. (1963). *Islam in Focus*. Edmonton: All-Rashid Mosque. Republished Indianopolis: American Trust Publications, 1975.

21. *The Ismaili Canada* (March 1996). Published by Insha Canada, ste. 786, 789 Don Mills Rd., Don Mills, ON. M3C 3L6, p. 24.

22. *The Bulletin* published by the Islamic Council of Montreal, P.O. Box 142, Station TMR, PQ. HEP 3B9. See also *The Message* ICNA Canada publishing office, Brossard, Quebec.

23. Niyazi, K. (1992). *Zulfiqar Ali Bhutto of Pakistan, Last Days*. New Delhi: Vikas Publishing House, 1992. See also Antonio Gualtieri (1989). *Conscience and Coercion Ahmadi Muslims and Orthodoxy in Pakistan*. Montreal: Guernica.

24. Adams, C. (1983). "The Development of Islamic Studies in Canada." In E. Waugh, B. Abu-Laban, and R. Qureshi, eds., *The Islamic Community in North America*. Edmonton: University of Alberta Press.

25. Sachedina, A. (1981). *Islamic Messianism*. Albany: State University of New York Press.

26. Zarqa Nawaz was the woman interviewed.

9

Sikh Religio-Ethnic Experience in Canada

Joseph T. O'Connell

Immigration History of Sikhs in Canada

Sikh history in Canada thus far breaks neatly into two broad periods, each roughly half a century long and each divisible again into a briefer turbulent and a longer calm phase (Buchignani and Indra 1985; Johnston 1979, 1988; N. Singh 1994). For the first (nearly) half of this century (1902–1947), Sikh (like other Asian) immigrants in Canada, concentrated almost exclusively in the west coast province of British Columbia (B.C.), faced hostility and discrimination. The half century since 1948, by contrast, has been marked by removal of racial barriers to immigration and to exercise of legal rights and by dramatic increase in immigration and settlement of Sikhs throughout Canada.

Initially, Sikh numbers in Canada expanded rapidly, to about 5,000 by 1908, only to face mounting hostility, legal/civic disabilities, economic depression, and violent conflicts—epitomized by the expulsion from Vancouver harbor in 1918 of the *Komagata Maru* with over 350 would-be immigrants from India (nearly all of them Sikhs). The Sikh population in B.C. declined to less than 2,000 by the end of what Buchignani and Indra call the "Early Years" (1902–1918). Then followed the "Quiet Years" (1919–1947), during which the remaining, predominantly male, Sikhs struggled, with some success, to bring wives from India and establish a small but enduring Canadian Sikh community. These Sikh pioneers focused their collective lives upon their *gurdwaras* (i.e., temples) in Vancouver and a few other places in B.C. Many became involved in the lumber industry and some in agriculture. Along the way, they modified their Punjabi Sikh way of life in the direction of prevailing Canadian sociocultural norms.

After the Second World War, Canada begin to dismantle its policy of excluding and/or disenfranchising Asian immigrants. Immigration from South Asia steadily rose from a handful in 1947 to a high of 12,868 from India alone in 1974. In the 1950s, the bulk of the small but expanding quota of Indian immigrants were Sikhs, mostly assisted kin or friends of those already in Canada. In the 1960s, when immigration rules were changed to favor highly skilled professionals, non-Sikhs from throughout India began to share the immigration to Canada, but even then Punjabi Sikhs continued to account for about half the Indian immigrants. In the 1970s, as the criteria for migration shifted to semiskilled workers, Sikhs, thanks to the chain-migration process, still accounted for nearly half of immigrants from India.

The arrival of Sikhs and other Asians in increasing numbers in the 1950s in B.C., where the bulk of the new immigrants were settling, set off renewed alarm over an impending "tide" of Asian immigration. But, this time, harassment could be successfully resisted and contained, though not eliminated entirely. South Asian immigrants arriving in the 1960s, by contrast, brought professional credentials, fluency in English, and cultural experience akin that of their Canadian neighbors. They found settlement relatively congenial, all the more so as most came to localities with no prior history of hostility to Asian immigrants. However, as the immigrant profile in the 1970s shifted to semiskilled laborers—and as immigration increased despite an economic slowdown and unemployment—anti-Asian prejudice and hostility sprang up right across the country. Sikhs, among the most visible of "visible minorities," were prime targets of racist abuse. Countering this, however, were official policies of "multiculturalism" and human rights—with the tacit approval, if not whole-hearted enthusiasm, of the bulk of the Canadian population. By the early 1980s, overt hostility to South Asian immigrants was abating and the latter were steadily building up the economic, social, and political bases for themselves and their children in Canada. In the Census of 1991, the number of men, women, and children designated as Sikh by religion was 147,440, a gain of 118 percent since the 1981 Census. Of these, 74,550 resided in British Columbia (49,450 in greater Vancouver) and 50,090 in Ontario (41,450 in greater Toronto) (Statistics Canada, *Religion in Canada* 1993, Table 2). One would estimate about 200,000 Sikhs in Canada in 1997.

What made 1984 a watershed in Canadian Sikh history was the protracted conflict between the government of India and important sectors of Sikh leadership and population in the Indian state of Punjab. In June 1984, the Indian army overran the most sacred of Sikh shrines, the Harimandir, or Golden Temple, at Amritsar, to root out armed militants and their inflammatory charismatic leader, Jarnail Singh Bhindranwale. That assault brought outrage from Sikhs around the globe. It was seen as an act of sacrilege, brutality, and contempt, a sign that the government of India was poised to destroy the Sikhs and their religiocultural heritage. Prime Minister Gandhi was soon assassinated by her own Sikh bodyguards (and many Sikhs celebrated); Sikhs in Delhi were massacred (and many Hindus seemed not to care). Sikhs overseas, notably in England, Canada, and the United States, had by 1984 the numbers, security, and resources to mobilize effective support for their fellow Sikhs in India—and for what they felt was the survival of Sikh religion and ethnic identity—and they did so.

The conflict in India, epitomized by the assault on the Golden Temple and subsequent assassination and massacres, brought dramatic reaffirmation of Sikh solidarity and identity from many Canadian Sikhs who till then had been preoccupied with the demands of settlement in a new country. Many Sikh men began to wear turbans, whether they had ever taken Khalsa initiation or not. Women as well as men sought Khalsa initiation—or returned to practice of lapsed Khalsa vows. Sikh youth became intensely aware of their familial ties to Sikhs in India and concerned with their cause—and wanted to know better what being Sikh was all about. *Gurdwaras* grew in number, size, and attendance and in pace of activity therein.

Selected themes of the Sikh tradition came to the fore: the valor and martyrdom of Sikh warriors, the heroic leadership of Guru Gobind Singh, the strategic importance (especially in crises) of the Khalsa order of "baptized" Sikhs. Beneath the overt symbols of identification with the Sikh cause stirred changing attitudes and the ways individuals understood themselves as being Sikh: not in a vague, taken-for-granted, perhaps even receding way, but as the central, emotionally gripping, challenged-and-reaffirmed personal identity and basis for communal solidarity.

Canadian Sikh publications, meetings, sermons, lobbying, and so on, took up the cause of Sikhs in India and denounced the government of India, the Congress Party, the Gandhi family, and whoever or whatever could be seen or suspected as being hostile toward the Sikhs. Friendships cooled as Sikhs and Hindus avoided one another's religiocultural, social, and even educational associations and events. There was political and financial support from Canadian Sikhs for Sikh interests in India, including the secessionist struggle, the extent and character of which support are hotly contested matters (Blaise and Mukherjee 1987; Mulgrew 1988; Kashmiri and McAndrew 1989), which we need not try to resolve here. However, for understanding the character of Sikh religioethnic life in Canada since 1984—both collective Sikh activities and individual Sikhs' mental/emotional experience—it is crucial to realize how powerful a factor has been—and still is—Canadian Sikhs' identification with the cause of their fellow Sikhs in India.

The Current Situation in Sikh Religion and Punjabi Sikh Ethnic Identity: Universality and Particularity; Assimilation and Retention

The volume in which this chapter appears is concerned explicitly with the religious experience of South Asians in diaspora. But, for most Sikhs in Canada, being Sikh is at least as much a matter of ethnicity as of religion. And for some, that ethnic identity is tantamount to a political/national identity. To say "most Sikhs," of course, is hazardous as there is as yet no study of a representative sample of Canadian Sikhs extensive and systematic enough to establish conclusively all but the most general observations. However, cumulative evidence and impressions over several years point in this direction. And when we consider what Canadian Sikh leaders and spokesmen (most are indeed male) say and do—in *gurdwaras*, associations, conferences, and community publications—

what we find is a very strong emphasis on ethnic identity, even when appealing to explicitly religious beliefs, symbols, and rites to support that identity.

The ethnic identity of Canadian Sikhs is by and large a distinctly Punjabi Sikh identity. Within the category of Punjabi Sikh, there is considerable variation, reflecting among other things the region of origin within the Punjab—or localities outside the Punjab and even outside India (East Africa, South Africa, South East Asia, Britain, etc.) from which immigrants or their forebears have come. The majority of Canadian Sikh immigrants are from the Punjab, disproportionately from the home districts of the early pioneers, who began the long and ramifying chain of Punjabi Sikh migration. There are also variations of endogamous group, that is, so-called caste or *zat* (*jati*) (and of clans within a *zat*), but a large majority are of the dominant agricultural *zat* in the Punjab, the Jats. There is always the fundamental distinction between initiated Khalsa Sikhs and non-Khalsa Sikhs, a distinction that has been the focus of serious conflict within some Sikh congregations, especially in British Columbia, where "new" Punjabi immigrants insisting on Khalsa standards have challenged the accommodations by "old" Canadian Sikhs to prevailing Canadian customs. At present, those upholding Khalsa norms—whether they constitute a majority or not—are dominant in most *gurdwara* management and other community affairs, and in the image presented to the Canadian public as to who is a Sikh. Ideally the voluntary Khalsa initiation transcends both caste and ethnicity. But in practice there is a tendency for the Khalsa symbols to serve as markers of a Punjabi Sikh ethnic identity. Also, in some Sikh families, intense pressure is brought to bear on boys and young men not to cut their hair, notwithstanding the voluntary ideal of Khalsa dedication.[1]

There are, however, some Canadian Sikhs, including a number of converts of European-North American background, for whom being Sikh does not imply an ethnic identity. The Western adherents to Sikh Dharma, otherwise known as 3HO (Healthy, Happy, Holy Organization), founded by Harbhajan Singh (Yogi Bhajan), are the most visible among the small minority of "*gora*" (white) Sikhs (Dusenberry 1988). Their presence among Sikhs brings the question of whether Sikh religion is or should be bound up with ethnicity at all. The Sikh Dharma members themselves adopt (while adapting) some Punjabi cultural customs, as in dress and in food, but insist that it is the principles of Sikh Dharma in Khalsa form that are crucial. They sometimes criticize Punjabi Sikhs for confusing Punjabi sociocultural practices with Sikh *dharma* (religion, duty,

law) and for slackness in maintaining the Khalsa code, as interpreted by Harbhajan Singh. However, 3HO Sikhs in Canada sometimes represent a Sikh position in human rights cases involving
the five Ks (the outward emblems of the Khalsa Sikh: *kes*, uncut
hair (with turban); *kanga*, comb; *kara*, steel wristband; *kirpan*,
sword; *kacch*, shorts) and in interfaith dialogues. They often are
called on to instruct young Sikhs in the principles of Sikh religion.
There are a number of other white (*gora*) converts, including spouses
of Punjabi Sikhs, but their impact on Sikh community life seems
to be minimal and not well documented.

Another category of Canadians who consider themselves Sikhs,
but for whom being Sikh does not constitute an ethnic marker,
consists of immigrants from India (and their offspring) for whom
being Sikh is an important part of their devotional or spiritual life,
but who in sociocultural aspects of life might consider themselves
Hindu. They do not identify with a Punjabi Sikh ethnic community
and its particular social, economic, and political interests. There is
at present little documentation on such "religious only" Sikhs in
Canada, and they have little or no overt organization or public
voice. But one continues to encounter such self-professed Sikhs
among students as well as among older persons. They may shade
off into the traditional category of Sahajdhari ("innate," i.e., not
marked by outward symbols) Sikhs—who also are little studied
and are marginalized in Canadian public discourse on who is a
Sikh. Their claim to being Sikh might well be challenged by the
more ethnically determined Sikhs and by those for whom the Khalsa
is the only valid mode of being Sikh. Yet both the immigrant "religious only" Sikhs and the Western Sikh converts test the claim
that Sikh religion is (potentially?) a universal, though comparatively young, "world religion."

Gurdwaras and Related Sikh Institutions: Their Rituals, Social Services, and Politics

By far the most vibrant institution among Canadian Sikhs is the
gurdwara ("door to the guru," that is, temple for the sacred book,
Sri Guru Granth Sahib), with attached community kitchen, *langar*,
and ancillary facilities. While a room in a private home may serve
as a small *gurdwara*, the standard pattern in Canada, begun in
Vancouver at the turn of the century, has been for a community
gurdwara to be established once there is even a modest number of
Sikhs residing in a locality. Functionally, the typical *gurdwara* in

Canada is more like the large urban *gurdwaras* in Indian cities where Sikhs are in the minority (like Delhi and Calcutta), than like village *gurdwaras* in rural Punjab. In the Punjabi village, the *gurdwara* is set within a traditional all-encompassing sociocultural milieu that is permeated with Punjabi-Sikh patterns of life. But in cities outside the Punjab, the *gurdwara* becomes not only the sacral focus of Sikh life, but the hub around which otherwise disconnected aspects of diaspora ("scattered") sociocultural life—even the basics of economic and political survival—of Sikhs may be reassembled and a coherent way of life reconfirmed. It serves thus to reinforce ethnicity while emphasizing a transcendent religious orientation.

As numbers grow, additional *gurdwaras* are built, sometimes reflecting differences of *zat* ("caste"), politics and/or factional rivalries, sometimes to allow for differing conceptions (e.g., Khalsa or Sahajdhari) of being Sikh, but often enough for sheer demographic pressure and geographic convenience. On weekends, and more so on Sikh festival days, such as *gurpurbs* (anniversaries of the birth or death of the historical gurus, especially Gurus Nanak and Gobind Singh) and the spring Baisakhi commemoration of the founding of the Khalsa, *gurdwaras* are abuzz with activity, centering on the *gurdwara* liturgical service with its popular *langar* (common meal). Hundreds (thousands in the larger *gurdwaras*) of Sikhs (and others—*gurdwaras* traditionally are open to all well-meaning persons) congregate to prostrate before the Guru Granth Sahib, listen to *kirtan* (sometimes sung by professional *ragis* from India, sometime by local Sikhs), hear sermons (usually in Punjabi) by local and visiting Sikh preachers, recite in unison the *ardas* prayer and share the sacramental *kara prasad* (a thickened sweet porridge) in the temple room proper and enjoy the traditional vegetarian meal, *langar*, in the adjacent refectory. Ancillary activities—clubs, classes, managing and planning sessions, and all sorts of personal conversations and scampering around by children—go on outside the temple hall proper. During the week, there may be special religious services (praying for the deceased, naming children, celebrating holy days) as well as numerous auxiliary functions. On the great spring festival of Baisakhi, there may well be large processions jointly organized by several *gurdwaras* and culminating (in Toronto or Vancouver) in massive outdoor assemblies addressed by Sikh spokesmen and public officials.

The traumatic events of the 1980s and 1990s in the Punjab and Delhi, however, have had a powerful impact on *gurdwaras* in Canada. Canadian Sikhs have felt motivated to identify themselves more strongly as Sikhs and to participate more intensely in Sikh affairs, with the *gurdwara* as the focal point for most such activity. The Sikh liturgy itself, which includes references to Sikh martyrs and allusions to Sikh victory (*raj karega khalsa*, "the Khalsa shall rule"), provides a sacral context for the political discussions and exhortations that may feature prominently within a *gurdwara* program (and for the songs and pictures of martyrs and banners advocating Khalistan that adorn some *gurdwaras*). For over a decade, major *gurdwaras* in Canada have enabled their congregations to identify themselves emotionally and practically with the struggles of Sikhs in India and thereby to internalize the sense that Sikhs are oppressed and in danger—primarily in India but overseas as well. With the decline of the Khalistani insurgency and the recent shift of Sikh politics in Punjab state toward Indian constitutional democracy, the crisis mentality and priorities within Canadian *gurdwaras* too may be expected to change, though not without resistance and confusion—as signaled by the violent resistance to a recent change of leadership and policy in a major *gurdwara* in Surrey, B.C., in January 1997 (*The Globe and Mail*, 25 January 1997, D 1–2).

Nevertheless, throughout the post-1984 years of Sikh history in Canada, *gurdwaras* have not failed to provide for immigrant Sikhs much of the same broad repertoire of sociocultural services they had been providing for as long as there have been Sikh immigrants in Canada. In a very basic sense, the *gurdwara* is a meeting place, a physical place with psychic space for greeting friends (an especially valuable function for recent immigrant women, who otherwise might have little scope for socializing beyond the home). It is a place for making useful business, social, and political contacts and for bringing together Sikh playmates for children and Sikh friends (and prospective spouses) for Sikh youth. The *gurdwara* is a place for sharing and assessing news of Sikhs elsewhere in Canada and abroad; and for informing and mobilizing the congregation to face problems and opportunities affecting the community at large.

One of the tasks of the *gurdwaras* is teaching the young, especially those born in Canada, the basics of the Sikh way of life—including respect for Sikh gurus, admiration for the heroes and highlights of Sikh history, and appreciation for Punjabi Sikh customs and values. Crucial to all of the above, in the judgment of many Sikhs, is enabling the young to use the Punjabi language, above all to read and understand the sacred language of the Granth. Most *gurdwaras* of any size will offer classes and programs intended to teach Punjabi language, Sikh religion and history, and other aspects of Punjabi Sikh sociocultural heritage. What is also apparent, however, from reports of concerned adults and, more tellingly, from remarks by young Sikhs, is widespread disappointment till now with much of these educational efforts. Classes are reported to be, with some bright exceptions, lacking in structure, attuned more to the Punjab/India milieu of the volunteer teachers than to the Canadian milieu of the children and youth, relatively few of whom attend regularly. There are libraries in *gurdwaras*, but generally they are poorly stocked. The problem is surely not lack of resources, but one of priorities. *Gurdwara* buildings typically are impressive: new, large, attractive, functionally well designed—thanks to generous donations from members. Nor is there a lack of capable teachers, social workers, and others, among professionally trained young adult Sikhs—who might be recruited and hired to lead such work, supplemented by part-time volunteers.

The dominant priorities of most *gurdwara* administrators—as measured by commitments of time, effort, and funds—seem not to be understanding and educating the young. Rather, the priorities are building, controlling, and managing the *gurdwaras* themselves, assisting immigrant members to settle, aiding yet others to immigrate, lobbying governments in the interest of Sikhs, and so forth. These, of course, are all justifiable concerns in themselves, but they reflect more the concerns of the immigrant adults than the needs of the Canada-born young. Since 1984, support for Khalistan and other aspects of the Sikh cause in India has, of course, absorbed a great deal of the attention and resources of Canadian *gurdwaras*.

Where there have been some concerted Sikh attempts to address Canada-focused educational and other sociocultural concerns—including religious education and language retention—and to provide a forum for serious intellectual exchange among Sikhs (and between Sikhs and non-Sikhs), these have generally occurred outside *gurdwaras*. Sikh societies, associations, or institutes (not infrequently with substantial ad hoc "multicultural" funding from governments) have held conferences, published informative reports, and set out possible courses of action.[2] As yet, these efforts have had relatively little impact. Some provincial, regional, and even national bodies have come up, to serve umbrella functions for Sikh societies within their respective zones. The Federation of Sikh Societies of Canada (proposed at Ottawa in 1980 and inaugurated at Calgary in 1981), in its heyday, lobbied successfully for such Khalsa Sikh concerns as wearing turban and carrying *kirpan*. It also organized (from 1983) the campaign for the Chair of Punjabi and Sikh Studies at the University of British Columbia and (from

1984) coordinated Canadian Sikh support for a Sikh homeland, Khalistan (N. Singh 1994).

It is the *gurdwaras*, however, that remain the only really influential and deeply rooted Sikh organizations in Canada. There have been some attempts to organize networks of *gurdwaras* and there have been calls for reform and restructuring of *gurdwara* management. But such proposals have been controversial and none has gained much ground. Nevertheless, basic questions face the currently vibrant *gurdwaras*. Will most second-generation Sikhs continue as adults to attend and support *gurdwaras*? Will they find satisfaction in Punjabi-language liturgy and sermons and with priorities that reflect the concerns of immigrant Sikhs? Will women insist on a share in *gurdwara* management? Should there be centralized control of Canadian *gurdwaras* on a national basis? or direction of Canadian *gurdwaras* by Sikh institutions in India, for example, the traditional, but relatively ineffectual, *takhts* (seats) or the modern, but intensely politicized, Shiromani Gurdwara Prabandhak Committee (S.G.P.C.)?

Unlike earlier generations of Canada-born Sikhs in B.C., who were few in number, minimally educated, only precariously established in Canada, and isolated from the old country, the rising generation of Canada-born Sikhs will be securely based—economically, educationally, legally, even politically—in Canada. (There are already two Sikhs in the federal Parliament, and, at the provincial level, Sikhs can be found in parliament, cabinet, and supreme court.) Canada-born Sikhs are now closely tied to the Punjab in ways undreamed of by the pioneer Sikhs in B.C.—by easy travel, instant communication, joint economic ventures, substantial continuing immigration, and so forth. So, while the pressures to conform and assimilate into secular Canadian life are pervasive and powerful, countervailing pressures and resources—from family, kin, and religio-ethnic community—are also pervasive and powerful. There is clearly much scope for tension, but also for mutual accommodation and compromise, in forging creative ways of being Canadian and Sikh.

Personal Piety

There is as yet little scholarly work treating the personal piety of Sikh individuals in Canada. One such study (Goa & Coward 1986) offers a phenomenological interpretation (supplemented by interviews in Calgary) of Sikh practices (e.g., *amrit* initiation and taking guidance [*gurdwaravak lao*] from the sacred word of Guru Granth) and notes modifications to these practices (due to pressure of time, innovative technology, critical mentality) in the contemporary Canadian context. There are available also some illuminating personal reminiscences (e.g., Bains & Johnston 1995) and essays or book(let)s of testimony to personal spirituality, the representative nature of which is difficult to determine. There are published speeches, essays, and books, including studies of *nam-simaran* meditation (e.g., Sethi 1972, 1988), by Canadian Sikhs on what Sikh piety and morality ought to be, but these do not necessarily reflect widespread actual practice. A handful of films (e.g., Hayter & Pettigrew 1992) on Sikh families in Canada offer glimpses of personal practices, beliefs, and values. Much of the considerable social science research on Canadian Sikhs, especially on Sikh women, alludes to religion while explicitly examining other issues, but shies away from directly addressing more intimate feelings and private devotional practices.

There are available to me, fortunately, two unpublished surveys of religious views and practices of small samples of respondents—Sikh families (Lamba 1990) and Sikh (mostly Jat Sikh) women (Baath 1995)—in the Toronto area. As both the researchers are women and as Baath's more elaborate study dealt exclusively with women, it is possible to speak with somewhat more precision and confidence about Sikh women's personal piety than about men's. Both studies report more extensive involvement in private religious practices by the grandparent generation than by the parent generation and least by the generation of children born in Canada. With the exception of some immigrant male grandparents, it is female Sikhs generally who pay more attention to private Sikh devotional practices than do males.

Very few male Sikhs of the "parent generation" indicate that they engage in lengthy prayers or extended periods of *nam-simaran* meditation, though some do. Many others, men as well as women, manage to keep in touch with Sikh spirituality and sentiments by such means as brief morning and/or evening prayers and listening to recorded *kirtan* or sermons while driving to work or managing the home. Khalsa Sikhs, men as well as women, typically observe at least the minimal morning and evening rites and prayers expected of Khalsa initiates. It seems likely that most Sikhs, male and female, if asked, would affirm their faith in the divine and their conviction that there are divinely established religious and moral norms. Many among the parent generation men might apologize that the busyness of modern life distracts them from doing more in devotional matters. Many among Sikh youth might also apologize that they do not yet understand the religion very well and that, though they affirm the basic tenets and try to maintain weekly or occasional *gurdwara* attendance, they find themselves doing very little in terms of daily prayer or meditation.

As for the Jat Sikh women studied by Baath and Lamba, it would seem that, despite their move to Canada (whether as young wives or as mothers of adult immigrants), most manage to maintain quite vibrant personal devotion in traditional Sikh ways. Both studies report that most adult Sikh women interviewed maintain a daily regimen of basic Sikh prayers, many listen to recorded *kirtan* and/or sing live *kirtan* during the week, and value the *gurdwara* experience on weekends and festivals. Quite a few keep some Sikh religious books on hand and read or recite passages from the Granth or other Sikh texts. Many tell of their sympathy for Sikhs martyrs (past and present) and display a strong sense of devotion to Guru Nanak and Guru Gobind Singh (especially feeling sympathy for the latter over the death of his four sons).

Younger Sikh women, especially those born in Canada, typically do not read the Granth in its original language (though some do). Some memorize passages and may sing *kirtan* and do some reading of Sikh prayers and traditions in English, but not necessarily on a daily basis. There is a widespread conviction that the divine is a real presence, not anthropomorphic but spiritual, the cause of the world, the lawgiver and guiding force behind human actions, as summarized by Baath:

> All of the others have more or less the same observation or feeling about God. They all believed in the presence of God. All of them believed that God is beyond one's description. He is present in his creation. All of these statements are in tune with Guru Nanak's philosophy of God. Sikhs do not tend to see God's explicit visibility but they do relate the existence of God to their day to day life. (Baath 1995, 13)

This basic sentiment, I suspect, would be echoed in comparable studies of male Sikh religious convictions, were these available.

Among the more engaging ways that some Sikhs try to involve their children in their own spiritual practices is arranging for *gurdwara* services to be performed in the home with older children and youth as officiants while the adults and small children form the congregation. There are also occasional visits to Canada by Sants, spiritual advisers having their own circles of followers for whom they prescribe certain devotional and/or meditational practices. The influence of these spiritual Sants appears to be marginal at present. Whether they are fading away or represent a type of religious ministry that may yet flourish among Sikhs in the Canadian diaspora is a subject worth looking into.[3]

Public Policy Issues Regarding Religious Education

Religion and the Public Schools

Nearly every school-age Sikh child in anglophone Canada attends public school. For most, this means no formal instruction in Punjabi language and culture nor in Sikh religion during school hours, though in localities with concentrated Sikh population there may be Heritage Language options. The Sikh child may be exposed to some version of Christian-Jewish religiomoral outlook shared by his or her teachers or, more likely, to a milieu wherein all religiocultural traditions are formally respected but marginalized from a "neutral" secular humanist perspective. Certain Catholic and Protestant schools, however, do receive government funding thanks to Canadian constitutional guarantees dating back to 1867. A recent suit by the Multi-Faith Coalition for Equity in Education in Ontario (in which there is Sikh participation) to require that government funding be extended to religious schools other than Catholic ones failed, but has been appealed (Sweet 1996). There is no legal bar to operating private schools on ethnic or religious grounds, provided the schools meet government guidelines (at least one Khalsa school operates in B.C.), but these are costly.

Sikh proponents of separate Sikh schools decry the unfairness of subsidizing only Catholic (or Protestant in Quebec) schools and appreciate the opportunity for fostering Punjabi language and Punjabi Sikh religiocultural values and behavior that Sikh schools would provide. Sikh opponents of separate Sikh schools, however, argue that separate Sikh schools would tend to create a ghetto mentality in Sikh children, making difficult their relating as adults to the rest of Canadian society. What may well eventuate are less drastic alternatives: optional, but substantial, components of Punjabi language and/or Sikh religiocultural education within the public school curriculum; more effective Sikh weekend schools, educational and resource centers and camps; better instruction within *gurdwaras* themselves. Edmonton, Alberta, interestingly, is experimenting with denominational and/or ethnic schools organized within the government-funded public school system itself. Canada, it may be noted, has never been bound by the rigid "separation of church and state" doctrine that developed in the United States.

French Language and Sikh Religious Education

Canada is unique among the three countries treated in this volume by being officially bilingual. In the province of Quebec, children of all immigrants are required to attend French-medium schools. It would, in any event, be advisable to become fluent in French, if one is to prosper as an adult in Quebec (whether Quebec remains within the Canadian federation or not). In many cases, however, this linguistic situation may impose considerable strain, as very few Sikhs in Canada can claim French as a mother tongue or have fluency in French before immigrating. Various solutions have been broached, but none as yet found satisfactory and feasible (M. Singh 1996, 37–43). For those Sikhs who do become fluent in French but not in English, learning more about Sikh matters can be frustrating, unless they know Punjabi well. There is very little good publishing on Sikh topics in French. The one striking exception, however, concerns the most important text of all, the Guru Granth Sahib. A French translation of the entire text, a labor of love by a Canadian immigrant Sikh, Dr. Jarnail Singh of Toronto, has just been published!

Postsecondary Sikh Education

In the mid-1980s, while the crisis of Sikhs in India was at its height, the government of Canada, to foster multiculturalism, was helping to establish chairs of ethnic studies in Canadian universities. In these circumstances, the Federation of Sikh Societies of Canada raised $350,000 from Sikh donors—to be matched by a government grant—for a Chair of Punjabi and Sikh Studies at the University of British Columbia. But, faced with escalating violence in India and Canada—and the terrible crash of the Air India plane in 1985—amid charges of Sikh terrorism and countercharges of Indian agents-provocateurs, the government of Canada withheld its share of the funds until 1987. The university then appointed a talented young social historian, Harjot Oberoi, an Indian Sikh trained in Australia. This selection disappointed some communally active Sikh leaders, who urged the university to remove him, which it refused to do. Once Oberoi's doctoral thesis was published—as a prize-winning book on the transformation of Sikh communal identity at the turn of this century—he became the object of unremitting criticism and reproach orchestrated by a network of Sikhs (ideologically guided from Chandigarh and financed from southern California) opposed to academic research on Sikh history and religion (Giani 1994; O'Connell 1996). In the summer of 1996, Oberoi resigned from the Sikh chair, though he continues to serve in the university's Department of History. The vacated chair will continue to function in a truncated fashion for the present, supporting language courses in the night school and perhaps a series of visiting professors or lecturers.

A similar scenario played itself out at the University of Toronto, where W. H. McLeod and J. S. Grewal, highly regarded scholars of Sikh religion and Punjab history, served as visiting professors from 1988 to 1993, thanks to donations by Sikhs and the university's own funds. The same network opposed to academic research on the Sikhs succeeded in dissuading Sikh donors from supporting the Toronto initiative only after getting Sikh authorities at Amritsar to declare the first recipient of a Toronto Ph.D. in Sikh religion, Pashaura Singh (a Canadian immigrant Sikh and former *granthi* at Calgary) to be a blasphemer—based on tendentious interpretations of his unpublished Ph.D. thesis. The ability of the University of Toronto to offer courses and support doctoral research on Sikh history and religion has been severely curtailed, though not eliminated.[4]

Potential Influences in Canadian Sikh Life: Grandparents and Canada-Born Sikh Women

Till now, elderly immigrant Sikhs (usually sponsored by adult children in Canada) have been disproportionately few and relatively marginal to the activities of Sikhs in Canada, with the exception of the small concentration of old Canadian Sikhs on the west coast. There is, however, considerable scope for the elderly to function as transmitters of the Indo-Punjabi-Sikh heritage—even to their own children, who may have left India as young adults and have been preoccupied ever since with establishing their families in the new country. But it is as grandparents living in their children's homes (the usual Sikh practice) that the senior generation may be most crucial as religiocultural transmitters, especially of spoken Punjabi language. Sikh children also may learn from their grandparents their prayers, legends of the past and customs of family, clan, and region, as well as fundamentals of Sikh religion.

The situation of senior citizens among old Canadian Sikhs in B.C. is rather the reverse of that of the recently immigrated elderly. They are, in cultural terms, among the least Punjabi and the most Canadian of Sikhs in Canada. They are not dependent on their children for sponsorship and support; indeed some are wealthy and prominent in public as well as domestic and community affairs. If the immigrant elderly are the authorities on Punjabi Sikh experience, the old Canadian Sikh seniors are the authorities on Canadian Sikh experience reaching back to the hard years of survival in the face of prewar racial discrimination.

On the other hand, in Canada at present, equal opportunity for women is at the forefront of public policy and individual aspiration. It is safe to say that in doctrinal and liturgical terms, and in the symbolic motifs of the Adi Granth, Sikh religion is relatively gender neutral (N.G.K. Singh 1993; Grewal 1993). Moreover, women are eligible for, and many undergo, Khalsa initiation; they are entitled to touch and read from the Granth and to conduct *gurdwara* services. On the other hand, all incumbents of traditional Sikh *takhts*, virtually all officers of the S.G.P.C., and nearly all officers of Sikh *gurdwaras* and Sikh associations in Canada (apart from exclusively women's groups) are males.

Canadian Sikh women, however, have been anything but alienated from Sikh community life. They share with men such tasks as singing *kirtan*, fanning the Granth, preparing *langar*, and teaching children and youth. Occasionally, they address the congregation at *gurdwara* services. For Sikh women who grew up in India, this distribution of functions may not be problematic. But will the male monopoly of organizational and symbolic leadership roles continue to be acceptable to younger Sikh women born and educated in Canada? If Sikh women come forward to share community leadership, will they be welcomed or resisted? If women do indeed emerge into leadership positions, will that mean significant change in ethos and policy of Sikh community life?

At present, a number of young Sikh women are active in voluntary women's causes quite independently of Sikh community activities. And a growing number are being trained in law, medicine, social service, teaching, and so on. These women will have an impact on the lives of other young Sikh women as much by their example as by the causes or policies they advocate. Such Sikh women with reformist energies generally are, no doubt, sympathetic to the concerns of Sikhs in India, and some in principle may support Khalistan. But the causes they find most tangible and compelling are those that affect them as women. Their fellow activists are women—usually including women of Indian background (not excluding Hindu women) along with other "women of color" and women of European background. Whereas the dynamics of the male Khalistani activist's commitment tend to narrow his purview (to exclusively Sikh solidarity and suspicion of Indians, Hindus, and "neutral" third parties), the dynamics of the Sikh woman activist's causes draw her outward—to solidarity with women of any ethnic or religiocommunal background. Indeed, she may find a special rapport with other women of Indian or Punjabi (including Hindu) background—who may have experienced firsthand and become disenchanted with comparable patriarchal (and religiously legitimated) sociocultural systems. If the emerging generation of Sikh women educated in Canada choose to direct their energies toward Sikh community affairs, and are not rebuffed and alienated in so doing, it could mean dramatic new developments in the Canadian Sikh religio-ethnic experience at the turn of the new millennium.

--------------------- NOTES ---------------------

1. There is concern among Sikhs in the Toronto area, though as yet virtually no public discussion of the matter, about several recent suicides by boys who had been under severe family pressure to maintain uncut hair and/or take Khalsa initiation against their will.

2. For two decades, the most productive sponsor of such conferences and publisher of proceedings has been the Sikh Social and Educational Society, 70 Cairnside Cres., Willowdale, Ontario M2J 3M8.

3. See Harold Coward's chapter in this volume for an analogous type of ministry currently popular among Hindus in Canada.

4. The university, from its own resources, offers a semester course on Sikh religion in alternate years and, thanks to Sikh donors, an alternating pair of two-semester courses on the language of the Granth. One Ph.D. student currently is preparing a thesis on a Sikh topic.

———————————— BIBLIOGRAPHY ————————————

Baath, J. (1995). "Sikh Women's Interpretation of Their Religious and Cultural Traditions: A Survey." Unpublished University of Toronto graduate paper, 74 pp.

Bains, T. S. and H. Johnston (1995). *Four Quarters of the Night: The Life-Journey of an Emigrant Sikh*. Montreal and Kingston: McGill-Queen's University Press.

Blaise, C. and B. Mukherjee (1987). *The Sorrow and the Terror: The Haunting Legacy of the Air India Disaster*. Markham, Ontario: Viking.

Buchignani, N. and D. Indra, with R. Srivastiva (1985). *Continuous Journey: A Social History of South Asians in Canada*. Toronto: McLelland and Stewart.

Dusenberry, V. (1988). "Punjabi Sikhs and Gora Sikhs: Conflicting Assertions of Sikh Identity in North America." In O'Connell et al. (eds.) (1998), 334–55.

Giani, B. S. (ed.) (1994). *Planned Attack on Aad Sri Guru Granth Sahib: Academics or Blasphemy*. Chandigarh: International Centre of Sikh Studies.

Goa, D. and H. Coward (1986). "Ritual, Word and Meaning in Sikh Religious Life." *Journal of Sikh Studies* Vol. XIII, no. II, 13–31.

Johnston, H. (1979). *The Voyage of the Komagata Maru: The Sikh Challenge to Canada's Colour Bar*. Delhi: Oxford University Press.

———. (1988). "Patterns of Sikh Migration to Canada." In O'Connell et al. (eds.), 296–313.

Kashmiri, Z. and B. McAndrew (1989). *Soft Target: How the Indian Intelligence Services Penetrated Canada*. Toronto: James Lorimer.

Lamba, S. (1990). "A Study of Nine Sikh Families and the Maintenance of Their Religious Heritage." Unpublished University of Toronto undergraduate paper, 37 pp.

Mulgrew, I. (1988). *Unholy Terror: The Sikhs and International Terrorism*. Toronto: Key Porter Books.

O'Connell, J. T., et al. (eds.) (1988). *Sikh History and Religion in the Twentieth Century*. Toronto: Centre for South Asian Studies, University of Toronto.

———. (1996). "Fate of Sikh Studies in North America." In P. Singh and N. G. Barrier (eds.), *The Transmission of Sikh Heritage in the Diaspora* (pp. 269–88). New Delhi: Manohar.

Pettigrew, D. (Producer) and R. Hayter (Director) (1992). "Gurdwara, House of the Guru" (documentary film). Vancouver, Temple Films Ltd.

Sethi, A. S. (1972). *Universal Sikhism*. New Delhi: Hemkunt.

Singh, M. (1996). "Religious Education in Canadian Schools: A Sikh Perspective." In J. Singh and H. Singh (eds.), *Proceedings of the Third Sikh Educational Conference 1995* (37–43). Willowdale, Ontario: Sikh Social and Educational Society.

Singh, N. (1994). *Canadian Sikhs: History, Religion, and Culture of Sikhs in North America*. Ottawa: Canadian Sikhs' Studies Institute.

Sri Gourou Granth Sahib (Traduction Française) (1996). Jarnail Singh. Providenciales, British West Indies: Intellectual Services International.

Statistics Canada (1993). *Religion in Canada*. Ottawa: Industry, Science and Technology Canada.

Sweet, Lois (1996). *The Fourth "R": Religion in Our Classrooms*. Toronto: Atkinson Charitable Foundation.

PART III

South Asians in the United States

Introduction

Raymond Brady Williams

The United States is a country of immigrants," is a constant refrain taken up by new arrivals because it affirms their rights and helps define their relations to new neighbors. The Statue of Liberty symbolizes an open door, but immigration has been neither constant nor uniform, suggesting, perhaps, a swinging door or one mostly ajar. Although the first immigrants from South Asia entered in 1820, it was not until the beginning of this century that more than 275 persons immigrated from South Asia in a single decade (INS 1982:2–1). The first major migration links the United States with Canada because Punjabi farmers moved from British Columbia into Washington, Oregon, and California to escape the aftermath of an anti-oriental riot in Vancouver on 7 September 1907, eventually establishing a thriving farming community in California. They were denied opportunity for citizenship in 1923 by a decision of the United States Supreme Court that South Asians, who had previously been treated as Caucasians, were not "free white persons" within the law. They were defined as Asian under immigration and naturalization procedures.

The door was closed to Asians by a series of laws culminating in the Immigration Act of 1924, which codified the "Asiatic Barred Zone," placed the first permanent limitation on immigration, and established the "national origins" quota system. In fact, the numbers of people immigrating from all countries dropped precipitously after 1924 and did not return to previous levels until 1989. A number of additional factors, including the Great Depression and the Second World War, restricted immigration, producing a 40-year lull in immigration. Indeed, in some years more people left the United States than arrived. The lull had profound effects on American society and religion. South Asians were not a major factor because from 1820 to 1960 a total of only 13,607 persons immigrated into the United States from South Asia, and an unrecorded number of these departed (INS 1982:2–4).

The Immigration and Nationality Act of 1965 changed all that dramatically by (1) abolishing the national origins quota system, eliminating national origin, race, or ancestry as a basis for immigration so that each country had the same quota and (2) establishing a detailed preference system based on professional or occupational skills needed in the United States and on family reunification. The seven categories of preference were: first, unmarried sons and daughters of U.S. citizens and their children; second, spouses and unmarried sons and daughters of permanent resident aliens; third, members of the professions of exceptional ability and their spouses and children; fourth, married sons and daughters of U.S. citizens, their spouses, and children; fifth, brothers and sisters of U.S. citizens (at least 21 years of age) and their spouses, and children; sixth, workers in skilled or unskilled occupations in which laborers were in short supply in the United States, their spouses, and children; and finally, nonpreference: other qualified applicants (INS 1991:17, Table A). Subsequent legislative and administrative measures revised the details of numbers and categories, but the two main characteristics of equal quotas and preference categories continue to define legal immigration to the United States. Until recently very few people from South Asia sought refugee status, and then only a small number from conflicts in the Punjab, Kashmir, and Pakistan.

The newly opened door had dramatic results few had anticipated. In 1991 some 1,827,167 persons were granted permanent resident status, the highest total ever recorded (INS 1991:12,18). Immigration shifted from Europe to Asia so that for the period of 1981–1990 nearly 50 percent of those naturalized as citizens were born in Asia. Those born in South Asia share in the growth of immigration, with 53,448 gaining admission in 1993 (India 44,121; Pakistan 8,927, Bangladesh 3,291, and Sri Lanka 1,109). Those arriving in the first decade were part of the brain drain, not "Your tired, your poor/Your huddled masses yearning to breathe free" that described earlier immigrants in words enshrined on the Statue of Liberty. Rather, they were the physicians, engineers, scientists, nurses, and computer specialists needed in the growing American economy. Of the 46,000 employed Indian immigrants in 1974, 16,000 were engineers, 4,000 were scientists, and 7,000 were physicians or surgeons; the next year 93 percent of the Indians admitted were classified as either "professional/technical workers" or their spouses and children (I. Singh 1979:41). Nine out of ten were high school graduates and two out of three were college graduates. South Asian immigrants in the 1970s were among the best educated, most professionally advanced, and successful of any immigrant group, and their income recorded in the 1980 census ranked second highest among ethnic groups in the country.

A major shift has taken place from the 1970s and early 1980s, when a majority of immigrants qualified by meeting professional and educational criteria, to the current situation when a large majority qualify on the basis of family reunification. Of the 44,121 persons of Indian origin admitted in 1991, over 35,000 were sponsored by members of their families already resident in or citizens of the United States (INS 1991:40–45, Tables 6–8). Most waited for several years between application and admission. Their experience of immigration is very different because they come to join families and networks already established. Fewer of those arriving in 1993 enter under professional and occupational categories—India 43 percent, Pakistan 28 percent, Bangladesh 30 percent, and Sri Lanka 65 percent (INS 1993:40, Table 6). The early immigrants were predominantly young professionals, many of whom are now bringing their parents to live in retirement.

The growth of the South Asian community in the United States has been dramatic, up from 371,630 persons recorded in the 1980 census to 919,626 in 1990 (those from India 815,447 up 125.6 percent in the decade, Pakistan 81,371 up 415.3 percent, Bangladesh 11,838 up 800.9 percent, and Sri Lanka 10,970 up 275.3 percent). These percentages reflect the fact that Pakistanis and Bangladeshis were relatively slower at moving through the open door in the 1970s but arrived in relatively greater numbers in the 1980s.

They constitute distinct configurations of South Asians not duplicated elsewhere because of the particular selection processes of the preference categories and the ad hoc networks set up by early immigrants. Hence, they are "Made in the USA" in ways that make them distinct from analogous groups in Canada, the United Kingdom, and even in the countries of South Asia. They create new social, professional, political, and religious organizations and institutions in their new places of residence, and they relate in different ways to their new neighbors. One cannot find in India, or perhaps elsewhere in the diaspora, social or religious groups identical to the South Asian groups in the United States.

South Asians moved rapidly throughout the country. Predictably, the areas with the largest concentrations are in the metropolitan areas of New York and New Jersey, Illinois, Texas, and California, but by 1980 only 3 of the 370 urbanized areas and only 20 of the 680 towns and cities in the United States census did not include some South Asians. Unfortunately, the census records do not contain clear data regarding the regional-linguistic diversity of South Asian immigrants, who certainly do not represent a uniform reflection of the geographical, ethnic, or religious distribution in South Asia. They have continued to be successful, as the 1990 census records: the mean family income for foreign-born Asian Indians was $65,381 compared to the mean family income for the total population of $43,803 (CP-3–5:141,153, Table 5). The best estimate is that 40 percent of Asian Indians are Gujarati and another 20 percent Punjabis. Since 1957, federal regulations prohibit the government from keeping records of religious affiliation of citizens. And it is not possible to determine how many South Asians have taken the opportunity provided by emigration to discard or change religious affiliation. Hence, data regarding religious affiliation are less precise than those available about South Asians in Britain or Canada.

Nevertheless, religious affiliation is an important, socially accepted marker in the United States, because members of each American immigrant group have had to re-create their personal and group identities in America. Religion has functioned for many as a transcendent basis for developing identity, especially for new immigrants because migration is enormously disruptive as plausibility structures for both personal identity and group cohesiveness are threatened. New immigrants are establishing a plethora of religious organization and institutions in the United States, some of which are the foci of the following chapters. They are creating new forms of transnational or world religions at the same time that they are changing the landscape of American religion. The most important fact about the new immigration is that it continues unabated. Even though the numbers of immigrants change year by year and new regulations revise the preference categories slightly, the door remains open, and new immigrants from South Asia arrive every year in large numbers both to join the established communities and religious groups and to transform them—and they will continue to do so for the foreseeable future. That is what continues to give the United States its special defining characteristics as a country of immigrants.

10

Negotiating Hindu
Identities in America

Diana L. Eck

New England's First Hindu Temple

I n May of 1990 in a suburb of Boston, not far from the starting
point of the Boston Marathon, New England's first traditional
Hindu temple was consecrated with the rites called *kumbhabhisheka* in which sanctified waters from hundreds of waterpots
(*kumbhas*) were showered (*abhisheka*) over the temple towers and
the divine images within. For nearly a week fires had been kindled
at several fire-altars in the ritual arena called the *yajnashala*—a
great yellow-and-white striped tent pitched next to the new temple.
Priests from India and a dozen American temples had invoked the
Divine at these fire altars, pouring offerings and chanting Vedic
hymns that have been preserved in memory for three thousand
years. After a week of rituals, New England Hindus carried the

water pots out of the tent-sanctuary and around the new temple. They bore the waters of India's Ganges River mingled with those of the Mississippi, the Missouri, the Colorado Rivers of America. Priests nobly bearing the heaviest pots on their heads rode a hydraulic hoist to the temple rooftop to sprinkle the consecrated waters over the elaborately carved towers. More than three thousand Boston area Hindus cheered, stretching their hands heavenward to catch the blessings of the water.

The newly installed images of the Gods were also blessed with a shower of water that day. In the central sanctuary of the temple sits the image of Lakshmi, the Goddess of wealth and good fortune. To the right is a shrine housing the image of Vishnu, the transcendent Lord and husband of Lakshmi, and to the left is a shrine housing the image of Ganesha, the auspicious elephant-headed remover of obstacles. These dark granite images had been made in India at the artist colonies at Mahabalipuram south of Madras and shipped to Boston. During this week of ceremonies, they were symbolically "bathed" in countless Sanskrit hymns, in tubs of flowers and grains, in milk, honey, and water. Their eyes were ritually opened, their breath ritually activated.

Installing deities in this way is no small commitment, for from this time on priests must be in attendance and worship must be offered, every day of the week whether anyone but the priest is present or not. On this Sunday morning in May of 1990, Lakshmi, Vishnu, and Ganesha became the permanent divine residents of Ashland in suburban Boston. After years of makeshift worship— renting halls, setting up tables as altars, invoking the temporary presence of the Divine in small images—the Hindu immigrant community of New England brought to America the most important immigrants of all: the divine embodiments of the Gods. Without visas, green cards, or citizenship papers, Lakshmi, Vishnu, and Ganesha have settled permanently in Massachusetts.

The story of the growth of the Sri Lakshmi Temple is typical of that of many American Hindu communities in the 30 years since the passage of the 1965 Immigration Act. In the 1970s, new Indian immigrants—mostly professionals who settled in the United States early in their careers—began to raise families and realized that their children would have no cultural or religious roots at all unless they began to plant the seeds. In this case, a group of Tamil families met occasionally in their homes for worship and special festivals. In 1978 they incorporated as the New England Hindu Temple Inc., with an eye toward building a temple. For a few years they worshiped in temporary rented halls—a Knights of Columbus

Hall in Melrose and the Village Club in Needham. Glossy colored prints and small metal images of the deities sufficed. By 1981, the group had collected $30,000 in donations, enough to buy a parcel of land set back from the road in suburban Ashland.

These Hindus were engineers and doctors, metallurgists and biochemists, not scholars of religion or temple builders. Few thought of themselves as actively religious and none would have been involved in building a temple back home in India. So to build a temple in Boston, their lives as Hindus took a new, intentional, and practical form. They brought a traditional temple architect from India to survey the site and to orient and design the temple—all according to the ritual canons of the *Shilpa Shastras*. Plans in hand, the community was faced with the challenge of explaining the proposed temple to the members of the municipal zoning board, most of whom had no idea what a Hindu temple would be like. Then the ritual design had to be translated into working drawings by a Wellesley engineering firm that excavated the foundation and constructed the huge temple shell of concrete block. Then came the Indian artisans called *shilpis* who lived in the temple for months and painstakingly cast and installed all the ritual ornamentation that covers the temple spires and the several sancta of the temple within.

The sequence of ritual events that accompanied the building of the Sri Lakshmi Temple has been repeated in dozens of American cities: from the ceremonial groundbreaking (*bhumi puja*) to the consecration of the temple (*kumbhabhisheka*) and the establishing of deities (*prana pratishtha*).[1] In many American communities, the critical *kumbhashisheka* rites are staged over the course of several days. Whether in Nashville or Atlanta, Chicago or Boston, the completion of a newly constructed Hindu temple in America draws Hindus from across the country. For the past two decades, these have become the pilgrimage events (*yatras*) and the religious fairs (*melas*) of America, with the sponsoring of waterpots for the consecration a form of temple fund-raising.

For Hindu immigrants to America, the process of building a temple is simultaneously the process of building a community. In New England, the consecration rites became the occasion for drawing hundreds of volunteers—men and women, children and elders—into creative participation in the life of the new temple. They applied themselves to tasks sublime and mundane: assisting the dozen priests with their ritual duties, chanting hymns and devotional songs, stringing lights, threading a multitude of flower garlands, cooking lemon rice for thousands of visitors, sweeping and cleaning at the end of each day, at the outset of each phase of the ritual. Specific roles fell to lucky ones. A group of little girls were chosen to be the first to see the deities when their eyes were ritually opened. A contingent of elderly ladies—mothers of children and wives of living husbands—were consecrated and worshiped as living embodiments of Lakshmi. During the climactic weekend of the consecration rites, North Indians celebrated with devotional *bhajan* singing, while those from the South sang the songs of the Tamil poet Tyagaraja. By the time the sacred waters were sprinkled at the end of the week of ritual, a richly variegated Hindu community had come together at New England's first temple. In a real sense, building a temple had begun to build a new Hindu community.

Negotiating Hindu Identities

The Sri Lakshmi Temple in Massachusetts is but one of more than 400 Hindu temples in the United States. Most are located in quarters transformed from other uses and would be quite invisible to the passing eye: a huge warehouse in Edison, New Jersey, that has become a Swaminarayan Hindu Temple, a suburban home in Maryland that is a Chinmaya Mission center, a former church in Minneapolis that serves the Hindu community of the Twin Cities. In the past two decades, however, more than 30 new temples have been built from the ground up and many more are underway. The first temples to be built as such were the Sri Venkateswara Temple in Pittsburgh, dedicated in June of 1977, and the Ganesha Temple in Flushing, Queens, dedicated on 4 July 1977. Within a few years Hindu "temple societies" like the one organized in New England were forming in a dozen American cities. In Pearland, south of Houston, Hindus built an enormous temple to the goddess Meenakshi. In Chicago's western suburbs, they dedicated a temple to Lord Rama high on a hill in Lemont and to Sri Venkateswara in a sprawling residential neighborhood in Aurora. In the 1970s, Hindu temple societies were formed and began working toward the building of temples in such places as Albany (Hindu Temple of the Capital District), Detroit (Bharatiya Temple in Troy), Los Angeles (Sri Venkateswara Temple in Calabasas), Livermore, California (Shiva-Vishnu Temple), Lanham, Maryland (Shiva-Vishnu Temple), Liberty, Ohio (Sri Lakshmi Narayan Temple), Nashville, Tennessee (Sri Ganesha Temple), and Flint, Michigan (Paschimakasi Sri Viswanatha Temple).

Hindu temple life is but part of the diverse and textured life of the Hindu tradition. In the United States, as in India, the topography of Hinduism is highly nuanced. Most important and most invisible to the observing eye are the multitude of home altars—in a kitchen cupboard, a coat-closet, a corner of the living room sanctified for domestic worship. Hindu homes are also the site of Gita study groups, ritual observances such as a Satyanarayan Puja, and devotional bhajan singing. Equally important is the fluid life of small communities, like the families that formed the core of the Sri Lakshmi Temple: they coalesce for a Sunday afternoon in the Knights of Columbus Hall and disperse after the puja and the potluck dinner. The regionally based cultural organizations such as the Marathi Mandal, Telugu Association, Bengali Association, or the Tamil Sangam are also part of the rhythm of American Hindu life, gathering in rented halls, then dispersing once again. Although these groups define themselves in secular terms, they often time their local or regional gatherings to coincide with the observance of regional Hindu festivals. The Telugu Association of the Boston area, for example, meets thrice yearly: for Ugade, the Telugu New Year, for a park picnic during the summer, and for Divali in the fall. All this is part of the Hindu religious life of the United States—variegated, dynamic, with the many distinctive rhythms of India's regional cultures.

However, the most visible markers of a new Hindu presence are the newly built Hindu temples. To move beyond makeshift weekend quarters to permanent temples has required a much more intentional and complex level of negotiation—both within the immigrant community and with the structures of American public life that govern religious institutions. The building of temples is but one measure of the life of immigrant Hindu communities, but it is a significant measure. Despite America's vaunted individualism, religious institution-building is also an important marker of the public presence of an American religious community. German Jews, Swedish Lutherans, and Italian Catholics have all signaled their arrival with visible institutions that both nurture the community and place it visibly on the map. Unlike early Swedish Lutheran immigrants, however, Hindu immigrants from India are not an homogeneous group, but bring many different regional and sectarian traditions with them. As Raymond Williams has pointed out, their patterns of negotiating a common identity are more likely to resemble those of various European Catholic groups in the formation of the American Catholic Church (Williams 1988, p. 41). The astonishing proliferation and multiplicity of new Hindu temples on the U.S. landscape provides an important set of data through which to view the ongoing negotiation of Hindu American identity.

In the United States, first-generation Hindu immigrants have met in a context that is the home-terrain of no one group. The term "diaspora" is often used loosely to describe the dispersal of a religious or ethnic community from its homeland to other parts of the world, taking its meaning from the Jewish diaspora. The very notion of a diaspora requires a strong locative sense of a homeland, and most Hindus from India have that sense, not only culturally as Indians, but religiously as Hindus.[2] But the dispersal of Hindu communities outside India is considerably more complex than the term diaspora might convey, for these communities were already "dispersed" in the varieties of regional and sectarian traditions that compose Hindu religious life in India. One might even argue that Tamils, Bengalis, and Gujaratis have become more proximate than scattered in this "diaspora." In American cities and towns the diaspora often brings people together who may never have had to cooperate in a project like temple building in the scattered communities of the homeland.

Of course in some areas there are sufficient numbers of immigrants or a sufficiently strong sectarian identity to enable a regional or sectarian group to form a temple that virtually replicates what they have known back home. Among the Gujaratis, the Swaminarayan sect, extensively studied by Raymond Williams, has developed a network of over 30 centers and 10 major temples. So homogeneous is the community that the large new temple in Edison, New Jersey, posts its announcements and publishes its brochures in Gujarati. The Pushtimarga sect devoted to Lord Krishna is also largely Gujarati and maintains a strong sense of regional and sectarian identity at its center in Vraj, Pennsylvania, or at its new temple in Sayreville, New Jersey. There are also temples—such as the Sri Venkateswara Temple in Pittsburgh or the Balaji Temple in Chicago—where the dominant languages are Tamil and Telugu and the ritual idiom that of South Indian brahmins. In other temples, such as the Sri Hanuman Mandir in Hempstead, Long Island, the lingua franca is Hindi and the ritual idiom that of North Indian *bhakti*.

In many American cities, however, Hindu immigrants from all parts of India have had to negotiate a wider sense of "we" in the creation of temples. Among the first questions the temple committee must ask is which of the Hindu deities will occupy the central shrine, or should there even be a central shrine? Most temples whether in India or the U.S. have multiple shrines and deities, but ordinarily there is a central shrine for a particular deity, for whom the temple is named and consecrated, the others occupying subsidiary shrines. American Hindu temple societies have negotiated several responses to this question. Some have managed to agree on a central deity. In Nashville, the founding committee sent a ballot to area Hindus, easily achieving consensus around the popular Ganesh, who occupies the central sanctum, with Shiva and a series of Shaiva shrines to one side and Vishnu and a series of Vaishnava shrines on the other. In Boston, the largely Tamil founding community proposed a temple to Sri Lakshmi, the auspicious goddess of fortune and wealth, rightly suspecting that the choice would elicit little opposition. She too is flanked by Ganesh of the Shaiva family on one side, and Vishnu as Sri Venkateswara on the other. Other temple societies have negotiated a different and more unusual solution and consecrated two primary deities: Shiva and Vishnu. Such is the case, for example, at the Shiva-Vishnu Temples in Lanham, Maryland, and Livermore, California. A third approach has been to give the temple a more inclusive and generic name—the Bharatiya Temple (Detroit), the Hindu Worship Society (Houston), or the Hindu Temple and Cultural Center of South Carolina (Columbia)—and include a number of shrines within.

In both Pittsburgh and Chicago, negotiation over the name and inclusivity of the temple has resulted in the building of two separate temples. In Pittsburgh, some South Indian leaders were committed to Sri Venkateswara as the central image, an interest that was also supported by the Tirupati Tirumalai Devasthanams in India that provided an initial loan for the temple.[3] Other Indian immigrants, however, envisioned a temple with many different deities. The site for the temple had already been purchased: a hill in suburban Monroeville. As the two differing visions became clear, the South Indian contingent bought another parcel of land: the Penn Hills tract where the Sri Venkateswara Temple is located today. Another group built the Hindu-Jain Temple in Monroeville, a more ecumenical temple that includes altars dedicated to the Jain *tirthankaras* as well as to various Hindu deities. In the Chicago area, the Balaji Temple in Aurora is dedicated to Vishnu as Balaji, an affectionate name for Sri Venkateswara, while the Hindu Temple Society of Greater Chicago in Lemont has both a Ram Temple built in South Indian style, with subsidiary shrines within the temple for many deities, and a Siva-Durga-Ganesha built in the style of the Bhubhaneshvara temples of Orissa.

Negotiating an American Identity

In the process of temple building, Hindus have to negotiate not only Hindu identities, but also an American identity as they encounter a set of distinctively American expectations. The twin principles of the "nonestablishment" of religion and the "free exercise" of religion enshrined in the First Amendment to the American Constitution have created an operative framework for American religious institutions.[4] Alexis de Toqueville observed in the early nineteenth century that in America the "spirit of religion" and the "spirit of freedom" do not march in opposite directions, as in France, but in the same direction (Toqueville 1835, 1990, p. 308). He noted to his astonishment that the lack of state support for religion, far from diminishing its vibrancy, seemed to make religious communities more energetic, even in the public sphere. Toqueville pointed to what American religious historians have called the spirit of "voluntarism" distinctive of American religious life. With no government support and the freedom to flourish, religious communities have had to compete for and gather adherents, building religious institutions by the voluntary contributions and energies of their constituents. This has leant a distinctive shape to religious life in the United States, with religious communities organized for fundraising purposes as nonprofit corporations, with the requisite boards of directors and membership lists required by the U.S. Internal Revenue Service for tax-free contributions.

Thus as Hindu communities constitute themselves for the purpose of building temples, they too develop a pattern of participation that few are likely to have encountered in India. They must incorporate, elect officers, solicit members, keep records, and garner volunteers for temple activities. All this falls to the largely lay leadership of temple communities. As they approach the task of finding or building a temple home, these new temple societies must undertake pledge campaigns, sponsor fund-raising events, develop temple publicity, and produce community newsletters. The first fruits of this American religious identity are not only the temples themselves, but the documentary record of newsletters and commemorative publications that provide the primary-source material of a new era of Hindu history.[5] The visitors' guide published by the Sri Venkateswara Temple in Pittsburgh provides a temple history and a brief explanation of Hinduism and its gods. "The temple is more than a religious institution," the brochure begins, "It is a cultural center, a place for dialogue, a place for Indian adults to reaffirm their heritage, for their children to discover who they are. For all

Americans, it is a reminder of
country."

Varieties of American Hinɑ.

It is important to recall that the Hindu immig.
the United States in the 1960s and 1970s came
already had a number of Hindu institutions and a c.
sure to Hindu ideas and spiritual disciplines. For new
affirming a Hindu identity in the United States has a.
encountering the Vedanta societies, the yoga movemen.
ashrams and gurus that have attracted many Euro-Americans
the years, shaping a particular and in some ways peculiar imaɓ
of Hinduism in the minds of many Americans.

By the mid-nineteenth century, the wisdom traditions of India's
Upanishads and Vedanta philosophy had attracted the American
writers and intellectuals such as Ralph Waldo Emerson, Henry
David Thoreau, and other Transcendentalists. In the 1890s, Americans who had encountered Hindu religious ideas only through the
writings of the Transcendentalists had the opportunity to hear their
first Hindu: Swami Vivekananda. One of the most eloquent Hindu
spokesmen of the day, Vivekananda came to the United States in
1893 for the World's Parliament of Religions and stayed on to travel
and lecture, eventually leaving to America its first Hindu institutions: the Vedanta Societies in both New York and San Francisco.
In the subsequent decades, the number of Vedanta Societies gradually grew, each center led by a monk of the Ramakrishna Order
sent from the Belur Math in Calcutta. With the new post-1965
immigration, these Vedanta Societies—for decades the outpost of
Euro-American stalwarts—began to attract Indian-born immigrants
who found there a congenial home for their Hindu faith. Today the
Vedanta Societies are in the midst of negotiating a new identity
with mixed Euro-American and Indian-American congregations.
Their retreat centers in Ganges, Michigan, or Olema, California,
now have a wider spiritual clientele, including many immigrant
families. There is also a new set of Vedanta institutions such as the
wide network of Chinmaya Mission centers, with their many summer camps, and the Arsha Vidya Gurukula in Pennsylvania, which
provides a year-long series of weekend and week-long family camps
for the study of Vedanta.

The practice of yoga had also become part of the religious fabric
of America long before the current generations of Indian immigrants

nsing that America's hunger for spiritual vision was
ith a spirit of practicality, Vivekananda focused much of
ing on yoga, especially what he called *raja yoga*, the "royal
vhich he described as both "mystical" and "psychological."
iblication of *Raja Yoga* in 1900 provided, in summary form,
ction in the postures of the body (*asanas*), the control of the
th (*pranayama*) and the stages along the path of realization.
Vivekananda did not live long enough to tend the path of yoga
the United States. That task fell to another teacher, Paramahansa
ogananda, who came from Bengal to a meeting of the International Congress of Religious Liberals held in Boston in 1920 where
he spoke on "The Science of Religion." He insisted that religious
life, like science, must be confirmed in experience. Yogananda explained the practical appeal of yoga in the language of experiment
and experience, attracting those who were interested in science
and healing as well as in spirituality. By 1925, Yogananda had
established the Self-Realization Fellowship, which became the most
widespread Hindu movement in the United States before the 1960s.
In following decades, the "mind-body" connection he had espoused
began to fertilize the soil of a multitude of "New Age" movements.

One of the most enduring of the many gurus who came to the
U.S. in the 1960s was the Maharishi Mahesh Yogi, in some senses
the heir of Yogananda in his ability to "market" a form of meditation that was distinctively appealing to Americans: Transcendental
Meditation or TM. Its practical appeal stands in the tradition of
yoga that had been cultivated in the United States by both
Vivekananda and Yogananda. Indeed, the Maharishi emphasized
so heavily the practical aspect of meditation that he ceased to use
the term "Hindu" at all, employing instead the language of science
to present TM in the American context. With TM and the research
of Dr. Herbert Benson of the Harvard Medical School and, later, Dr.
Deepak Chopra, the term "meditation" made its way into the world
of medicine. By the 1990s practices that had been previously pro-
pounded only by gurus in orange robes were being taught by doctors in white coats, as American hospitals began to include
mind-body clinics and meditation classes in their repertoire of
options for patients.

Among the Hindu teachers who first benefited from the new
U.S. immigration laws was an elderly Bengali, Swami A. C.
Bhaktivedanta, who launched what was, in many ways, the most
notable Hindu movement that took root in the United States in the
late 1960s: the International Society for Krishna Consciousness
(ISKCON). His story is, in one sense, a great "American" story—

arriving nearly penniless in New York in 1965, chanting "Hare Krishna, Hare Rama" in Tompkins Square Park, and opening America's first Krishna temple in a storefront on Second Avenue. Within five years, there were "Hare Krishna" temples in 30 cities in the United States. The complex history of ISKCON is a separate story, but in one essential respect that story is also important to the story of South Asian Hindu immigration: when the new immigrants arrived, these Krishna temples were almost the only temples in America, and they soon became the first temple-homes of many new Hindu settlers. In some cities—Chicago, Dallas, Denver, and Philadelphia, for instance—Hindu immigrants have continued to participate in the life of the ISKCON temples, transforming these temples into multi-ethnic Hindu communities.

Temple-centered devotional Hinduism was really introduced into the United States by the Krishna Consciousness movement. While a century ago the seeds of Vedanta and yoga were transplanted in the United States, ISKCON began the process of transplanting a more specific idiom of Hindu worship, liturgy, art, and symbol, hitherto rooted primarily in the cultural soil of India. New immigrants have continued this process on a much larger and more complex scale, bringing temple Hinduism to America.

Hindu Sacred Geography in America

In naming their temples and establishing the deities within, Hindu immigrants have replicated the sacred geography of India in the American landscape. Perhaps nowhere on earth have myths been so extensively inscribed in the landscape and the land so profusely storied as in India, where pilgrimage to sacred shrines, called *tirthas* or "crossings," is still one of the most common forms of travel. Of course, European immigrants had also brought the place-names and associations of their homelands in Europe to America. Hindu immigrant communities have continued this pattern, linking their temples to the associative power of the *tirtha*s of India. The Pushtimargi tradition, emphasizing Krishna's "path of grace," has established its new home near Schuylkill Haven, Pennsylvania, an area which it calls Vraj, the name of Krishna's homeland in central North India. The stream that runs through the temple property has been named Yamuna, after the holy river that runs through the land of Vraj in India. In Austin, Texas, the International Society for Divine Love has established Barsana Dham, named for Barsana, the hometown of Radha, Krishna's beloved. In Austin both Euro-Americans and new Hindu immigrants participated in the gala consecration of the "Queen Radha Temple" in 1995. Sushree Meera Devi, a western devotee, wrote of the meaning of duplicating the land of Krishna in Texas: "It is not possible for everyone to visit Vraj in India. For many people family and business commitments or economic considerations make travel to India difficult. With the Grace of Shree Swamiji, Barsana Dham has been established in Texas, U.S.A., where the same Divine-love vibrations of Vraj may be experienced by the devotees" (Meera Devi 1994).

As we have seen, several of the new, large South Indian style temples are named for Sri Venkateswara, also called Balaji, who is Lord of the hilltop shrine called Tirupati in Andhra Pradesh. The immense popularity of Tirupati in India today resonates in the many representations of this deity in the United States, such as the Sri Venkateswara Temple in Pittsburgh, the Balaji Temple in Chicago, and the Sri Venkateswara Temple north of Los Angeles. The Pittsburgh temple in particular—because of its age, its magnificence, and its hilltop location—has attracted Hindu pilgrims from throughout the United States at the rate of more than 20,000 a year.

Other famous temples and *tirthas* of India area also replicated in the United States. In Houston, the temple of Sri Meenakshi specifically recalls the goddess of the holy city of Madurai in Tamilnadu. In Flint, Michigan, the Paschimakasi Sri Viswanatha temple, the "Kashi of the West," is named for the city of Kashi or Banaras in India and houses the particular form of Shiva known as in Kashi Vishwanatha, "Lord of the Universe." The newly opened Divya Dham Temple in Queens, New York, also includes a *linga* of Kashi Vishwanatha, along with an entire set of the twelve *jyotirlingas* that signify the self-manifest presence of Lord Shiva in the sacred geography of India. The Divya Dham has also replicated a powerful goddess shrine of northwest India: Vaishno Devi, located in a cave on a hilltop near Jammu and attracting hundreds of thousands of pilgrims yearly from across North India. In one corner of the Divya Dham, a hilltop has been created and worshipers are invited to climb a set of stairs to enter into a cave-chamber for the darshan of Vaishno Devi.

Perhaps the most eclectic pilgrimage-temple in the United States is the Shiva-Vishnu temple, in the suburbs of Washington D.C. in Lanham, Maryland, which duplicates virtually the entire sacred geography of South India: Sri Venkateswara Balaji from the hilltop shrine of Tirupati in Andhra Pradesh; the reclining image of Vishnu called Anantapadmanabha from Trivandrum in Kerala; Ranganathaswami Vishnu from the Srirangam Temple at Tiruchirapallai; Shiva as he appears at Rameshvaram where the coastline stretches out toward Sri Lanka; Lord Rama from the pilgrimage temple at Badhrachalam in Andhra; Krishna as he is known in Udipi in the coastal region of Karnataka; and the six forms of Murugan as they are found in the popular cycle of six temples. Most recently, the temple dedicated an image of Ayyappa who resides on a remote hilltop in Kerala, one of the most sought after pilgrimage destinations in India. The pilgrimage to the hilltop of Ayyappa, called Shabarimalai, requires the ascetic discipline of a long journey through the forest and up the hill on foot before climbing the final eighteen sacred steps to the temple. In Maryland, the eighteen steps are replicated, bringing pilgrims to the shrine of America's Ayyappa, chanting "Swamiye Ayyappa!"

Sacred rivers also have symbolic importance and water of the Ganges is brought to America for ritual use. Drops of the Ganges water are used to sanctify the waters used in domestic and temple rituals. For large consecration rites, the waters of the Ganges are mingled with the waters of America's own rivers. Pittsburgh is not only the home of two major Hindu temples, but also the auspicious confluence or sangam of three rivers: the Allegheny, Ohio, and Monongahela. One Indian American who has lived in Pittsburgh for over twenty years, noted in a 1993 interview, "We have come to love Pittsburgh because of these rivers. In India all of our holy places were built on the banks of rivers or at the place where rivers join. We think of these as holy places, spiritual crossings." He added with a bit of humor, "Of course we don't bathe here in Pittsburgh, but the meeting rivers are still a reminder that this is an auspicious place."

Losing the Lunar Perspective:
The Festivals of Hindu America

American Hindus have also brought a kaleidoscope of festival celebrations with them from India. Most are based on the Hindu lunar calendar, with an extra month added every few years to keep the months and their festivals in roughly the same seasonal location. Most American Hindu temples publish newsletters announcing their regular weekly *pujas* and the upcoming festival celebrations. Some temples convey their calendars in wholly traditional terms, marking the *amavasyas* (new moon days), *ekadashis* (elevenths in the fortnight), and *purnimas* (full moon days). Others have omitted all reference to the precise lunar location of a festival, listing only the date, often a weekend, on which it will be observed at the temple. The tension between a lunar calendar and an American workweek with its weekends is evident in variety of American Hindu festival calendars. The Ganesha Temple in New York is explicitly committed to observing holy days and festivals on the precise lunar date on which they fall, but it also holds more family-oriented observances on the nearest weekend. If Mahashivaratri falls on a Wednesday, the temple will have its all night observances midweek, but is also likely to have a Mahashivaratri program on the weekend. Many temples cannot do both and the community has to chose between the auspicious dates of the lunar calendar and the convenience of the weekend.

Festivals are important magnets for gathering the dispersed community. Even observances that would be primarily domestic in India, such as the Divali festival, will include a major temple-based component in the United States, offering the community an opportunity to celebrate together. In many temples the celebration of a festival is combined with an educational program about the importance of the festival for the benefit of the younger generation.

New kinds of festival observances have also emerged. Among them is what I would call the "gala festival," such as the observance of Holi at the Trump Palace Hotel in Atlantic City—a cultural and social event with its analogues in new forms of festival observance in India. The most popular of the gala festivals is the New Jersey Navaratri, celebrating the "Nine Nights" of the Goddess. Launched in 1990 by a group of New Jersey Gujaratis, the Navaratri has now become one of the largest festival events of any religious tradition in America, attracting more than 10,000 people every weekend night for four or five weeks. The event takes place at the Raritan convention center in Edison, New Jersey, where a huge tent is erected, with some 80 tractor-loads of beams and plywood for the dance floor. The main attraction is the *garbha*, the quick-moving dance with hand-held wooden sticks that has become the staple of the Indian American community, especially the younger generation. In 1993, the event combined high-energy social life of the *garbha*, with the worship of Amba Mata, and fund-raising for victims of India's recent earthquake. It has drawn Indian immigrants from all parts of the subcontinent—including Muslims, Sikhs, and Christians. What is noteworthy in the New Jersey Navaratri is not only its size, energy, cost, and multicultural patronage, but its wholesale transformation of a nine-day festival into a month-long festival of nine weekend-days.

While we cannot survey the rich range of festivals in such brief compass, the observances of Navaratri alone provide a window into their variety. Other Hindu communities have adapted the "Nine Nights" of the goddess in quite different ways. The Hindu Temple of Metropolitan Washington has two "All-Night Mata's Jagrans," from 8:00 P.M. until dawn on two consecutive Saturday nights. The Sri Ganesha Temple in Nashville simplified the entire nine-day festival holding its Navaratri or "Durga Puja" program on a single Saturday, beginning with a 9:00 A.M. program in the auditorium and proceeding through a breathtaking array of *pujas, abhishekas,* and *aratis,* lunch, a cultural program, and ending finally with an 8:30 P.M. dinner. Yet all these very different public observances of Navaratri do not necessarily displace home observances. Indeed many South Indians observe the festival by visiting one another's homes to see the elaborate home altars that are decorated in this season.

The Americanization of the Hindu festival calendar has taken another form as well: the addition of American holidays. One temple calendar lists its fall holy days, moving seamlessly from Pitri Paksha Tarpan, to Ashtami Sraddha, to Columbus Day; from Kartik Purnima, to Guru Nanak's Birthday, and the First Sunday in Advent. In Bridgewater, New Jersey, New Year's Day on 1 January is observed with a special *arati.* During May, children gather at the temple in Bridgewater for a Mother's Day Puja. Finally, many ritual and fund-raising events of the Hindu immigrant community are organized around America's special long-weekends—Presidents Day, Memorial Day, Fourth of July, Labor Day, Columbus Day, and Thanksgiving.

Hindu Identity: Defining Hinduism

What does it mean to be a Hindu? Does Hinduism define a cultural identity? an ethos or worldview? a set of beliefs? a range of practices? Both adherents and scholars who speak of Hinduism emphasize its multiple forms and textures, so various as to undermine any very substantive referent for the term at all. At the same time, the pressing questions of Hindu identity in the United States have begun to lend a more substantive definition to the term "Hinduism." Hindus in America are asked in countless casual encounters what it is that Hindus "believe." Even Hindus who have a deep sense of the complexity and multivocality of the Hindu tradition are forced to abbreviate and simplify, to distill from centuries of textured human experience a few principles that can be readily apprehended. A Harvard College researcher, Badsah Mukhopad-hyaya, doing research in the Bay area where he grew up, wrote, "Most immigrant Hindus living in the Bay Area are constantly forced to explain their religion to people totally unfamiliar with the subject. In doing so, they consciously or subconsciously rework definitions to make them both comprehensible to the Western mind and as inclusive as possible of various kinds of Hindu beliefs and practices" (Mukhopadhyaya 1993).

In the United States one can begin to see the emergence of a simplified articulation of Hinduism by Hindus of the diaspora. The Northern California Hindu Businessman's Association has published the "Nine Beliefs of Hinduism," a statement of Hindu belief first created by the Himalayan Academy in San Francisco. It includes belief in an all-pervasive Supreme Being, the soul evolving toward union with that One, karma and reincarnation, personal commun-ion with the gods, the guiding importance of the gurus, and finally ahimsa and religious tolerance. Temple newsletters often include one-page essays on the Sanatana Dharma, the "eternal principles" of the tradition. The book, *Am I a Hindu?* has been published by a leader in the New Orleans Hindu community, writing as an immigrant father in response to a set of questions posed by an American-born child. Scholars and Hindus alike will insist that Hinduism has never been a "creed," but a culture and a way of life. Yet in the United States, Hindus are articulating their "belief" in such principles as pluralism, tolerance, and nonviolence.

The Vishva Hindu Parishad of America and its loose affiliate the Hindu Students Council are well aware that the issues of "Hindu identity" that have perplexed the soul of India and generated the Hindu nationalism of the 1980s are, in a very different context, the issues with which Hindus wrestle in the United States.[6] The Hindu Students Council has developed what is unquestionably the widest network of Hindu college students in the United States, with cam-pus and regional conferences, summer camps, and work projects— all emphasizing the formation of a strong sense of Hindu identity. While many American Hindus would explicitly reject the religious nationalism of the VHP in India, they have developed no alterna-tive organizations to address the issues of Hindu identity in the United States.

Individual temples, however, are beginning to develop the kind of temple life that will enable young people to "grow up in a temple" through education programs and rites of passage. At the Hindu Temple Society of Greater Chicago in Lemont, Illinois, the youth program called "In the Wings" brings young people together for weekend classes and summer camps to enjoy the company of one another and learn about their tradition. Hindu Heritage classes abound in temples all over the country, some with makeshift curricula and others making use of materials that are being explicitly produced to teach Hinduism in the west.[7] In addition to traditional ritual enactments like the *upanayana*, Hindu temples are evolving new ritual forms such as the "Graduation Puja," a special *puja* held for high school seniors.

On the rural road that winds through the hills into Saylorsburg, Pennsylvania, is a Hindu camp called Arsha Vidya Gurukulam, set in a grove of tall pines. Here weekend and week-long Hindu family camps provide educational programs for Hindus of all ages. One might find the adults sitting in the carpeted temple room where Swami Viditatmananda is teaching a short philosophical treatise called the *Tattva Viveka*. In the temple basement, children might be learning about the parts of the *puja*. Outside, teenagers, fresh from a discussion group, might be practicing football passes in a grassy meadow. Arsha Vidya Gurukulam hosts family camps not only in the summer, but at Thanksgiving, Christmas, and over the Fourth of July weekend. And there are youth camps for high school and college students, Vedanta camps for adults, and stress-management camps for busy professionals.

One hundred years after Swami Vivekananda came to the United States and began planting the seeds of Vedanta in American cities, the Hindu tradition has truly taken root in America—and in ways Vivekananda would not have imagined. Were he to return to tour the United States in the late 1990s, Vivekananda would perhaps not be surprised to find these Indian professionals seriously studying Vedanta under the pines in Pennsylvania. But he would be quite surprised to find Bengali summer picnics in Boston, practitioners of Ayurvedic medicine in Seattle, a temple youth choir learning Hindi devotional songs in suburban Maryland, a group gathering to sing the Hindi Ramayana straight through in Chicago, and the procession of Lord Ganesh through the streets of San Francisco. Had he returned to Harvard during commencement week in 1993, he would have been surprised to hear the first marshals of the Harvard and Radcliffe graduating classes, both American-born Hindus, the children of first-generation immigrants, chanting from the Vedas at Harvard's baccalaureate service. In the late twentieth century, all across the United States, a new and somehow "American" Hinduism is coming into being.

—————————————— NOTES ——————————————

1. The temple consecration in 1990 was but the first stage. In the next six years, the temple ornamentation was completed, new altars to the Navagrahas and to Ayyappa were installed, the temple entry was extended, and finally the tall ornamented tower called the *rajgopuram* was erected over the main gateway. Its *kumbhabhishekam* was performed in June of 1996.

2. The distinctive similarity of the Hindu and Jewish traditions as highly locative is interesting in considering the notion of diaspora. It would make little sense to speak of a Muslim, Christian, or Buddhist diaspora, for these religious traditions are ideologically translocal, not linked foundationally to the topoi of any particular place, even though places like Mecca, Rome, or Bodh Gaya have centering force in their various ways.

3. It should be noted here that there was also wide Indian American financial support for the Pittsburgh temple and the loan to T. T. Devasthanams was quickly repaid. While the Tirupati counterpart sends trained priests to American temples, even the many Sri Ventakeswara temples are almost wholly built and supported by the Indian American community.

4. First Amendment to Constitution consists of sixteen words that have been the sturdy, but continually contested, basis of "church-state" relations in the United States since the 1790s: "Congress shall make no law respecting an establishment of religion or prohibiting the free exercise thereof."

5. One of the contributions of the Pluralism Project at Harvard University has been to document and maintain files with the newsletters, solicitations, and commemorative publications of the first-generation American Hindu temples.

6. The VHP had its first conference in the United States in 1970. Its stated purpose is "To unite Hindus with a view to instill in them devotion to the principles and practices of the Hindu Way of Life. To cultivate in them a spirit of self respect for themselves and their way of life and respect for the people of all colors, creeds, races, and religions. To establish and reinforce contacts with Hindus all over the world." Both the VHP and HSC have extensive web sites.

7. The most extensively used curriculum seems to be the *Vedic Heritage Teaching Program*, developed under the direction of Swami Dayananda and his staff at the Arsha Vidya Gurukula retreat center in Pennsylvania.

It includes several levels of instruction, with both student workbooks and teacher's guides. The Hindu "catechism" developed by the American-born Satguru Sivaya Subramuniyaswami is Shaiva in orientation: *Dancing with Siva, Hinduism's Contemporary Catechism.*

―――――――――――――― **BIBLIOGRAPHY** ――――――――――――――

Agarwal, P. (1991). *Passage from India: Post 1965 Indian Immigrants and Their Children.* Palos Verdes, CA: Yuvati Publications.

Baumann, M. (1995). "Conceptualizing Diaspora." *Temenos* 31:19–35.

Eck, D. (1990). " 'New Age' Hinduism in America." In Sulochana Raghavan Glazer and Nathan Glazer, eds., *Conflicting Images: India and the United States.* Glenn Dale, MD: Riverdale Publishers.

Jackson, C. T. (1994). *Vedanta for the West: The Ramakrishna Movements in the United States.* Bloomington: Indiana University Press.

Meera D. (1994). "Radha-Krishn and the Land of Braj." Souvenir Booklet, Shree Raseshwari Radha Rani Temple. Austin, Texas: Barsana Dham.

Mukhopadhyaya, B. (1993). "Hindu Communities of the Bay Area." Pluralism Project Research.

Ramaswamy, S. and S. (1992). *Vedic Heritage Teaching Program.* Saylorsburg, PA: Arsha Vidya Gurukulam.

Subramuniyaswami, S. (1993). *Dancing with Siva: Hinduism's Contemporary Catechism.* Kapaa, Hawaii: Himalayan Academy Publications.

Thomas, W. M. (1930). *Hinduism Invades America.* New York: Beacon Press.

Toqueville, A. de (1835, 1990). *Democracy in America*, 2 vols. The Henry Reeve (trans.) text as revised by F. Bowen, with a new introduction by D. J. Boorstin. New York: Random House.

Viswanathan, E. (1992). *Am I a Hindu? The Hinduism Primer.* San Francisco: Halo Books.

Vivekananda, S. (1900, 1973). *Raja Yoga.* New York: Ramakrishna-Vivekananda Center.

Williams, R. B. (1988). *Religions of Immigrants from India and Pakistan.* Cambridge: Cambridge University Press.

Yogananda, P. (1946). *Autobiography of a Yogi.* Los Angeles: Self-Realization Fellowship.

―――. (1958). *Scientific Healing Affirmations.* Los Angeles: Self-Realization Fellowship.

11

At Home in the *Hijra*

South Asian Muslims in the United States

Yvonne Yazbeck Haddad

One of the most prominent characteristics of the Muslim community in North America is its diversity.[1] While it includes a significant number of Muslims whose forebears immigrated between 1870s and World War II and who are in various processes of integration and assimilation,[2] the majority of Muslims in America today are foreign born, socialized and educated overseas, whose identity has been shaped by the various nation states fashioned by European colonialism during this century or by the nationalist reactions of the postcolonial period. It includes immigrants who chose to move to the United States in quest of economic opportunities or political and religious freedom; émigrés and refugees forced out of their homelands reluctant to

239

relinquish the dream of returning to help in the restoration of the order left behind, as well as a large number of converts, both African American and white, who through the act of conversion are opting out of the dominant American cultural identity.[3] They represent over 60 nations with the various ethnic, racial, linguistic, tribal, and national identities they bring.[4]

Within this conglomeration of identities, the Muslim immigrants from South Asia form what appears to some as a distinct group with its particular experience in the Indian subcontinent, one that colors and influences its perceptions of what it means to be Muslim and minority, shaping its strategies for survival in an increasingly hostile environment. At the same time, it is evident that the particular experience of the different national groups, whether Bangladeshi, Indian, or Pakistani continues to produce a variety of responses. These are further impacted by the diversity in age, income, occupation, language, education, and sectarian allegiances in the population under study.

The professionals who emigrated from the Indian subcontinent to the United States since the middle of the 1960s have placed their trust in two competing visions of the revitalized future of their community and the means of bringing it into reality. The majority had fashioned their identity from a concept of shared history, religion, language, and culture within a national border in order to create a viable state. Others grounded their identity in a larger umbrella ideology that saw itself as initiating the re-creation of a viable Islamic nation encompassing the whole world.

The community displays a variety of perspectives, interests, and commitments. The early migrants were on the surface a more socially homogeneous group, young peasant or working-class men willing to put up with hardship in order to vindicate the trust and hope of those left behind. The students who came in the 1960s were from more diverse economic, religious, social, and professional backgrounds. The majority were raised in the nation state that had fashioned their identity and had some commitment to a national identity. Besides sharing their recently acquired affluence with their families left behind, they dreamed of sharing their newfound knowledge with their homeland.

Unlike the established patterns of earlier waves of immigrants to the United States such as Jews and Catholics, most recent South Asian Muslims have not had to climb up the ladder of economic mobility. Rather, they have been dropped into the middle and upper-middle classes through their professional achievement without their parents having to pay the price of toiling in the sweatshops of

America. There has been very little effort on the part of Americans to integrate them socially, or on their own part to press for such integration. Nor do they appear to have the connections, the skills, or the will to do so.

Putting Down Roots

A variety of associations have been organized in the United States for the specific purpose of serving the Indo-Pakistani community, ranging from inclusive cultural clubs that are shared with others from their original countries deemed more compelling than religious ties. The Bengali language, for example, provides an option for community identity outside the mosque. The language as well as the rich cultural heritage of literature, music, and dance of the area are shared with the Christians, Hindus, and Buddhists from Bangladesh as well as Hindu immigrants from the Indian state of West Bengal. Thus several cultural organizations that celebrate the heritage have been formed. They tend to attract the secularist Bengalis as well as some of the more liberal mosqued individuals who do not share the Jamaati Islami teachings about the sinfulness of music and art or those of the Tableeghi Jamaat who see them as distracting the believer from concentrating on total devotion to the worship of God. Other national or ethnic organizations include: Committee of Indian Muslims in the United States and Canada, the Pakistani League, and the Pakistan Student Organization of America.

South Asian Muslims are also served by the numerous Muslim organizations in America that for some function as a kind of survival mechanism, a way in which to seek refuge from the pain of prejudice and injustice that many of them feel is placed on them by the larger culture. Such organizations provide them with a context in which their own cultural and religious identity can be affirmed rather than rejected, and a way in which they can see themselves as fortified so as to be able to participate in the broader American culture.

The Muslim Student Association (MSA), organized in 1963 by a small group of Muslim students from the Indian subcontinent as well as the Arab world, has had a revolutionary influence in redefining Islamic identity in the United States.[5] Their most important contribution is the publication and dissemination of Islamic literature in English advocating their particular interpretation of Islamic values concerning economic, social, cultural, and political issues.[6] Grounded in the ideology of the Muslim Brotherhood of

Egypt and the Jamaati Islami of the subcontinent, the group has been able to create the largest Muslim organization in the United States and Canada committed to developing an authentic and modern Islamic identity that supersedes linguistic, tribal, regional, ethnic, and national allegiances. Once the students decided to settle in the United States and began to raise families, they reconstituted themselves as the Islamic Society of North America that was focused on preserving and perpetuating Islam in North America with a declared agenda of transforming America into an Islamic society. They have brought into existence a successful network of Islamic institutions including a large number of mosques/Islamic centers, 321 by 1984. Since then the number has increased to over 1,250 mosques and Islamic Centers that service the Muslim community.

Mosque construction was especially vibrant in the 1970s and 80s because of generous donations from Saudi Arabia, Kuwait, and other oil producing countries. This financial support coincided with the beginning of the real establishment of the Muslim community in America as more and more students opted to seek employment in the United States, began to raise families and think about a future in America. It has been marked by a concerted effort to establish places of worship that can also function as community centers. Mosques and Islamic centers continue to be voluntary associations of believers coming together in a common cause. They are a very important means for the concretizing of an American form of identity. Just as the Jews have their synagogues and the Christians their churches, the Muslims have their mosques. The Sunday schools and weekend schools associated with the mosque organizations have been established to promote Islam, maintain its tenets into the next generation, and preserve the religious and ethnic identity and culture of the parents. Mosques provide instruction in values that promote upward mobility and educational achievement. More important, in the American context, the mosque/ Islamic organization provides the opportunity to build community out of a diverse peoplehood. Members of the mosque are called brothers and sisters in the faith such that often it serves the function of the extended family.

The mosques built in the seventies tended to be ethnically pluralistic. The driving force in many communities came from Indian Muslims who had the experience of being a minority in a non-Muslim majority community and who had a special understanding of the role a mosque can play in fashioning and maintaining community as well as the importance of the initiative of the believers in creating such institutions. New roles were added to the mosque/ Islamic center since it was clear that it could provide additional services for the immigrant community and their families.

Among the most important of these roles has been the preservation of an Islamic culture and identity. Religious instruction in many cases has been delegated to the mosque and the Sunday School. The mosque has become a place where children can meet others inculcated with the preference for Islamic family values. The teaching of the mosque thus not only affirmed the uniqueness and supersession of Islam over other "infidel" faiths of America, it confirmed the divine commandment to obey one's parents and not question their authority since they have a special knowledge of the faith that is essential for survival in profane American society. The Islamic institutions, whether mosques, schools, literature, or media, became vehicles for re-creating a modern Islam relevant for American life, a normative tradition that can accommodate the wishes of the founders while maintaining control over their offspring.

The mosque institutions as developed in America face many challenges, paramount among them the fact that they depend on private charity and volunteer services. While tithing is one of the foundational prescribed pillars of Islam and contributing to the building of mosques is guaranteed to provide a place for the giver in the Garden in the hereafter, this has not translated into a practice of generous donations for the support of the mosques and Islamic centers. Most donors give for the initial construction of mosques and schools and will periodically respond to a specific emergency fund-raising drive such as providing an ambulance for one's village back home or for relief in Kashmir, Chechniya, or Bosnia. Giving generously for the maintenance of the services of the mosque, such as the salary of the imam, custodian of the mosque, teacher in the school, or for heating does not seem to have a high priority among members. Another serious issue that appeared in the late eighties is the development of the ethnic mosque, despite the fact that earlier mosques were depicted as an ideal implementation of Islamic community that supersedes local, regional, ethnic, or linguistic distinctions. This was due to several reasons, the most important of which is the immigration of the extended family the majority of whom are not fluent in English and for whom the mosque functions primarily as the social center for celebrating ethnic culture and customs.

Life in America has brought about a variety of new problems including intermarriage, mostly of Muslim men marrying out of the faith and thus precipitating a crisis situation in the number of unmarried Muslim women.[7] Other issues include whether it is necessary to implement Islamic law;[8] whether there is a proper way of living an Islamic life in a non-Muslim environment;[9] whether Muslims can accommodate to the American economic system based on interest;[10] whether the need to promote dialogue is in accord with the necessity of propagating the faith;[11] whether America dictates a new kind of Islamic leadership;[12] whether to anglicize their names or hold on to distinctive Islamic name,[13] and whether American law guarantees full rights for the community.[14]

American Muslims do not have a Mufti who can provide informed Islamic opinion on how to live according to Islamic precepts in the American context. A survey of several groups shows that most would not recognize or pay attention to such an authority. While some Indian Muslims may pay allegiance to a specific mulla imported from India, the majority do not tend to take his teachings as authoritative. The immigrants did not bring their imams with them initially and are not looking to import them now. What has been created in America is a kind of "congregational" Islam with the imams being elected, credentialed, and fired by the local congregations. Serious questions are being asked concerning the nature of their authority and how it is acquired. Currently there are moves to build seminaries in the United States to train imams and religious leaders who have knowledge of America and are not prone to replicate what obtained in India, Bangladesh, or Pakistan.

The result is that in many instances the mosque in the United States is a hybrid institution. It is not so much a transplant as a new creation with a revitalized function and role in society. But the fact that it is seen as an Islamic space, a way of being on the map, of being formally part of America has been reflected in mosque design. Great care has been taken to give mosques a distinctive recognizable Islamic architectural feature. At the same time, the mosque has begun to serve new functions such as a place one can go to if one wants to have a wedding or a funeral.

The mosque has brought revolutionary change in Muslim women's religiosity in the United States. It has become the custom in most mosques to build a segregated place for women that they generally attend during Sunday family services. The absence of wali shrines (there are only two in North America) to service women's needs, has given rise to new organizations for women and new forms of worship. There are over 100 Muslim Women's organizations and almost as many Qur'an study groups for women. In some cases, old world customs of women's weekly visits have been turned into special occasions for learning about Islam. There are a number of women experts on Islamic subjects who are in high demand.

The roles of Muslim women and the family in the American context has received special attention from contemporary Muslim writers.[15] These roles have subtly changed and shifted over the years as more clearly defined Islamic expectations have been laid on Muslim women, especially the immigrants among them.[16] Muslims have also written critically about American women, American culture, and American family values that are usually dismissed as the primary cause for the collapse of the social order. The superior role Islam affords women is seen as a potential contribution to the saving of America from the social crisis in which it is mired.

Many Muslims in America, including South Asians, emphasize traditional roles for women and imported imams from India continue in some cases to insist on confining the women to the house. Nonetheless there are many professional Muslim women, doctors, psychiatrists, professors, social workers, and engineers who have been active in founding and operating Islamic institutions. In some cases they have even helped organize the fund-raising for the construction of mosques.[17] Some have volunteered to teach in the Sunday school. On the whole, the ethnic mosques associated with Indians and Bangladeshis continue to be a male domain, especially among the recently arrived undereducated immigrants, while some Pakistani women have been able to break past traditional restraints. One Pakistani woman is the elected president of a mosque organization in New York.

Today young women are still being taught at home, in the Sunday Schools, and the youth conferences sponsored by the Muslim Youth of North America (MYNA) that they have been endowed by God with the responsibility of maintaining an Islamic home and nurturing children in the faith, reinforcing the role of the woman as wife and mother. Since for the most part they have mostly been encouraged to seek higher education and a profession, however, there is now a growing number of American-born young women entering the legal and medical professions, as well as becoming journalists and university professors. They are veterans of the double message. At the mosque and at the MYNA-sponsored conferences strict segregation is enforced leading one prominent Mosque president to comment: "We tell them that there are two kinds of boys: Those they can talk to but cannot marry and those they meet at the mosque who they cannot talk to but will marry."

The rise of the ethnic mosque has revealed some tension in the Muslim community, between the identity of the Muslim *umma*, a peoplehood united in religious affiliation to the message of Muhammad as the only one of divine origin, and the various ethnic, linguistic, tribal, and national identities that comprise the Muslim population. Besides distinctive preferences for language and local customs, there are residual transplanted feelings of distrust among the various constituents of the Indo-Pakistani Muslim community. Indian Muslims feel betrayed and unappreciated because of the compromises they had to make for survival as a minority in India. They tend to blame the Pakistani exodus as the cause of undermining Muslim power in the subcontinent; they display an acute alertness to the vagaries of negative attitudes toward Islam and Muslims in the majority press, fearing discrimination leading even to genocide. Pakistanis view themselves as pioneers in formulating a viable modern Islamic nation. The Bangladeshis recall their experience at the splitting of the nation and are at times suspicious of other Muslims from India/Pakistan.

The differences between the religious culture of people from South Asia and those from the Middle East with whom they initiated the mosque movement in the United States sometimes become an issue. Muslims from South Asia in some cases have introduced the tradition of reciting *taraweeh* every evening in the mosque during the month of Ramadan. Other celebrations include *milad al-nabi*, where passages from the Qur'an and from the hadith recalling narratives and teachings of the Prophet Muhammad are recited. This custom is highly frowned on by many Muslims from the Arab world, especially those from Saudi Arabia.

Thus while freedom to define Islam and its cultural framework and the search for a uniform ideal in the American context have worked to fuse together disparate national cultures into the culture of the mosque/Islamic center, at the same time national distinctions have served to foster the promotion and appreciation of different cultures, as well as in some instances intolerance for what one presumes to be un-Islamic accretions. Pakistanis, Indians, and Bangladeshis resist the pressure to Arabize their culture in order to become "authentic" Muslims. Ethnic diversity comes up against, and in many ways is resistant to, conformity and pressure to adhere to the norms identified by the leadership.

Still there is often a sense of disappointment that consensus cannot be reached on everything. Differences in opinions on what is of crucial importance still plague the community. The young men who braved America and sought to change the world are now married to wives who were not necessarily part of the struggle and have children who were raised in the United States who do not share their parents' experience or identity. This has produced a generation that is aware of the parents' struggle but does not necessarily identify with it. While they have experienced American hostility and racism, most of the children feel comfortable in American society and know how to operate in it.

Another factor that has a pull on this generation is the growing reality of the extended family as more of the relatives of Muslims living in America manage to immigrate to the United States. Recent immigrants and parents continue to represent the pull of a culture left behind, one that may be deliberately eschewed by Muslims here as prohibiting Muslims in America from becoming assimilated or successfully competing on the American scene. Thus the questions of what of the home culture to maintain and what to reject as un-Islamic continue to be matters of daily decision.

Muslims as Minority

While the context of American society leaves room for the division and subdivision into small organizations, the same context, given its negative image of Muslims and the variety of pressures they have experienced, pushes them for collective action as a strategy of survival despite the many elements that may cause tensions among them. The crisis of Muslim life in a hostile context has become the driving force in maintaining the push for common ground, common cause, and unity.

Since the middle of the 1980s the American Muslim community has expressed deep concern about American tolerance of negative depictions of Islam and Muslims.[18] Anti-Muslim sentiment has generally become more evident in the wake of what Muslims believe to be the unbalanced coverage given events overseas by the American press. The press had a heyday reporting on the Salman Rushdie affair, the World Trade Center bombing, and some in its corps insisted that the Oklahoma City bombing had the *modus operandi* of Middle Eastern terrorists despite the fact that the investigation showed that it was the work of Christian Americans.[19] As a consequence of such biased coverage, Muslims report a series of attacks on mosques and Islamic institutions. In addition to the vengeful acts of some isolated Americans inflamed by media reports about Islam, Muslims fear the more organized hostile activities of certain groups. Recent hate crimes include the bombing of a mosque in Texas as well as the burning of mosques in Indiana and California.

Casting the veil of negativism over Islam are a variety of interest groups including officials of the American government seeking support for various policies,[20] officials of Arab governments affirming their legitimacy against opposition political groups in their countries, members of the Israeli government and their American defenders,[21] the so-called experts on foreign policy who need a threat in order to sell their expertise,[22] as well as certain elements of the press who increasingly delineate Muslims as outside the "national character" of "shared American culture" or the "mainstream." Questions are raised concerning the compatibility of their religious practices and cultural preferences with the American lifestyle, especially as pertains to issues of dress, roles for women, sexuality, child rearing, free time, alcohol, gambling, educational needs, private hygiene, occupation, and their scrupulousness in financial transactions that involve interest.

Muslims are also concerned about deliberate falsifications about Islam that are perpetrated by those who appear to have declared Islam as the "enemy." The community is also afraid of becoming a target of Christian missionary Crusades. The demonization of Islam as perpetrated by Christian fundamentalists depicts Muslims as major actors in hastening Armageddon and bringing about the imminent end of time when Jesus will come to initiate the rapture. Muslims are depicted on Christian television programs as warmongers, bent on destroying Israel.[23]

While some segments of the American press have managed to create the image of the Muslim as the consummate terrorist, Muslims surveying the history and experience of the Muslim community worldwide often see themselves as victims of forces of Judeo-Christian hatred. They trace this victimization from the Crusades and the Reconquista, through the age of imperialism, and see it reinforced in contemporary events in Azerbaijan, Chechniya, Palestine, and Bosnia.

Other solutions have been proposed that can guarantee social and political empowerment.[24] Muslims are not to accept minority status as a permanent condition in which they accommodate and acquiesce to those in power since that will perpetuate their weakness. They must perceive their "minorityness"[25] as a challenge to be transcended. Muslim communities should seek residence in certain enclaves. There they could establish a truly Islamic community based on the brotherhood of Islam, an organization that is not elitist, sectarian, partisan in politics, or divided into racial or pro-

fessional distinctions. Such enclaves, if governed by Muslims through
the principle of *shura*, consultation, would not be ghettos but specially created communities empowered to serve as a means of fostering and maintaining Islam. Their social, economic, political, and
cultural life would revolve around the mosque and the Islamic
school. Such enclaves are necessary to protect the community from
the dangers of assimilation and disintegration. Only through the
maintenance of control over their children's education will Muslims
be able to insulate themselves from the pressure to discard their
Islamic identity and integrate into society. Thus for Kettani, maintaining cultural distinctions such as language, dress, and Islamic
names is crucial.[26]

The efforts of a variety of interests in the United States to
orchestrate a negative response to Muslims in the United States,
from outright demonizing of Islam to declaring Muslims as the
enemy, are increasingly acting as an important agent in forging a
cohesive Islamic identity. Muslims who are the target of disinfor-
mation and stereotyping are being urged to participate in efforts to
counter their false accusers. The struggle to rectify the public image
at times seems elusive, if not impossible. The defense of Islam is
creating a reinterpretation of the faith fostering a sense of identity
increasingly based on two foundations: a history of victimization
perpetuated by a variety of enemies of Islam and a current sense
of impending danger. The menacing accusations and the facile stereotypes are instigating a reassessment of the meaning of the faith
vis-à-vis Christianity and Judaism, and inspiring creative new
ventures in combating what is perceived as clear demonstrations of
Judeo-Christian hatred. Islam must be utilized to bring about the
well-being of the Muslim community as well as its social and political empowerment. Muslims must not accept minority status as
a permanent condition. They must seek to alter such a condition
and transcend it.

There is no unanimous Muslim understanding of the American
challenge or of how to respond to it, what strategy to employ or
what kind of identity to foster. Questions persist as to whether as
Americans, Muslims should participate in the political arena,
support a particular party or candidate, vote, or run for office;
whether to build umbrella political organizations or organize political action committees as well as explore and negotiate coalitions
with other interest groups; whether to risk participation in interfaith activities and dialogue or refrain from such activity, which is
often seen as trying to undermine Muslim unity; whether to relinquish authority in running the mosque to a trained leadership, and

whether this leadership should be American home grown or dependent on religious leaders trained overseas who bring ideas that are not compatible with the reality of the American context.

The cutoff of aid from the Gulf countries as punishment for the refusal of immigrant Muslims to support American intervention in the Gulf War led the Muslim community to turn to itself to reassess its mission and its goals as well as to generate resources to maintain the institutions it had carefully established during the preceding two decades. The Gulf War made it evidently clear to the Muslim community that they lack political power in the United States. It reconfirmed their marginality and inability to influence American policy. Muslim weakness became more evident when the Congress passed new immigration laws restricting immigration of people from Muslim countries and when various segments of American society launched a relentless campaign against Islam and Muslims. This drove some Muslims to seek security by further isolation from the dominant society. Others took refuge in further Islamization, while still others have continued the quest for a negotiated place on the American scene.

Concern over the continued marginalization and demonization of Muslims in American society, as well as what was seen as the failure of the models projected by the leadership of the 1970s and 1980s, has led to the formation of the North American Association of Muslim Professionals and Scholars (NAAMPS) in April 1993, whose leaders called for dramatic changes in the way Muslims choose to live in North America. At the same time, the leadership of Islamic Society of North America, Islamic Circle of North America, the American Muslim Alliance, and the American Muslim Council have called for new realistic interpretations of what it means to live in *hijra* in North America.

Muslims should gain the confidence of other people by their positive contributions to the growth of the contemporary civilization, which is universal, and by participating in the concerns of all the fellow human beings. This surely does not mean being lost in mere imitation of others. Muslims should have their own understanding and stands, but with regard to the interests of humanity at large and restricted to their own selves, however numerous and extensively distributed all over the world they may be. There are areas of cooperation where Muslims should not hesitate to work with others without compromising on their differences. Sometimes Muslims talk about social justice in a totalitarian way which is rejected by the world. We should be careful about our words and pay attention to the limitation of our audiences. We have to consider the importance of modern thinking and not try to underestimate or ignore it because of its shortcomings. We may not agree with many contemporary ideas and thinking, but we cannot also rule out that they have also led to achievements. If our thinking is so oversimplified that it considers every modern institution as superficial, and every emphasis of human right as hypocritical, then how can we be a partner in this world and how can we benefit from these international institutions and documents for our peoples and for the whole world?[27]

A number of factors come to play in terms of the degree to which Muslims, and in this case those from South Asia, choose to identify with and participate in American culture. Certainly there are significant differences between Muslims who feel at home in America and find Islamic justification for participating in the various dimensions of its life and those who for many reasons decide to be more isolationist. The latter tend to view the United States as a land of *kufr* (unbelief) and urge their fellow believers to live protected lives away from the evils that they associate with American culture. One manifestation of the difference is evident in discussions about whether Muslims are free to eat the food of Christians and Jews or must have their own *Zabiha* meat. While the isolationists place a great premium on maintaining a *halal* kitchen, for example, the accommodationists argue that "any nourishing diet, any decent dress, and any type of architecture for their houses and mosques" is acceptable if it does not violate the tenets of the faith, since religion and culture are finally not identical.

To some extent decisions about acculturation are related to emotional ties to the home culture. "There was a romance and mystique about our Pakistani origin," said one man. Children are taught that Pakistani social habits are different from those of American children, and that Muslims do not drink alcohol or eat pork. Many Pakistani children are taught Urdu and taken to Pakistan for vacations so as to reinforce their identity, and sometimes this reinforcement is more at the hands of grandparents who cling to the home culture than of parents who themselves are finding ways to acculturate. The differences in family feelings, as well as interaction with American children in the contexts of schools and other occasions underscore for them the reality of differentness.

They mingle with children who are not of their complexion and whose social behaviors are different: American children are free, Pakistani children are wary. American children are independent, Pakistani youngsters are directed by their parents. American kids have no inhibitions with the opposite sex, our kids are more held back. Any attempt to change results in confusion and guilt complex.[28]

The temptation to acculturate may be accented for South Asian Muslims given the fact that so many come to America as well educated professionals. Pakistani, Indian, and Bangladeshi doctors, for example, can choose to participate in the larger society, join country clubs and generally participate in the culture to a degree that is not possible for many Muslim immigrants without their educational and economic advantages. They have entered American society at the top of the professional ladder, moving into the academy and the medical and engineering professions. Their income puts them not only into the upper middle class of society, but occasionally enters them into millionaire circles.

Despite these advantages, however, many of these same professionals opt to constrain their relationships to others of the same ethnic origin, socializing with South Asians only and participating in Islamic activities that might not have had any appeal to them at an earlier time, including going to the mosque. No matter which direction they choose, however, the reality is that immigrants from South Asia do face a color barrier. They experience this not necessarily in terms of professional or economic integration, but as a factor in social relations. Regardless of their professional achievements, they often experience an American society that finds it impossible to view Indians, Pakistanis, or Bangladeshis as other than "brown." At the same time they come to the American scene with a distinct South Asian color consciousness with all its attendant baggage defining themselves as brown.

Access to academic presses has increasingly given Muslim academicians an opportunity to define themselves and their community. To some that task has appeared daunting. Not only have they had to assess how and in what ways to participate in American society, they have also had to deal with the fact that Islam is increasingly framed in negative contexts. As Muslim intellectuals they have had not only to reflect and write on Islamic topics, but also to break out of the prevailing academic discourse that has traditionally been associated with things Islamic, to cope with the anti-Muslim prejudices and the tendency for people to dismiss what they write as propaganda defending their own beliefs, and the social pressure to conform to an ideal of "melting" or assimilating that is often not desirable and ultimately seldom attainable. It is not surprising that many have opted to maintain their own distinctiveness, as assimilation would symbolize an abandonment of the faith as well as apparently slipping into the morass of what is perceived as a pornographic American culture that appears to have accepted a warped model of family values aimed at destroying the support system necessary for survival in an increasingly troubled environment. Caught on the horns of a dilemma, they find themselves approving of the family values advocated by the Christian right at the same time that they are well aware that it is these same groups that malign Islam.

Thus much of what these Muslim academics write tries to affirm and advocate Islamic values aimed at defining an ideal and supportive community that is able to remain compelling to the youth. This community is grounded in Islam as a religion which—while it proscribes the choice of living outside of the group—nonetheless presents Islam as a universal ideal. The emphasis thus is not on finding ways in which Muslims can be Americans, but rather on extolling the virtue of the community and awaiting the day when America will become Muslim. Aware that the larger society looks askance at their values and customs, they try to turn the tables by declaring these customs and values to be superior, of divine imperative, and ultimately to be attested to as valid by the rest of American society.

NOTES

1. For studies illustrating the diversity of Muslims in North America, see: Yvonne Yazbeck Haddad and Jane I. Smith, eds., *Muslim Communities in North America*, Albany: State University of New York Press, 1994. Cf. Yvonne Yazbeck Haddad, *The Muslims of America*, New York: Oxford University Press, 1991.

2. For a comparative study of five mosques on questions of integration and assimilation, see Yvonne Yazbeck Haddad and Adair Lummis, *Islamic Values in the United States*, New York: Oxford University Press, 1987.

3. See for example: Essien-Udom, E. E. *Black Nationalism*, Chicago: The University of Chicago Press, 1962; Eric C. Lincoln, *The Black Muslims*

in America, Boston: Beacon Press, 1961; Akbar Muhammad, "Muslims in the United States: An Overview of Organizations, Doctrines, and Problems," in *The Islamic Impact*, Yvonne Yazbeck Haddad, Byron Haines, and Ellison Findly, eds., Syracuse: Syracuse University Press, 1984, pp. 195–218.

4. Yvonne Yazbeck Haddad, "Maintaining the Faith of the Fathers: Dilemmas of Religious Identity in the Christian and Muslim Arab-American Communities," in *Arab-American Communities*, ed. Ernest McCarus, Ann Arbor, University of Michigan Press, 1994.

5. Gutbi Mahdi Ahmed, "The Muslims of the United States," in Haddad, ed., *The Muslims of America*, New York: Oxford University Press, 1991, pp. 11–24.

6. Abul A'la Maududi, *The Role of Muslim Students in the Reconstruction of the Muslim World*. Kuwait: I.I.F.S.O., 1978.

7. Jon C. Swanson, "Mate Selection and Intermarriage in an American Arab Moslem Community." M.A. thesis, University of Iowa, Iowa City, 1970; Nielsen, J. S. "Islam and Mixed Marriages." *Research Papers: Muslims in Europe*, 20 (1983) pp. 8–17 (Legal aspects.); Dawud Assad, Mixed Marriages. *Research Papers: Muslims in Europe*, 20 (1983), pp. 3–7; Rabiah Hakeem, "Cross-Cultural Marriages among Muslims: A Word of Caution." *Islamic Horizons* XIV, 10 (1985); Ilyas Ba-Yunus, "Muslims in North America: Mate Selection as an Indicator of Change." *Muslim Families in North America*, eds. Earle H. Waugh, Sharon McIrvin Abu-Laban, and Regula Burckhardt Qureshi. Alberta: The University of Alberta Press, 1991, 232–49.

8. D. F. Forte, "Islamic Law in American Courts." *Suffolk Transnational Law Journal*, (1983), pp. 1–33; Ebrahim Sulaiman Sait, "Muslim Personal Law." *Muslim Communities in Non-Muslim States*. London: Islamic Council of Europe, 1980, pp. 109–24.

9. Akbar Muhamad, "Some Factors Which Promote and Restrict Islamization in America." *American Journal of Islamic Studies* I, 2 (1984), 41–50; Monzer Kahf, *The Calculation of Zakah for Muslims in North America*. Plainfield, IN: The Muslim Student Association, 1978; Ahmad Hussein Sakr, *Dietary Regulations and Food Habits of Muslims*, New York: The Muslim World League, n.d.; Yusuf al-Qaradawi, *The Lawful and the Prohibited in Islam*, Kuwait: I.I.F.S.O., 1984; Malik B. Badri, *Islam and Alcoholism*. Indianapolis: American Trust Publications, 1976.

10. Ali F. Darrat, "Are Checking Accounts in American Banks Permissible Under Islamic Laws?" *American Journal of Islamic Social Sciences* II (1985), 101–4; Sulayman S. Nyang, "Muslim Minority Business Enterprise in

America: An Economic Historical Perspective. *The Search* 3, ii (1982), pp. 42–65; M. Raquibuz Zaman, "Banking, Investment, Insurance and Muslims in North America." *Journal Institute of Muslim Minority Affairs* V, 1 (1983–1984), 71–76; Monzer Kahf, *The Islamic Economy*, Plainfield, IN: The Muslim Student Association (1978).

11. Marston Speight, "Christian-Muslim Dialogue in the United States of America. *Islamochristiana* 7 (1981), pp. 201–210; Larry Poston, "The Future of *Da'wah* in North America," *American Journal of Islamic Social Sciences*, 8 (1991) pp. 501–11; Ahmad Hussein Sakr, "Islamic Dawa: Some Problems." *The Journal: Rabetat al-'Alam al-Islami* VIII (June 1979), 14–16; Zaheer Uddin Nazim, *Manual of Da'wah*, Montreal: Islamic Circle of North America, 1983.

12. Earle H. Waugh, "The Imam in the New World: Models and Modifications." In *Transitions and Transformations in the History of Religions*, Frank E. Reynolds and Theodore M. Ludwig, eds. Leiden: E. J. Brill, 1980, pp. 124–49; Abdur Rahman Shad, *Duties of an Imam*. Revised by Abdul Hameed Siddiqui. Chicago: Kazi Publications, 1978.

13. M.A. Qazi, *What's in a Muslim Name*, Chicago: Kazi Publications, 1974; Sam Hamood, *Dying with the Wrong Name*, New York: Anthe Publication, 1980.

14. Kathleen M. Moore, *al-Mughtaribun: American Law and the Transformation of Muslim Life in the United States*, Albany: State University of New York Press, 1995; Sidney Rahim Sharif, *Crime and Corrections: An al-Islamic Perspective*, Chicago: Kazi Publications, 1983; Abdeen Jabara, "Operation Arab: The Nixon Administration's Measures in the U.S. after Munich." In *The Civil Rights of Arab-Americans: The Special Measures*, M. D. Bassiouni, ed. North Dartmouth, MA: Arab-American University Graduates, 1974.

15. Gamal A. Badawi, *A Muslim Woman's Dress According to the Qur'an and Sunnah*, Plainfield, IN: MSA Women's Committee, n.d.; Melody, "Hijab in the Eyes of a New Muslim." *Islamic Order* IV, 4 (1982); Regula Burkhardt Qureshi, "Marriage Strategies among Muslims from South Asia." *Muslim Families*, 185–213; Saleem Qureshi, "The Muslim family: The Scriptural Framework." *Muslim Families*, 32–67; Hammudah Abd al-Ati, *The Family Structure in Islam*, Plainfield, IN: American Trust Publications, 1977; Muhammad Abdul-Rauf, *The Islamic View of Women and the Family*, New York: Robert Speller & Sons, 1977; "Muslim Family Life in America." *The Journal: Rabetat al-'Alam al-Islami* VIII (June 1979), pp. 50–53; Rabiyah Y. Abdul-Khabir, "Prevalent Problems in Muslim Marriages." *Al-Ittihad* XIX, 3–4 (1982), 15–26.

16. Zahr Munir, "Being Muslim and Female." *Journal Institute of Muslim Minority Affairs* V, 1 (1983–1984), 77–80.

17. Safia Haddad, "The Woman's Role in Socialization of Syrian-Americans in Chicago." In *The Arab Americans: Studies in Assimilation*, Elaine C. Hagopian and Ann Paden, eds. Wilmette, IL: Medina University Press International, 1969, pp. 84–101.

18. See for example: Ahmad Yusuf, "Al-Hajma al-Sihyoniyya `ala al-Muslimin fi al-Wilayat al-Muttahida. Mawjat al-Tahrid al-Thalitha: al-Jihad fi America," *Filastin al-Muslima*, January 1995, pp. 38–40.

19. Besides producing the controversial documentary "Jihad in America" aired on PBS, Steven Emerson testified before the House International Relations Committee where he asserted that "Radical Islamic networks now constitute the primary domestic—as well as international—national security threat facing the FBI and other law enforcement agencies." Steven Emerson, "Testimony of Steven Emerson: Subcommittee of Africa House International Relations Committee, U.S. House of Representatives, 6 April 1995, p. 4. He has also published an article and is in the process of writing a book on the subject. Steven Emerson, "The Other Fundamentalists," *The New Republic*, 12 June 1995, pp. 21–30.

20. In an interview with *Time* magazine, president Reagan said, "Lately we have even seen the possibility of, literally, a religious war—the Muslims returning to the idea that the way to heaven is to lose one's life fighting the Christians and the Jews." *Time*, vol 116, #20, p. 37, 17 November 1980.
In responding to Reagan's accusation the Council of Masajid adopted a unanimous resolution expressing indignation over the "slanderous travesty of and a fallacious distortion of the teachings of Islam." The resolution affirmed that Islam is the "religion of peace and stands against injustice and tyranny," and stressed that in fact Islam makes a special point of urging its followers to be polite and kind to Christians and Jews. (See S. 3:64.) The President's statement was further condemned because it was perceived as potentially inciting to violence against Muslims in the U.S. "Mosque Council Condemns Reagan's Attack on Islam," *Majallat al-Masajid*, vol. 2, no. 2, February 1981, 17–18.

21. Daniel Pipes, "Fundamentalist Muslims," *Foreign Affairs*, Summer 1986, 939–59; Daniel Pipes, "The Muslims Are Coming! The Muslims Are Coming!" *National Review*, 19 November 1990, 28–31; Bernard Lewis, "Islam and Democracy, *The Atlantic* (February 1993), 87–98; Martin Kramer, "Islam vs. Democracy," *Commentary* (January 1993), 35–42. The late Israeli Prime Minister Yitzhak Rabin is reported to have told American Jewish young people that the United States must support Israel in order to combat

the Islamists, the enemies of peace who also threaten America. In an address to the American Israel Public Affairs Committee Annual Conference on 21 March 1993, Israeli Prime Minister Yitzhak Rabin said: "Thank you very much for your decision to go [to Capitol Hill] and to try to convince the senators, the congressmen in the need of Israel in this period . . . to ensure that the United States will support these efforts by Israel, as the president said, by minimizing our risks, by military aid, economic aid, understanding of the threat of the Islamic extremist terror groups not only to Israel . . . It's a threat to all moderate regimes . . . The United States has to continue to support and to prove to the region, to the peoples, to the countries, that its readiness to assist those who seek peace and ready to bring economic and social reform and to try to contain . . . the dangerous trend of the Islamic fundamentalistic [*sic*] terrorist organization and the country that backs them." as quoted in Ahmad AbulJobain, *Islam Under Siege: Radical Islamic Terrorism or Political Islam?* Annandale, VA: United Association for Studies and Research Inc., Occasional Papers Series No. 1, June 1993. Other Israeli leaders have expressed similar sentiments. Haim Hertzok is reported to have said that while the world today is concerned about the atom bomb and weapons of mass destruction in the region, a more sinister and dangerous development is the growth of Islamic fundamentalism. Shimon Peres told a White House audience that the United States must increase its aid to Israel because it is engaged in a war against Islamic extremism. *al-Mujtama`*, 1078, (December 1993), p. 6.

22. See Yvonne Yazbeck Haddad, "The 'New Enemy'? Islam and Islamists after the Cold War," in *Altered States: A Reader in the New World Order*, edited by Phyllis Bennis and Michel Moushabeck (New York: Olive Branch Press, 1993), pp. 83–94. Cf. John L. Esposito, *The Islamic Threat*, New York: Oxford University Press, 1995; Patrick J. Buchanan, "Is Islam an Enemy of the United States?" *New Hampshire Sunday News*, 25 November 1990.

23. Donald E. Wagner, *Anxious for Armageddon*, Scottdale, Pa: Herald Press, 1995; Grace Halsell, *Journey to Jerusalem*, New York: Macmillan and Company, 1982; Grace Halsell, *Prophecy and Politics*, Lawrence Hill Books, 1986. See also: Dwight Wilson, *Armageddon Now*, Tyler, TX; Institute for Christian Economics, 1991; Hal Lindsey, *Countdown to Armageddon*, New York: Bantam Books, 1980.

24. M.A. Kettani, *Muslim Minorities in the World Today*, London: 1986, 9–13.

25. The term was coined by Syed Z. Abedin in his foreword to Kettani's book, *Muslim Minorities*, xiii.

26. Kettani, *Muslim Minorities*, pp. 9–13.

27. Mohammad Fathi Osman, "Towards a Vision and an Agenda for the Future of Muslim Ummah," in *Islam: A Contemporary Perspective*, ed. Mohammad Ahmadullah Siddiqi, Chicago: NAAMPS Publications, 1994, pp. 16–17.

28. Zeenat Anwar, "But We Are Americans Now! Our Youth, Our Families, Our Future," 30 July 1995 NAMPPS.

12

Sikhism in the United States of America

Gurinder Singh Mann

The history of the Sikhs is primarily associated with the Punjab, a region in northwest India they call their home land (Grewal 1990). Situated among the dominant communities of the Hindus and Muslims, the Sikhs have, historically, remained a minority even within the Punjab. Beginning in the seventeenth century, groups of Sikh traders moved into other parts of the subcontinent and established small communities in far-off cities; the number and size of these communities outside the Punjab remained rather small. The annexation of the Punjab by the British in 1849 opened doors for the Sikhs to migrate to distant countries as members of the imperial work force. In the closing years of the nineteenth century, we see the emergence of small but distinct Sikh communities in East Africa and Southeast Asia (Barrier and Dusenbery 1989).

At the turn of the twentieth century, the Sikhs expanded their range of travel farther and began to arrive in North America. They constituted a large majority of what Raymond Williams in his introduction to this section calls "a thriving farming community in California." Despite great personal and legal hardships in the midtwentieth century, the Sikhs persisted in their efforts to settle in the new land and today they constitute a vibrant community of over 200,000 spread throughout the United States, with distinct concentrations in California, Chicago, Michigan, and the greater New York and Washington, D.C. areas.

La Brack (1988) made a pioneering study of the history of the Sikhs in the United States. Williams (1988) initiated a significant effort to discern the religious experience of South Asians in the United States including the Sikhs; Diana Eck (1997) has expanded this area of study further. Building on the previous research and my past ten years' work with the community, I attempt to present, in this chapter, what it is to be a Sikh in the United States in the closing years of the twentieth century.

The chapter comprises three sections. I begin with a discussion of the composition of the Sikh community in the United States. In the second section, I present Sikh religious life in the new country, both at personal and communal levels. In the third, I trace the challenges facing the community in the United States and the tentative solutions that the Sikh leadership is offering to meet these challenges.

The Sikhs of the United States

The present-day Sikh community in the United States possesses considerable internal diversity. Its oldest segment constitutes the descendants of the early immigrants who were from small landowning families in the Punjab and had initially come to the United State to make money but later decided to stay permanently. These people are settled primarily on the West Coast and include second- and third-generation Sikhs.

The second segment of the Sikh community to arrive in the United States comprises Sikhs who came for higher education in the middle decades of the twentieth century and stayed on after completing their studies. Unlike their predecessors who worked as laborers, saved money, bought lands, and began to farm, these Sikhs prepared themselves for professional careers and garnered white-collar jobs. It seems that even when they had the chance to look for work in the states where they went to school, they preferred to move to the West Coast to be closer to the earlier Sikh settlements (Saund 1960).

The third and most prominent segment of the Sikh community consists of men and women who came to the United States after the passage of the Immigration Act of 1965. This group includes professionals with advanced degrees obtained in India in medicine, engineering, and other fields. From both rural and urban backgrounds, they arrived in large cities, reoriented themselves to American work demands, and located themselves wherever jobs in their areas of expertise were available.

The most recent arrivals include families who have come to the United States as a result of political persecution. They are divided into two groups. The first comprises those who have come directly from the Punjab. During the 1980s, the Punjab passed through a period of political turmoil, when a militant segment of the community attempted to secede from the Indian federation and establish an independent Sikh state called Khalistan. The Indian government's use of brute force to bring the situation under control prompted large-scale flight of rural Sikh youths to various Western countries. A large majority of these had obtained college degrees. After gaining legal residence through various channels, these men brought their wives, and are now in the process of settling down in the United States.

The second group to flee political persecution came from East Africa and Afghanistan. The ancestors of the Sikhs coming from East Africa were primarily from an artisan background and had gone there at the turn of the twentieth century to work in the railway system developed by the British (Bhachu 1985). Due to political upheavals in Kenya and Uganda in the 1970s, these families were subsequently forced to leave their homes. In addition, a number of Sikh traders who had lived in Afghanistan for over two centuries left that country when war broke out in the late 1970s. Both these groups arrived in the United States with considerable experience in business and quickly put down roots in large urban centers, such as New York.

The Sikh community in the United States also includes a small group of Americans of European descent who converted to Sikhism in the 1970s. They took up the Sikh path under the spiritual guidance of Harbhajan Singh Yogi, a Punjabi Sikh who had arrived in the United States in 1968 (Khalsa 1995). They constitute a small but visible segment of the community and are sometimes called American Sikhs, an epithet which is now increasingly used by all Sikhs living in the United States.

Sikhs in the United States differ in degree of religious observance. Amritdhari men and women have undergone the ceremony
of initiation (*khande di pahul*), and strictly observe the Khalsa
code of conduct (*rahit*). Kesdhari Sikhs keep long hair but have not
undergone the ceremony of initiation and follow the *rahit* partially.
Then there are Sikhs who freely cut their hair, but follow the *rahit*
in some basic ways.

With the exception of the followers of Harbhajan Singh Yogi, all
these groups have roots in the Punjab and most continue to identify
with their occupational heritage. Jats, the farmers who constitute
70 percent of the Sikh population in the Punjab, also make up the
largest segment of the community in the United States. They are
followed in numbers by the Ramgarhias (rural artisans) and the
Khatris (urban traders) (McLeod 1976).

At present, in the late 1990s, the Sikh community in the United
States includes people of varied levels of religious leanings, social
backgrounds, professional qualifications, and lengths of residence.
Although the early immigrants were mostly males, the post-1965
phase has balanced the gender ratio. First-generation Punjabi
immigrants still constitute the large majority of the population,
with the numbers of second- and third-generation Sikhs steadily
increasing. The Sikhs occupy a full range of occupational niches,
from highly trained professional positions to nonskilled labor.

Sikh Religious Life in the United States

In describing their way of life, Sikhs distinguish between two levels:
personal (*shakashi*) and communal (*panthak*). The first refers to
what happens in the course of daily living and especially within
the confines of the Sikh household; the second concerns communal
activity, with the institution of the gurdwara (Sikh temple) at its
center (*Sikh Rahit Maryada* 1950). Since little literature is available on the Sikh devotional life, I will try to describe it in some
detail.

The Personal Level

In their personal lives, Sikhs in the United States follow the traditions they followed in the Punjab before emigrating, making only
occasional modifications. Each day most Sikhs recite three prayers:
the *Japji* ("meditation") and a set of other hymns in the morning,

the *Rahiras* ("supplication") in the evening, and the *Sohila* ("praise"), a thanksgiving prayer offered just before going to sleep. The drive to work is often accompanied by recordings of the sacred Sikh hymns. The weekend brings local television programs with devotional singing (*kirtan*) and discourses on Sikh religious issues. On the first day of each month of the lunar calendar (*sangrand*), the *Baranmah* ("12 months"), a special prayer, is recited. While Amritdharis strictly adhere to this daily routine of prayers, others may modify the timing and the contents according to their convenience.

The Sikhs are a people of the book. Almost all Sikh families possess anthologies of selected sacred hymns (*gutkas*), which are used for recitation (over and above the daily prayers) and to teach young children. Families who can do so usually keep the Guru Granth Sahib, the sacred Sikh text, in their house. This requires some space, since the Guru Granth Sahib is normally kept in a separate room, to be opened (*prakash*) in the morning and put to rest (*sukhasan*) after sunset. The women in the family invariably assume this responsibility. Family members often undertake the complete reading of the text over a period lasting from six months to one year.

An unbroken reading of the Guru Granth Sahib (*akhand path*), which takes 48 hours, marks happy occasions such as moving into a new house, launching a new business, or the recovery from serious sickness of a family member. In major cities where the community has acquired a certain critical mass, a Sikh can call the local gurdwara, and arrange for the text of the Guru Granth Sahib to be brought to his or her house, along with professional readers (*pathis*) and those who lead devotional singing (*ragis*) when the reading is completed. In cities like Chicago and New York devotional items such as brocaded coverings (*rumalas*) for the Guru Granth Sahib are available in local markets.

Life cycle rites play an important part in the lives of Sikhs living in the United States. Soon after the birth of a child, the family visits the gurdwara, offers supplication (*ardas*) for his or her happy and healthy life, and takes "the command" (*hukam*) from the Guru Granth Sahib (the text is opened at random and the hymn that appears on the left-hand top corner is considered to be the divine reply to the supplication). The opening letter of the hymn is used as the first in the name of the newborn child. When the mother is able to visit the gurdwara, she brings the baby for a ceremonial submission to the Guru Granth Sahib (*matha tikaunha*).

Sikh marriage ceremonies are preceded by an unbroken reading of the Guru Granth Sahib. They takes place in the gurdwara itself or in a rented hall, with the bride and groom circumambulating the Guru Granth Sahib four times while a specific hymn of four stanzas is recited from its text. The usual day for marriages is Saturday, as it does not clash with the large Sunday services in the gurdwaras.

At the time of death, the body is taken to the mortuary and cremated. Following traditional Sikh religious practice, the ashes are invariably taken to the Punjab and dispersed in the river Sutlej—even in families who have resided in the United States for two generations. A reading of the Guru Granth Sahib is completed on the tenth day after the death, and relatives and friends gather on this occasion to pray for the peace of the departed soul.

The personal dimension of religious activity in the United States is often supplemented by a family pilgrimage to the Punjab, where parents and children visit the Darbar Sahib (popularly known as the Golden Temple) in Amritsar and other gurdwaras of historical importance. Recently, Sikhs in the United States have been visiting venerable gurdwaras in western Punjab, Pakistan. Every year a contingent goes to Nanakana Sahib, Pakistan, the birthplace of Guru Nanak (1469–1539), the founder of the Sikh tradition, to celebrate his birth anniversary.

Sikh habits of prayer have always been simple, and continue to be so in the United States—so simple that an average family does not gather for the daily prayers. The mother may well recite the *Japji* while preparing breakfast for the children, her husband doing so while having his morning shower. In some families, children also recite some daily prayers. The grandparents, if they live with the family, encourage children to pray with them on weekends. For the most part, the informality inherent in ways of praying makes it difficult for an outsider to observe daily Sikh devotional life.

The Communal Level

As if by way of contrast, however, Sikhs have a strong and vigorous tradition of community-based religious practice. The gurdwara serves as the major vessel for Sikh religious life at the congregational level. With only a single gurdwara in Stockton, California, up until 1947, there are now over 30 gurdwaras in California alone, and the number throughout the United States will soon reach 80. The rise of these new gurdwaras demonstrates the dramatic growth of the American Sikh community in recent years, both in numbers and in its economic well-being.

The strongly felt need for congregational worship among Sikhs in the United States has produced a fairly standard three-stage pattern that has been seen time and again as Sikhs have settled throughout the United States. As soon as Sikh families move into a given area, they begin to search for other Sikhs in the vicinity. Once a group is established, congregational devotion begins, with each family in turn offering its home for a gathering. If the family does not own the Guru Granth Sahib, the text is brought in for the occasion, and serves as the focal point of worship. A common meal (*langar*), an indivisible part of Sikh worship, is served at the end of the gathering. Sikhs do not have any specific taboos regarding food, but the meal served in this instance is always vegetarian and cooked in the simple Punjabi style.

As numbers of Sikhs in the immigrant communities increase, the group looks for a larger facility. Typically they find a church basement or use a large schoolroom where they can heat the food which is brought by a group of volunteer families. As time passes, the frequency of these meetings increases from monthly to fortnightly to weekly. As the congregation grows, so too do the donations, and once rental charges are paid, the remainder is deposited in the gurdwara account.

At this point, a single large donor or a group of donors commits to paying the downpayment on a large building considered suitable to become the permanent gurdwara. In some cases, representatives are sent to approach larger congregations for help. Once the building is bought, Sikh communal life begins in earnest. By this time the money in the gurdwara account, as augmented by regular donations, is sufficient to provide for maintenance and mortgage installments.

From the Sikh point of view the gurdwara is, first and foremost, the place of worship. The community gathers in the presence of the Guru Granth Sahib and participates in devotional activity that typically includes listening to the hymns recorded in the Guru Granth Sahib (*path*), singing them with musical accompaniment (*kirtan*), and attending to their exegesis (*katha*). Toward the closing of the devotional session, a supplication is made in which the Sikhs remember their history, seek divine blessings in dealing with their current problems, and reaffirm their vision of establishing a state in which Sikhs shall rule (Khalsa Raj). The service ends with a hymn read from the Guru Granth Sahib, which is interpreted to be the divine reply to the congregation's supplication.

Sikhs call the gurdwara gathering a *"diwan,"* a Persian word meaning "court." Having paid respects to the Guru Granth Sahib and participated in ritual glorification of God, they then discuss day-to-day problems facing the community. Activities at the gurdwara thus become a fair indicator of concerns and tensions within the community, and we can acquire a meaningful impression of Sikh communal life in the United States in the last quarter of the century by studying one of the more important gurdwaras, the Richmond Hill Gurdwara in New York.

The Sikh community began to develop on the East Coast in the late 1960s with a major center in the New York City's borough of Queens, where so many of the recent immigrants live. After performing communal worship in family houses and at the Saint Michael School in Flushing, the small community of Sikhs living there bought an old church building in 1972 for $65,000. The building was renovated, and then became the Richmond Hill Gurdwara—the first gurdwara on the East Coast.

The *diwan* was held on Sundays and local Sikhs conducted the services. The community soon felt the need for a full-time *granthi* (literally, "keeper of the book," but in practice, one who leads the devotional activity), and in 1976, one was brought from Southall, London. The service and the activities of the gurdwara expanded further. In the 1970s the local population was still small and the calendar of religious activities at the gurdwara was comprised primarily of celebrations of Vaisakhi (the festival associated with the institution of the Khalsa), the birth anniversaries of Guru Nanak and Guru Gobind Singh (1666–1708), and the days of martyrdom of Guru Arjan (1563–1606) and Guru Tegh Bahadur (1621–1675). These occasions brought together a large number of Sikh families from all over the East Coast, creating a semblance of vibrant communal life.

The steady expansion of the local New York community over the past 20 years has caused formal religious programs to expand. Similarly, from conducting one service on Sundays, the Richmond Hill Gurdwara now offers three services daily all though the week. There are currently four full-time *granthis*, and the leading groups of Sikh devotional singers from the Punjab visit the gurdwara regularly. Saturday is kept for marriages, and there is hardly a week when some special ceremony is not held. The gurdwara includes a large community kitchen, where over 5,000 men, women, and children take their meals on festival days.

Political activity is one facet of life in the gurdwara, and because of its size and its location in New York City, the Richmond

Hill Gurdwara rapidly emerged as a key Sikh center within the United States. By the late 1970s, Sikh politicians from the Punjab considered it an honor to be invited to Richmond Hill. The visitors included Gurcharan Singh Tohra, the president of the Shiromani Gurdwara Prabandhak Committee (SGPC), the premier Sikh organization based in Amritsar and responsible for managing the historical gurdwaras in the Punjab, and Hukam Singh, former speaker of the Indian Parliament. By 1983, the gurdwara had attained such prominence that Indira Gandhi, the Indian prime minister, took the time to go there while visiting the United States.

In the following year, however, in dealing with the Punjab problems, Mrs. Gandhi ordered government troops to attack the Darbar Sahib, and this left a significant impact on the activities of the Richmond Hill Gurdwara. Those people responsible for inviting Mrs. Gandhi to visit the gurdwara were forced out of the administration. (This group built a new gurdwara in Plainview, Long Island.) Jagjit Singh Mangat, a farmer-turned-businessman, emerged as the new leader, and under his direction, the gurdwara became the main center of support in the United States for the movement to establish Khalistan as an independent Sikh state in South Asia. Richmond Hill served as a place where Sikh leadership from England and North America could easily meet and approach forums like the United Nations.

By the early 1990s, the numbers of young rural Sikhs who had fled from the Punjab had increased substantially in New York. Perceiving themselves as victims of the Indian government, they were not satisfied with the level of Mangat's support for the cause of Khalistan. As the dream of Khalistan faded in the Punjab, these young men in their frustration forced Mangat and his supporters out of the gurdwara administration.

Mangat's departure created a void in the gurdwara leadership in which different groups among the recent arrivals, each with competing programs and none with administrative experience, brought effective political activity to a virtual halt. In the mid-1990s the congregation fragmented into many groups, but opinions tend to polarize at two extremes. Sikhs from urban backgrounds in the Punjab tend to stress the importance of devotional activity, while those from rural backgrounds are interested in the political agenda as well. In the absence of strong leadership, these tensions erupted in violence (*New York Times*, 23 July and 7 August 1994), and that, in turn, has led to a protracted litigation over the control of the gurdwara administration and its resources (*New York Times*, 20 October 1996).

For all its difficulties—and because of them, as well—the Rich-mond Hill Gurdwara symbolizes Sikh life in the United States. In political terms, as we have seen, it is a microcosm of Sikh life in the Punjab, except that as many have noted, sentiments for the creation of Khalistan seem to be even more strongly felt in the diaspora of Sikh life than at its center. As for the rhythms of ritual life in Richmond Hill, they too directly reflect the Punjab. Every care has been taken to replicate Sikh religious life as practiced in the Punjab, down to the smallest detail. If anything, the ambiance is more "Punjabi" than in the Punjab itself. Once inside the build-ing everything is essentially Punjabi in its flavor, and there is precious little to indicate that it is located in New York. Still, 25 years after the purchase of the erstwhile church, the stain-glass windows connect Punjabi-Sikh religious life with the world out-side—a world that is not entirely alien to the Sikhs in terms of its theology, but is a different world all the same. How can one recon-cile the multicolored light enlivening these beautiful windows with the integrity of Sikh identity? This is the great challenge hidden behind the rivalries that currently afflict the gurdwara in Rich-mond Hill.

The Challenges

Issues that confront the Sikhs living in the United States can be divided into three broad categories. The first set pertains to the community's relationship with the Punjab, the second concerns its relationship with mainstream American society, and the third deals solely with the internal dynamics of the Sikh community and its future aspirations.

Relationship with the Punjab

There are three aspects to this relationship—religious, political, and ethnic. The first involves the issue of religious authority and on this point the American Sikh community is split. A current expression of the struggle, which is unfolding itself in the Fairfax Gurdwara, is a case before the Virginia Courts (*The Sikh Founda-tion of Virginia v. Narinder Singh,* et al., 1993). The orthodox view represented by Narinder Singh and frequently expressed elsewhere, is that authority for all aspects of Sikh communal life lies in the SGPC, and consequently the SGPC should decide the constitutional set-up of all gurdwaras in the United States as well. In this view the Sikh community overseas is a satellite of the parent community in the Punjab. Gurdwaras in the United States therefore belong to a global hierarchy which has the Akal Takhat ("Throne of the Timeless") at its head. The Akal Takhat situated in the Darbar Sahib complex is traditionally recognized as the seat of Sikh temporal authority and the SGPC's formal decisions pertaining to Sikh religious life are announced from there. On the other side, however, are those such as the administrators of the Fairfax Gurdwara, who perceive themselves as an autonomous congregation. These Sikhs do recognize the authority of the SGPC, symbolic or real. But instead of taking orders from the SGPC, they seek to contribute to decision making at Amritsar and thereby hasten the process by which Sikhism is transferred from a religion based essentially in the Punjab to a one with truly worldwide following.

A second aspect of relations between American Sikhs and the Punjab is political. Overwhelmingly comprised of first-generation immigrants, adult Sikhs in the United States still think of the Punjab as their homeland. Their efforts in the 1980s to support the "Sikh struggle for Khalistan," as many of them put it, gave them a great sense of personal satisfaction. With the gradual collapse of that movement and the takeover in early 1997 of Punjab's state administration by the Shiromani Akali Dal, the Sikh political party, led by Parkash Singh Badal, a painful truth became evident: It is Sikhs living in the Punjab who are the primary arbiters of their own destiny. The Sikh community in the United States can support the political aspirations of the Sikhs in the Punjab, but it cannot define them. The realization is slowly dawning on many of these immigrants that the Punjab, with its historic gurdwaras, can serve only as the sacred land of diasporic Sikhs, and not as an instrument of their political will.

Third is the issue of Punjabi ethnicity. Sikhs in the United States continue to cling to the Punjabi elements of their identity, but it is not clear that this will always be the case, at least in the same way. I will address the problems generated by this type of allegiance to the Punjab in the section on internal matters below.

Sikhs and American Culture

Sikhs in the United States are deeply aware that they live in a country whose culture they did not create; and conflict between the wearing of Sikhs symbols and the law of the land reminds them

constantly of this reality. In the early 1910s, there was the case of
a Sikh named Veer Singh, who was denied citizenship because he
"refused to doff his turban while being sworn in" (La Brack 1988,
151). Despite their long hair and turbans, Sikhs were permitted to
join the U.S. army and fight in the First World War, but more
recently they have been barred from joining the army on those
grounds (Jensen 1988, 256). Similarly, Sikhs have suffered discrimination and have even been dismissed from their jobs for refusing to remove their turbans and wear the caps or hard hats assigned
to postal or construction workers (*Kalsi v. MTA*, 1995). Khalsa
children are currently not permitted to carry their ritual swords in
some school districts in California, and a legal battle is being fought
to gain permission for them to do so (*Cheema v. Thompson*, 1993).

Sikhs have been a minority all through their history and have
always faced these problems. Sometimes Sikhs have adapted to the
needs of the employer; in other cases they have been quite aggres-
sive in seeking legal redress for their grievances. The Sikh leadership is extremely sensitive to the need to help the American public
understand Sikh beliefs and its community's history.

Today, the Sikh community is in the process of making a place
in American society and it has adopted various means to accomplish this goal. Sikh Day parades were instituted in major cities; in
New York, the Vaisakhi parade was inaugurated in 1988 (*New York
Times*, 24 April 1988). Since then, it has become an annual event,
and more than 20,000 Sikhs from all over the East Coast gather in
downtown Manhattan. Floats representing facets of the Sikh tradition embellish the parade, and with great pride Sikhs explain to
the American passers-by the significance of *langar* in their belief
system, while inviting them to come and share food.

Several gurdwaras work on local levels to cooperate with other
religious organizations interested in interfaith activities. The effort
is to explain to these forums that the Sikhs constitute a separate
tradition. For instance, the gurdwara at Palatine, Illinois, played
an enthusiastic part in the World Parliament of Religions convened
at Chicago in 1993. The gurdwara at Rockville, Maryland, closely
works with forums involved in interfaith dialogue, providing Sikh
representation in their activities. The community is also working in
conjunction with other ethnic groups to address mutual social concerns such as discrimination, racially motivated violence, and hate
crimes.

One of the most ambitious methods the community has undertaken to establish its presence in the United States is to inaugurate the teaching of Sikhism and Punjabi language in American

universities. With the support of the Sikh Foundation, Palo Alto, the University of California at Berkeley initiated the process in 1977. W. H. McLeod, the leading Western historian of Sikhism, taught a course on the subject; in the same year, a major conference on Sikh Studies was organized, resulting in an important volume of essays (Juergensmeyer and Barrier 1979).

In the late 1980s community-sponsored programs in Sikh Studies were initiated at Columbia University and the University of Michigan. The University of California, Berkeley, began a program in Punjabi in 1992. Conferences on Sikh-related issues have also been held at Columbia University and at the University of Michigan, spurring new studies as a result (Barrier and Dusenbery 1989; Hawley and Mann 1993; and Singh and Barrier 1996). Beginning in 1997, Columbia University has a six-week summer program in Punjabi Language and Culture held in Chandigarh, which is intended to encourage scholars interested in Punjab Studies.

It was envisaged that these university-based programs would help to disseminate information about Sikhism in the United States among American students, and through them, to society at large. It has also been hoped that they would establish a tradition of Sikh scholarship outside the Punjab. In recent years, Columbia has emerged as a center for public information about Sikh issues.

This method of reaching the American public had not gone entirely smoothly. Debates have been waged about the university programs, and questions have been raised about the value of examining the Sikh belief system through the disciplines of anthropology, history, and textual studies. These tensions culminated in a controversy around Pashaura Singh's doctoral work completed at the University of Toronto (Giani 1994). He was pressured to appear before the Akal Takhat to explain his research results, and was forced to perform religious penance (*Indian Express*, 28 June 1994).

But for this extremely unfortunate detour, the production of an indigenous tradition of scholarship in North America is moving forward slowly but surely (Hawley and Mann 1993, 114). American scholars like Barrier, Helweg, Jensen, Juergensmeyer, La Brack, and Leonard, have made significant contributions, and a tradition of scholarship by Sikhs in the United States is also evolving. Parminder Bhachu of Clark University and Jane Singh of the University of California, Berkeley, have made important contributions in Sikh diaspora studies; Nikki Singh of Colby College has pursued a feminist interpretation of Sikh literature; and the research of Pashaura Singh and myself will produce a detailed history of Sikh scripture.

The University of Wisconsin-Milwaukee and the University of California at Santa Barbara have created new positions in Sikh and Punjab Studies with funding largely from their own resources. More recently, the department of Ethnic Studies at Berkeley has begun to take interest in issues pertaining to the Sikh Diaspora. The community's agenda of disseminating information about Sikhism at the university level seems to begin to bring important results.

Internal Matters

The large-scale move away from the Punjab has created a situation in which Sikhs must draw clearer lines between the religious and cultural elements of their identity. In my view, this process will bear significantly not only on the future of the Sikh community in the United States, but on the tradition in general. I present three instances of such issues, in increasing order of complexity.

In the vision of Guru Nanak, the founder of the Sikh tradition, women enjoy complete equality with men. The translation of Sikh doctrine into practice can be seen in the active role women play in family worship as well as in devotional practices in the gurdwara. In sacred activity both at home and in the gurdwara, gender distinctions do not play a significant role.

Nevertheless it would be inaccurate to say that this egalitarianism has filtered down to gender parity in all walks of Sikh life. Women may participate in gurdwara activities such as reciting scriptures, but in the management of the institutions their voices are not always heard. Sikh men leave relatively little space for women in gurdwara administration. In 1989, a group of women sought a place among the five leaders (*panj piaras*) at the head of the Vaisakhi parade in New York City; it was denied. More recently, however, women have been allocated prime spots in such parades. Some young women have asked to walk alongside the groom instead of following him while circumambulating the Guru Granth Sahib during the marriage ceremony. The ripple effect has reached Amritsar. In 1996, American Sikh women were allowed to participate in the ritual washing of the floor of the Darbar Sahib, Amritsar. This was traditionally a male privilege.

In the day-to-day activity of a Sikh family, however, Punjabi culture continues to assert itself in the United States. Gender roles continue to be defined by the patriarchal social structure prevalent in the Punjab. Even when a woman works full-time outside the house, she typically remains responsible for cooking and taking care of the children, roles that are reserved for women in Punjabi society. This generates stress in many families, and the tensions sometimes culminate in violence. Unfortunately, women who experience such problems often suffer alone and will not consider divorce, out of fear of hurting the family reputation, a cherished Punjabi cultural value. Young Sikh women educated in the United States, however, are becoming increasingly sensitive to these issues, and have begun to seek the unequivocal application of the principle of gender equality in both the sacred and mundane domains of Sikh life.

A second set of issues relates broadly to Sikh youth growing up in the United States. Beginning at the personal and family level, Sikh parents take great interest in their children's education, and try to help them in all possible ways. Yet, from the young people's point of view, this crucial support is often experienced as carrying with it a high level of expectations, and they find this highly stressful. During the adolescent years, these children are torn between gratitude for what their parents do for them and the need to make space for their evaluations of who they are and are capable of becoming.

In another area of conflict—education—cultural and religious issues are more closely intertwined than in matters of gender and generational negotiations. The concern of parents and the Sikh leadership at large is to transmit the Sikh heritage to Sikh children growing up in the United States. This agenda involves the teaching of Sikh doctrine and history, and crucially, the teaching of Punjabi in Gurmukhi script. In almost all gurdwaras, devoted volunteers gather children on Sunday mornings to instruct them in Punjabi and Sikh history, and summer camps have been established to accomplish the same ends.

The results, however, are not impressive. A large number of Sikh children growing up in the United States have extremely rudimentary knowledge of the Sikh belief system, and they do not speak or read Punjabi with any degree of confidence. Their lack of command of Punjabi understandably makes them uninterested in the family religious life as well as in what goes on in the gurdwara: they simply cannot understand. And this, in turn, results in a palpable fear among the Sikh leadership that if the children lack a clear understanding of Sikh ways of life they will eventually leave the community. The only proposal that I hear in the gurdwaras to solve this dilemma is that more efforts should be directed in the teaching of Punjabi, but little improvement seems to have been made.

For centuries, Sikhs have manifested an intense pride in the fact that their literature is written in Punjabi and in Gurmukhi script: these vessels of communications are close to the core of their sense of identity. Hence historically there has been little wavering from a doctrinal insistence on the importance of understanding the sacred Sikh writings in their own terms. These are not verses to be merely chanted, but understood; their contents matter in the daily lives of all Sikhs. With ever-increasing numbers of Sikhs born outside the Punjab, however, the traditional Sikh insistence that religion needs to happen in the vernacular—the common language and the common life—may have radically new implications. The diaspora experience has created a situation in which Sikhs may need to accept the Guru Granth Sahib in Roman transliteration or even in English translation, in place of or in addition to the original version. This will not be without precedence. In the early part of the twentieth century, editions of the Guru Granth Sahib in the Devanagari and Indo-Persian scripts were created for those who could not read Gurmukhi. Therefore it will be very interesting to see what reception awaits a new edition of the Guru Granth Sahib in which the original text, a Roman transliteration, and an English translation, appear side by side in three columns (Chahil 1995).

Conclusion

The movement of Sikhs to countries like the United States has opened doors to a new set of opportunities and challenges. Until now, Sikhs in the United States have been busy creating a religious life that is essentially a replica of what they knew in the Punjab. If any changes were made, they were largely cosmetic. This situation, in my view, cannot continue much longer. With domestic political pressures to control the number of new immigrants, the steady supply of Sikhs fresh from the Punjab will decrease. Children of immigrants reared in the United States will normally move into roles of leadership, and will make changes suited to their own needs.

The next few decades will be crucial in the history of the Sikh community. Challenging decisions will have to be made about issues of religious authority, sacred land, sacred language, and social practice. These decisions will have a lasting impact on the future shape of Sikhism, not only in places like the United States but also, owing to processes of rapid globalization and the sharing of Sikh leadership internationally, in the Punjab itself.

────────────── NOTE ──────────────

Acknowledgment: I am grateful to John S. Hawley and Jane Singh for their comments on earlier drafts of this chapter.

────────────── BIBLIOGRAPHY ──────────────

Barrier, N. G., and Dusenbery, V. A. (eds.) (1989). *The Sikh Diaspora.* Columbia, Missouri: South Asia Books.

Bhachu, P. (1985). *Twice Migrants: East African Sikh Settlers in Britain.* New York: Tavistock Publications.

Chahil, P. S. (1995). *Sri Guru Granth Sahib.* New Delhi: Crescent Printing.

Eck, D. L. (1997). *On Common Ground.* New York: Columbia University Press. CD-ROM.

Giani, B. S. (1994). *Planned Attack on Aad Sri Guru Granth Sahib.* Chandigarh: International Center of Sikh Studies.

Gibson, M. A. (1988). *Accommodation without Assimilation.* Ithaca: Cornell University Press.

Grewal, J. S. (1990). *The Sikhs of the Punjab.* New York: Cambridge University Press.

Hawley, J. S., and Mann, G. S. (eds.) (1993). *Studying the Sikhs: Issues for North America.* Albany: State University of New York Press.

Helweg, A. W., and Helweg, U. M. (1990). *An Immigrant Success Story.* Philadelphia: University of Pennsylvania Press.

Jensen, J. M. (1988). *Passage from India: Asian Indian Immigrants in North America.* New Haven: Yale University Press.

Juergensmeyer, M., and Barrier, N. G. (eds.) (1979). *Sikh Studies.* Berkeley: Berkeley Religious Studies Series.

Khalsa, S. K. (1995). *The History of the Sikh Dharma of the Western Hemisphere.* Espanola, NM: Sikh Dharma Publications.

La Brack, B. (1988). *The Sikhs of Northern California, 1904–1975.* New York: AMS Press.

Leonard, K. I. (1992). *Making Ethnic Choices.* Philadelphia: Temple University Press.

McLeod, W. H. (1989). *The Sikhs: History, Religion, and Society.* New York: Columbia University Press.

────── (1976). *The Evolution of the Sikh Community.* Oxford: Clarendon Press.

O'Connell, J. T., et al. (eds.) (1988). *Sikh History and Religion in the Twentieth Century.* Toronto: Centre for South Asian Studies.

Saund, D. S. (1960). *The Congressman from India*. New York: E. P. Dutton and Company.

Sikh Rahit Maryada. (1950). Amritsar: Shiromani Gurdwara Prabandhak Committee.

Singh, J., et al. (1988). *South Asians in North America*. Berkeley: Center for South and Southeast Asian Studies.

Singh, N-G. K. (1993). *The Feminine Principle in the Sikh Vision of the Transcendent*. New York: Cambridge University Press.

Singh, P., and Barrier, N. G. (eds.) (1996). *The Transmission of Sikh Heritage in the Diaspora*. New Delhi: Manohar.

Williams, R. B. (1988). *Religions of Immigrants from India and Pakistan*. New York: Cambridge University Press.

Tatla, D. S. (1991). *Sikhs in America: An Annotated Bibliography*. New York: Greenwood Press.

Conclusion

Trajectories for Future Studies

Raymond Brady Williams

There can be no conclusion to this work because South Asian religions are in the West to stay. The permanent presence and impact of South Asian immigrants and their religions are the most important conclusions of these studies, which impel us into a dynamic future. What started early in this century with migration to the West, small and unnoticed as the source of the Ganges, has resulted in strong communities of South Asian immigrants and well-established religious groups with temples, mosques, gurdwaras, prayer halls, churches, and other institutions as part of new religious landscapes. Studies in this book are timely for two reasons: (1) internally the immigrant communities and their religious institutions have reached a maturity in which they are in the process of passing on their traditions and their religious commitments to their children and grandchildren and (2) externally their religions have become visible to the public as a civic presence even to the point of appearing as alternatives to Judaism, Christianity, and secularism.

The authors of this book analyze the growth, triumphs, perils, and troubles immigrants experienced, and they provide nuanced family portraits of the religious groups in the West. The three country introductions reveal distinct demographies created by governmental immigration policies that set the stage for developments of religions. Policies of governments and their schools regarding religion, especially the official policy of multiculturalism in Canada, lead to variations such as those illustrated in the chapters on the Sikhs by Ballard, O'Connell, and Mann. The importance of media representations in establishing the public context for South Asian religions is shown in the work of Coney on New Religions and Haddad on Islam. Great diversity exists within the immigrant groups and among the religions. One need not accept Ballard's proposition regarding religion to acknowledge that South Asians are creating new forms of religions in the West—indeed different forms of Hinduism (Eck) and diverse forms of Islam (Haddad). Knott and McDonough reflect on the "protestantization" of South Asian religions in the West, and Eck refers to the phenomenon of a "simplified articulation of Hinduism." A striking aspect of South Asian religions in the West is the importance of the individual, which is demonstrated by the role of the individual laypersons in establishing the ethos of religious groups (Hinnells) and by the leadership of gurus in the West (Coward and Eck). South Asian women are reshaping their roles in ethnic and religious groups, a pervasive experience that Williams illustrates with the Christian nurses, and that Coward, McDonough, Haddad, and O'Connell record within other South Asian groups. Increasingly, institutions of higher education are serving the South Asian communities by training religious leadership (Lewis and Williams), by establishing centers for South Asian Studies (Mann, Coward, O'Connell), and by instructing young people of the second generation (Eck). The task in this conclusion is neither to repeat the major points from the past nor to predict the future, but to inaugurate the next group of studies needed to attend to the importance of both the new communities created by immigration from South Asia and the religions they situate in the West.

Future studies will build on the materials in chapters of this book, but scholars in the future will chart new trajectories, some not yet clearly perceived. The following trajectories already call for attention and suggest some of the rich possibilities: (1) the transnational development of the religions; (2) distinct religious groups and institutions; (3) future migration and its effects on religious groups; (4) racial, ethnic, and sectarian identities; (5) dynamics of interreligious contacts; and (6) new ways of study for new forms of religions.

Transnational Developments of the Religions

South Asian families and religious groups are experiencing a new form of transnationalism that changes the character of relationships between religious groups in several countries. Although religions have for centuries migrated, and adherents to religions have maintained relationships across considerable distances, both geographical and social—as is demonstrated in the first century letters of the Apostle Paul that connect Christians around the Mediterranean Sea–contemporary mobility and rapidity of communication create a new transnational experience. These studies situate several religious groups in the West in a comparative manner, leading to a next step to analyze the intricate networks of communication and relationship that characterize modern, transnational "world religions."

The national infrastructures and the juxtaposition of those in three countries that are the foci of the studies in this work are aspects of developing transnational infrastructures that are influencing the nature of these religions everywhere, just as multinational corporations influence how business is conducted everywhere, even for those not directly affiliated with multinational entities. The result is a challenge for scholars study to South Asian religions in the countries of the West, not as discrete national entities, but primarily as social groups without borders that maintain primary social contacts and affiliations that are transnational. The West is working its magic on South Asian religions—just as the new transnational networks enable the West to be involved in the transformation of culture and religion in South Asia—but South Asian religions are working their magic on the West as well.

Future studies will surely attend to complex religious networks and their effects in both South Asia and Western countries. Three examples illustrate the significance of these networks:

1. Leadership transfer is already a common experience in these religious groups. Leadership is imported from South Asia to serve the new religious groups, both as permanent employees of temples, churches, and other religious institutions, and as

temporary visitors on tour in the West throughout the summer months. Increasingly, people are returning to South Asia for training or to become religious specialists there. Swaminarayan Hinduism attracts young men from the United Kingdom and North America into the corps of sadhus. South Asian Christian "missionaries" travel in both directions. Leadership for many South Asian religions is becoming transnational in ways not possible earlier. Adjustments in administration of immigration laws and regulations sometimes inadvertently increase or decrease the flow of religious specialists or select particular types of specialists.

2. Transfer of money by migrants ranks second behind oil as the largest transnational movement of capital. Such transfer is a major aspect of the new transnational experience of religions, establishing relationships and strengthening institutional structures and, at the same time, profoundly affecting the shape of religious groups both in South Asia and the West. In previous generations the capital moved from strong Western churches to impoverished Eastern churches and religious institutions. Now capital moves from immigrants' homes and religious institutions to families and religious institutions in South Asia. However, these financial networks are very complex, somewhat hidden from public view, and, as a result, understudied.

3. Symbols also take flight as they are transformed from their original contexts and become recognized aspects of communication across regional and social boundaries. The almost universal accessibility of the Christian cross as a symbol is a clear example from earlier periods of migration, but the number and complexity of religious symbols that create the syntax of discourse about religions are becoming more numerous as the result of the development of new world religions—or, as one might better say, by the new transnational experience of religions. The reverse impact of these transnational networks on the experience of religions in South Asia is as important as the effects of South Asian religions in the West.

Distinct Religious Groups and Institutions

Hinduism is a family of religious traditions, each with its own scriptures, leaders, symbols, and social location, which causes some scholars to question if Hinduism is one thing or many. In truth, no one is a Hindu in general but only within specific traditions. Postcolonial scholars argue that Hinduism as a unifying concept is a Western creation dating from the time of British domination of India. Similar social construction is to some degree true of other religions as well, such as Christianity, Islam, Sikhism. Studies of Hinduism, Islam, and Sikhism in this work focus primarily on what is common to those within the various traditions and often results in universalizing Hinduism or Islam, as John Hinnells mentions in the introduction. In each Western country the South Asian community has grown sufficiently large and mature to manifest many forms of each religion. Many distinct groups within each religion have now grown to sufficient size and level of activity to warrant separate studies. Moreover, the networks of communication and influence described in the previous section trace the lines marked between outposts of these sectarian groups in several countries. They occupy separate social and cultural niches and link specific groups across great distances. Swaminarayan Hindus, Nizari Ismaili Muslims, and Syro-Malabar rite Catholics, for example, have vibrant and growing institutions in each of the three countries of this study and many others as well. Their transnational networks are strong and active, and they provide the primary loci for the formation and preservation of personal and group identity for many South Asians in the West. Analyses of these distinct religious traditions and comparisons of their modes of manifestation and transformation across all sorts of boundaries will provide information about the form and function of religions in the future.

Future Migration and Its Effects on Religious Groups

South Asian religions in the West are the product of twentieth-century migrations shaped by immigration laws in the United Kingdom and North America. Variations in size of the communities and their religious groups, their demographics of age, education, sex, and income, and their social locations in the three countries are determined to a large extent by administration of immigration laws. As the laws and their administration change, the communities and their religions undergo dramatic changes, often as unintended results of legislative or administrative revisions. Gates of immigration swing open and closed, moved by political winds. Gates are periodically opened for people from some countries, social classes, and ages, but closed to other specific groups. Immigrant groups are more attuned than the general population to the ways both minute and dramatic changes in laws and administrative regulations affect them. Hence, they become astute and active in influencing decisions in order to gain benefits for themselves, their families, and their compatriots. It makes an enormous difference to development of religious institutions whether they receive a constant stream of new adherents from South Asia or rely for survival of religious institutions only on natural growth, conversion, and the subsequent training of children and converts. Strong support for continued use of South Asian languages in religious and social gatherings is only the most obvious consequence of continuous arrival of new immigrants. Some families and religious groups make decisions about migration—between Western countries and from South Asia to the West—based on their perception of the receptivity of receiving countries, on their wager about which skills and professions are most likely to be valued in potential immigrants, and on their anticipation of future immigration possibilities. A task for scholars is to analyze how future variations in immigration regulations and the resulting migration of people affect religions in various countries and how the changing constellation of religions affects the cultural and religious context in and among countries.

Racial, Ethnic, and Sectarian Identities

In the introduction, John Hinnells indicates that some of the categories that are common in the media and in academic works are problematic. Studies of migrations in earlier periods established and codified both identities based on race, ethnicity, and sect allegiance and the categories and methods used in studying them. Immigrants have been both the subjects manipulating these categories and the objects of study and analysis.

Immigrants are active subjects as skilled manipulators of ethnic and sectarian aspects of personal and group identities. South Asians legitimately use these to their best advantage in establishing their social locations in a new environment and in mitigating negative responses, as immigrants have done throughout migration history. They adapt to markers of race, ethnicity, and sect in order to establish both boundaries and bridges and to maintain legitimate power in negotiations with other social and religious groups. Immigrants from South Asia early in the twentieth century claimed American citizenship as Caucasians, before the door was shut to them during the 1920s. A half century later, the new immigrants lobbied for inclusion of "Asian Indian" as an official designation in the 1980 U.S. census in order to qualify for special preferences as members of a minority. In other contexts, forms of allegiance and association related to regional linguistic divisions in India or other social distinctions prove useful in establishing social identities and boundaries (e.g., Gujarati, Sinhalese, Patel, Brahmin, or Hindu).

Scholars and governmental officials use the categories of race, ethnicity, and sect or analyze new immigrants and their organizations, thereby shaping the immigrants' experience and self-awareness into those categories. The new context of rapid mobility and transnational movement raises the possibility that these categories—as developed in the study of earlier immigrant groups and in a period prior to the new transnational situation—may no longer be adequate to the current experience. Nationality as a category may need some adjustment in a context where many individuals and families preserve a foothold in two or more countries and participate in social networks spanning boarders that enable them to live in two or more societies at the same time. Social and biological merging of cultures and peoples call into question the adequacy of racial and ethnic designations and the studies based on such designations, as recent debates about whether to use distinct racial categories for the 2000 census in the United States demonstrate. The new immigrants certainly change academic study of religions in the West by introducing religions and traditions not present before, but they also change the structures and categories of their research and analyses. South Asian communities and their religions pass through frames of a moving picture of time, but the picture changes the frame of projection as well. A future trajectory of research must include some revision of the categories and perhaps the creation of new categories and methods for study that will be more adequate for the new transnational context.

Dynamics of Interreligious Contacts

South Asian religions now occupy significant social locations alongside the religions that have long histories in Western countries, where Christianity, Judaism, and Deism had reached different levels of accommodation. The new landscape of religions, with its vivid, sometimes clashing colors, new sounds, and even new odors, requires a new series of negotiations among religions. The religious accommodation summarized as "Judeo-Christian" is being reshaped and expanded to include other religions and also different forms of Christianity. Earlier negotiations in Western countries between Protestants and Catholics, between Jews and Christians, and between religious people and secularists involved confrontations, hard negotiations, and unfortunate conflict, repression, and turmoil. Nevertheless, they eventually led to a general acceptance of modes of behavior that permitted and sustained civic life. That both religious freedom and civic order be maintained in the future is greatly to be wished and praised, but that will require great wisdom and skill by both religious and political leaders.

New immigrants, including South Asians, are often reticent to seek converts to their religions when they first arrive, both because they need to preserve boundaries until they are socially secure and because attempts at conversion, especially of young people from the rest of society, inevitably brings censure and opposition. Nevertheless, when new religious groups grow and become well-established, they begin to extend their reach into the rest of the population either through marriage or conversion. Islam now enters western countries in increasing strength as a primary alternative to Christianity in actively seeking converts. An example of the new negotiations necessary to the changed religious scene in the United States results from the conversion of many African Americans to Islam. In the first instance, the negotiation involves the relation of the Black church to the masjids and mosques associated with Louis Farrakan and Wallace Muhammed, but it also involves the relation of Black America to Islam around the world. That, in turn, affects the relation of African Americans and Jews in the United States and other countries in numerous ways. These relations are only a subset of more complex negotiations that establish the relationships and ground rules for intercourse among the religious and social groups.

Governments establish the grids along which these negotiations take place. Introductory sections of this book detail some of the differences between the United Kingdom, Canada, and the United States regarding the role of the government in encouraging religious groups and in supporting collaboration among them. The separation of church and state in the United States and the concomitant religious freedom from governmental intrusions into religious matters establishes a mode of negotiation between such groups different from that in either the United Kingdom or Canada. In every country, however, negotiations between religious groups take place officially as permitted by governments and at unofficial levels beyond the reach of governmental authority.

Interreligious organizations and commissions emerged out of the experience of earlier immigrants, primarily during the midcentury period of lull of migration to Western countries. They sustained the midcentury Judeo-Christian ethos in Western countries. More recently such organizations have been less effective in providing the contexts and forums for negotiations with the religions of more recent immigrants. Now other institutions seem to serve as mediating loci for interreligious dialogue and negotiation: schools, hospitals, city councils, social work agencies. Decisions on public policy issues—for example, regarding the status of religious schools—will influence the development of individual religious groups and the outcome of their interactions. "In God We Trust" and "One Nation Under God" are mottoes that emerged from the intense interactions between the religions of earlier immigrants in the Unites States. Mottoes, phrases, commitments that serve similar functions for uniting diverse populations are present in other Western countries. One trajectory for future study is analysis of the developing relations between old and new religious groups in Western countries to determine how such relationships evolve between diverse religious groups and how they shape the common life.

New Ways of Study for New Forms of Religions

New forms of religion develop on the margins created by migration. These new forms include modifications and reinterpretations of religious traditions that are responses to the new challenges and opportunities of the new homes of immigrants. The chapters on new religions analyze some new religions that have already developed in the West. Other forms include entirely new religious forms that develop at the point of contact between religions that previously were isolated from one another. These developments extend across the spectrum from the small incremental changes that a religion undergoes in a new cultural context to the development of new religions. The gestation and emergence of these new forms of religion into the new millennium constitutes an essential and challenging trajectory for the study of religion in the twenty-first century.

These trajectories of future study open the doors to new styles of interdisciplinary study because no single subdiscipline or mode of study is able to encompass all the new issues and topics generated by the new transnational character of migration and new reality of "world religions." Authors of this work are specialists in the religions of South Asia, but their work is of great significance to specialists in religion in the West, and what they have written will be judged by specialists in many disciplines and subject areas because of overlapping fields and the necessity of several angles of disciplinary vision. No longer can one adequately study any religion in one country or in isolation from the complex forces that propel the new migration and the transnational forms of religion.

Scholars who developed postcolonial studies argue that earlier studies of religions were shaped by the power relations between dominant and oppressed societies, with the result that scholars from colonial powers defined (and, they contend, often distorted) the religions of South Asia. They contend that scholars themselves propped up the intellectual supports for colonial domination. Studies of religion based on the methods of anthropology, sociology, history, and philosophy face harsh criticism. As the "jewel in the crown" of a major colonial power, South Asia was the object of much research that is attacked from a postcolonial perspective. Numerous and swift migrations at midcentury were an aspect of the postcolonial situation. However, the new transnational context for both the migration of religion and academic study of these religions opens the possibility for new modes of study beyond postcolonialism. The most accurate location for new studies of religions, including South Asian ones, is neither in colonial countries alone nor in previously colonized countries, but in the transnational realities experienced by participants in these religions across national boundaries. Moving beyond postcolonial categories does not mean that issues of power and dominance are absent. Issues arising from the power transnational elites exert to define religions and religious groups both from within as adherents and from without as researchers continue to be present. New trajectories for study must include attention to such dynamics, but they are now much more complex than colonial relations suggest.

This book marks a significant point in both the development of South Asian religions in the West and in scholarly research on immigrants and their religions. New scholarship will follow various trajectories in documenting and analyzing the future of South Asian religions in many locations worldwide. It is a challenging and exciting prospect, absolutely essential to understanding the human condition in the new century and, perhaps, contributing to greater understanding among peoples who are now close neighbors in ways not previously possible.

Contributors

Roger Ballard currently holds the post of Lecturer in Comparative Religion at the University of Manchester. Having taken his doctorate at the University of Delhi in 1969, he went on to explore developments within the Sikh community in Britain, during the course of which he also took the opportunity to make several ethnographic expeditions to the settlers' villages of origin in Punjab. In addition to his specific interest in the Sikhs, he also published many papers exploring the implications of the increasing salience of ethnic pluralism in contemporary Britain.

Judith Coney is Lecturer in the Study of Religions at the School of Oriental and African Studies in London, UK. She received her first degree from Lancaster University and her Ph.D. from the London School of Economics. Her specialist field is new religious movements (NRMs), with particular reference to South Asia. As well as writing articles on NRMs, she co-authored *The Way of the Heart: The Rajneesh Movement* (1986) and is engaged presently on a book about Sahaja Yoga, another South Asian movement. She is the editor of the Emerging Religions and Society Series published by Curzon Press, UK.

Harold Coward is Professor of History and Director of the Centre for Studies in Religion and Society at the University of Victoria, BC, and Fellow of the Royal Society of Canada. His main fields are Hinduism, Hindu-Christian relations, comparative religion, psychology of religion, and environmental ethics. He has directed

289

numerous research projects and published widely. His publications include *Jung and Eastern Thought* (1985), *Derrida and Eastern Philosophy* (1990, 1991), *Population, Consumption, and the Environment: Religious and Secular Responses* (1995). He is also the editor of the *Hindu-Christian Studies Bulletin*.

Diana L. Eck is Professor of Comparative Religion and Indian Studies at Harvard University. She received her B.A. from Smith College (1967) and her Ph.D. from Harvard University (1976). She is the author of *Darsan: Seeing the Divine Image in India* (1981), *Banaras, City of Light* (1983), and *Encountering God: A Spiritual Journey from Bozeman to Banaras* (1993). With Devaki Jain she edited *Speaking of Faith: Global Perspectives on Women, Religion, and Social Change* (1985) and with Francoise Mallison she edited *Devotion Divine: Bhakti Traditions from the Regions of India* (1991). Since 1991 she has been Director of the Pluralism Project, a student research project documenting the changing religious landscape of the United States, with special attention to Asian immigrant religious traditions. She is editor of the Pluralism Project CD-ROM, *On Common Ground: World Religions in America* (1997).

Yvonne Yazbeck Haddad is professor of History of Islam and Christian-Muslim Relations at Georgetown University. She is the former president of the Middle East Studies Association. Her published works include: *Contemporary Islam and Challenge of History, Muslims of America, Muslim Communities in North America, Islamic Values in North America, Women Religion and Social Change, The Contemporary Islamic Revival* and *Oxford Encyclopedia of the Modern Islamic World.*

John R. Hinnells is Professor of Comparative Religion in the University of London and founding head of the Department for the Study of Religion at the School of Oriental and African Studies. He is also Visiting Professor at the University of Derby. After studying at Kings College and the School of Oriental and African Studies, London, he taught religious studies at the Universities of Newcastle Upon Tyne and Manchester where he became professor in 1983 and later dean of faculty. His main area of research is Zoroastrianism, originally specializing on the ancient sources (*Persian Mythology* London: Newnes, 1985) and Mithraism (organizing international conferences, all published, in Manchester, Tehran, and Rome). In the 1980s he turned to studies of the Parsis in India and their global dispersion. In the course of this research he has made numerous visits to the Indian subcontinent, and also to Parsi communities on five other continents. He has published a number of books and articles, notably *Zoroastrians in Britain,* Oxford: Clarendon

Press, 1996. He is also committed to the dissemination of scholarly work for the general public and has edited several books for Penguin (*Who's Who of Religions,* 1996; *A New Dictionary of Religions,* 1997; *A New Handbook of Living Religions,* 1997). He advises Penguin Books on religious studies generally and Penguin (nonwestern) Classics.

Kim Knott is a Senior Lecturer in the Department of Theology and Religious Studies at the University of Leeds, England, where she also directs the Community Religions Project, a center for research and teaching that promotes the study of religious communities in Britain and publishes monographs and research papers. She works primarily on the religions of South Asian communities in diaspora, and religion and gender. She is the author of *Hinduism in Leeds* (1986) and *My Sweet Lord: The Hare Krishna Movement* (1986) and articles on neo-Hinduism and religions in Britain. Her current research is on women and destiny, and she is writing a short book for students on issues in the study of Hinduism. She is president of the British Association for the Study of Religions.

Gurinder Singh Mann is Associate Professor of Sikh Studies and South Asian Religions at Columbia University. He studied literature at Baring College, Batala, Punjab, and religion at Harvard and Columbia. He received his Ph.D. at Columbia in 1993. His research interests lie especially in the study of early Sikh manuscripts and the history and experience of the diaspora Sikhs. He has published *The Goindval Pothis: The Earliest Extant Source of the Sikh Canon* (1996), *Making of Sikh Scripture* (1993), and (with J. S. Hawley) *Studying the Sikhs: Issues for North America* (1993) and he is currently working on *The Sikhs of America.*

Sheila McDonough is a professor in the Religion Department of Concordia University in Montreal. She received her Ph.D. from the Institute of Islamic Studies at McGill University in 1963. She works primarily on modernism in South Asian Islam. Her books include: *Jinnah: Maker of Modern Pakistan* (1970), *Muslim Ethics and Modernity* (1984), and *Gandhi's Responses to Islam* (1994). She also teaches courses on Islam and women, and has several articles on various aspects of that issue.

Jørgen S. Nielsen is Director of the Centre for the Study of Islam and Christian-Muslim Relations at Selly Oak Colleges, Birmingham, UK, and Honorary Professor at the University of Birmingham. He has a Ph.D. in Arab history from the American University of Beirut (1978). Since then he has worked mainly on the contemporary situation of Muslims in Europe. He has written numerous articles, published *Muslims in Western Europe* (1992,

1995) and edited *The Christian-Muslim Frontier* (1997). He is joint editor of the journal *Islam and Christian-Muslim Relations*.

Joseph T. O'Connell is Associate Professor of Religion at St. Michael's College in the University of Toronto. He received his Ph.D. from Harvard University in 1970. He teaches on Hindu, Sikh, and Jain religions and does research on Vaisnava *bhakti* and on Islam in Bengal, on which topics he has published articles and translations. He has edited *Bengal Vaisnavism, Orientalism, Society and the Arts* (1985), and an issue of the *Journal of Vaisnava Studies* (1997) on the Gaudiya Vaisnavas. He has jointly edited *Bengali Immigrants: A Community in Transition* (1985), *Sikh History and Religion in the Twentieth Century* (1988), and *Presenting Tagore's Heritage in Canada* (1989).

Raymond Brady Williams is LaFollette Distinguished Professor in the Humanities, Professor of Religion, and Director of the Wabash Center for Teaching and Learning in Theology and Religion at Wabash College in Crawfordsville, Indiana. He received his Ph.D. from the University of Chicago in 1966. He is the author of works on the religions of India, including *A New Face of Hinduism: The Swaminarayan Religion* (Cambridge, 1984), and more recently on immigrants from India in the United States, including *Religions of Immigrants from India and Pakistan: New Threads in the American Tapestry* (Cambridge, 1996). He is editor of *A Sacred Thread: Modern Transmission of Hindu Traditions in India and Abroad* (Anima/Columbia, 1992), *The Community of the Humanities* (Wabash, 1992), and a new international journal, *Teaching Theology and Religion*, published by Blackwell Publishers in the UK, and by Cambridge in the United States.

Index

Proper names have been indexed where the people, places, etc. are discussed rather than mentioned in passing.

293

prejudice, 2, 51, 253. *See also*
     racism
priests. *See* religious leaders
professionals, 15, 38, 61, 81, 83,
     86, 122, 135–38, 148, 151,
     168, 173–74, 181, 186, 192,
     207, 214, 220–21, 235, 240,
     252, 260, 261
protestantization, 7, 18, 49, 52,
     82, 155, 158, 161, 278
public policy, 5, 49–51, 111, 118,
     166–68, 183–85, 203–205,
     221, 226. *See also* law
Punjab, 128–29, 152, 197, 259,
     268, 274
purity, 6–7, 10, 42, 43

Q-News, 122
Quebec, 174, 183
Qur'an, 122, 124, 176–77, 181,
     183

race, 2, 213, 283
  race relations, 2, 81, 148
  race relations legislation,
     Britain, 81
racism, 79–80, 116, 167, 191,
     193, 206, 252
Rajneesh, Osho, 58, 60, 61, 65–
     70, 93
Ramgarhias, 134–35, 143, 262.
     See also caste
recitation. *See* chanting
refugees, 148, 214, 261. *See also*
     East Africa
religious belief, 49, 124, 140,
     195, 201, 233–34
religious buildings, 2, 43, 92,
     114, 139, 149, 154–60, 265,
     277
  management of, 89–90, 94,
     141, 195, 199, 267–69, 272
religious education. *See* educa-
     tion, religious
religious identity. *See* identity,
     religious

religious leaders, 21–23, 29–30,
     47–48, 59, 94, 99, 113, 123,
     155, 174–75, 178, 185–87,
     197, 244, 249, 278–80
  training of, 94
religious practice, 5, 15, 31, 41–
     47, 141, 160–64, 233
religious studies, 1, 4, 7, 15, 31,
     109, 111, 119, 184–85, 187,
     199–200, 201, 234, 252, 271–
     72, 283, 285–86
remittances, 79, 112, 130, 131,
     169, 194, 243, 280
Réseau Ecuménique des Femmes
     du Québec, 183
Richmond Hill, 266–68
rites, life-cycle, 91, 92, 94, 96, 98,
     140, 263
rituals, 27, 41, 43, 45, 160–64,
     177–80, 201, 220, 262
rivalries. *See* tensions
Royal Canadian Mounted Police,
     166
Royal Commission of New
     Reproductive Technologies
     (Canada), 167
Rushdie, Salman, 116–20, 122,
     186, 247

Sachedina, Abdel Aziz, 187
Sahaja Yoga, 59, 63
Said, Edward, 8
sampradaya, 10, 57, 93
Sankar, Ravi, 164
Sanskrit, 94, 160–64, 165
Sant Mat, 59, 61
Sathya Sai Baba, 60, 61
scholarship. *See* religious
     studies
School of African and Oriental
     Studies, University of
     London, 5, 11
scriptures, 7, 94, 96, 97, 154,
     157–58, 160–64, 169
sectarianism, 97, 142. *See
     also* interfaith relations;
     tensions

U.K. Action Committee on
Islamic Affairs, 118, 119
U.K. Islamic Mission, 113
umma, 180, 246, 250, 253
undertakers. *See* funeral homes
unemployment. *See* employment
Union of Muslim Organizations
(Britain), 115
United Church of Canada, 69
United Kingdom. *See* Britain
United States
census, 216
immigration laws, 21, 65, 213–
14, 228, 250, 261
laws, 7, 65–66, 213
universalizing, 3, 281
universities. *See* education,
higher
University of British Columbia,
199–200, 204
University of California, Berkeley,
271
Uttar Pradesh, 152

values, 7, 176, 181, 201–202,
241–42, 253
Vancouver, 35, 148–49, 155–56,
178, 213
video, 10, 95, 164
Vishnu Mandir, 56
Vishva Hindu Parishad, 90, 92,
98, 155–56, 234
Vision TV (Canada), 184
Vivekananda, 227, 228, 235

Waco, 67
Westernization, 23, 52

women, 6, 16, 48, 79, 80, 91, 92,
96, 98–101, 102, 111–13,
122–23, 136, 152, 154, 168–
69, 177, 181–84, 192, 198,
200, 205–207, 222, 244–45,
272–73, 278
Women Against Fundamentalism
(Britain), 100
World Parliament of Religions
(1893), 9, 227
(1993), 270
world religions, 82, 286
World Trade Center bombing,
247
World War I, 78, 270
World War II, 79, 128–29, 214
World Zoroastrian Congress,
52
World Zoroastrian Organization,
37, 40, 48, 49
worship, 92, 102, 140, 154–60,
160–64, 232
communal, 262, 264–68. *See
also* religious buildings
home-based, 17, 43, 91, 154,
160–64, 168, 196, 232
individual, 5, 177, 200–203,
262

yoga, 59, 60, 63, 227–28
youth, 22, 92, 95–98, 102. *See
also* generational issues
youth camps, 49, 235, 273

Zoroastrians, 35–52
Zoroastrian Trust Funds of
Europe, 37, 48